The Da Vinci Code
Adventure

The Da Vinci Code
Adventure

On the Trail of Fact, Legend, Faith, & Film

Mike Gunn

with
Greg & Jenn Wright

HJ Hollywood Jesus Books
Burien, Washington 98166

For Donna,
My Faithful Wife

Contents

Part One:
Hidden Interconnectivity

> Langdon forced an awkward smile. "Well, folks, as you all know, I'm here tonight to talk to you about the power of symbols..."

The Power of Symbols

Mike Gunn, Lead Investigator

Staying right where you are is no adventure at all. The stimulating exploration of symbols that is Dan Brown's *The Da Vinci Code* asks us at least one very worthwhile question: are we satisfied with what we already know, or are we ready for an adventure?

Symbols are powerful tools, and the stuff of which language is made. Every culture's language and art has inherent symbols that point toward its myths, the stories that tell people who they are and where they have been. On the personal level, our

1

brains even work to classify information symbolically in order to function properly and make sense of the world before us. According to Edward O. Wilson, these mental concepts and symbols are ultimately "labeled by words."[1] Some symbols are layered and more difficult to verbally express and understand; these often require interpretation—even interpreters. In Seattle, for instance, we have rainbow triangles; I know what those mean, but you may not. But there are also straightforward symbols like stop signs and Mr. Yuck stickers which have a fairly limited range of interpretive parameters; we even have legal language (the law) that not only helps us interpret the signs, but restricts our interpretation. Where on that spectrum does the zymology of *The Da Vinci Code* lie?

What's in a Story

Dan Brown's action/mystery novel exists because of symbols and the "inside" information they may provide. But the book is not merely about the symbols themselves; it's more about various power bases struggling to be the dominant interpreter of the symbols. Dan Brown's hero, Robert Langdon, writer and Professor of Religious Symbology at Harvard, is in Paris as a guest lecturer at The American University. In the wee hours of the morning following his lecture, he is awakened by a visit from the French Judicial Police: a man has been murdered in the Louvre Museum—a man he had been scheduled to meet. Captain Bezu Fache has launched an investigation and wants Langdon on the scene. Elsewhere, an albino monk named Silas literally whips himself into a spiritual frenzy, while Bishop Aringarosa of the Vatican prelature Opus Dei jets from New York to Rome on a mission of utmost secrecy and importance. They are all on a collision course over historic struggles to control religious symbols and the manipulation of their power.

Historical symbols can be particularly confusing. According to one author, you have two options if you are going to teach students history: "you either lie to students or confuse them."[2] Throw fiction into the mix and the waters only get muddier. If Robert Langdon (or Dan Brown, for that matter) had it his way, he might have you believing that his interpretation of symbols is the most learned—and, of course, the "right" one.

Or would he? Perhaps you need to see the movie, or read the book, and figure that one out for yourself. In any event, Brown's novel presents an alternate history, a different one from the norm, so, in our quest for all things new, we may easily become intoxicated with its "gnostic" and apocryphal nature. But I hope that, after the hangover, and as the enjoyment of the book (or movie) as pure entertainment fades, your mind remains open to the truth—and that you find it somewhere between the first century and Dan Brown. After all, his story is an interesting one, if not entirely new.

Grail folklore has been part of our history's fabric since before the Middle Ages. Oddly enough, the Enlightenment had little interest in such tales, since mythological deconstruction required those "in the know" to conclude that only the merest fraction of any historic document was truthful or even accurate. When deconstruction failed to neuter religion, however, myths like those behind *The Da Vinci Code* began to resurface. For instance, the question, "What if Jesus really did have romantic relationships, and married Mary Magdelene?" was partly behind both novel and film versions of *The Last Temptation of Christ* (see our discussion in the next chapter). The theory that Jesus in fact fathered a bloodline that ended up as royalty in France was finally researched and presented as fact by Michael Baigent, Richard Leigh, and Henry Lincoln in their book *Holy Blood, Holy Grail* (1982). That relatively obscure volume, cited in *The Da Vinci Code* as "perhaps the best-known tome" on the subject, provides much of the grist for Dan Brown's mill—and *The Da Vinci Code* has actually become the international bestseller that *Holy Blood, Holy Grail* wanted to be. It is in fact one of the most successful books ever written, and was number one on the *New York Times* Best Seller list for over thirty-five weeks. The book certainly has its intrigue as conspiracy and secret societies abound, and mystery rules; but the question is still begged: how much of the book should we believe as "fact," and how much should just entertain us?

Where Fact Ends and Fiction Begins

Dan Brown's novel begins with a chapter titled "FACT," which describes two secret societies. One of them, Opus Dei, most certainly does exist, though quite possibly in a wholly different manner from what Brown would lead us to believe. The other, The Priory of Sion, may or may not actually exist; such is the nature of "secret societies": if we could confirm their existence, they'd hardly be secret, and if they were truly secret we couldn't confirm their existence. And here is where our adventure begins, where we begin our efforts to expand on what we already know—if we're willing to ask the right questions.

Has Opus Dei actually been the subject of controversy? Are reports of brainwashing and coercion wholly credible? What does Opus Dei have to say for itself?

Did the Bibliothèque Nationale actually discover documents relating to the fabled Priory of Sion? Were the so-called *Dossiers Secrets* actually secret, or is that merely the name given to them by romantically-minded researchers? Were they possibly a politically-motivated smear campaign? Are they even authentic? Can they be corroborated? Do they actually identify Sir Isaac Newton and Leonardo Da Vinci as members? And even if they do, does that constitute ironclad proof of the Priory's factual existence?

The answers we choose to such foundational questions— or the fact that we don't ask such questions at all—will undoubtedly affect the way in which we read the remainder of Brown's story. This opening chapter might even lead us to suspect that Opus Dei and the Priory might be the only two facts in the entire book. After all, Brown's characters make some dubious claims, such as the assertion that the Merovingians (Jesus' supposed royal bloodline—I told you, you've got to read the book!) "founded Paris."[3] This is about as accurate as Austin Powers' father's claim to inventing the question mark (again—see the movie).

But *The Da Vinci Code* is exciting to the public mind because it claims to uncover the big cover-up. It purports to unearth untold hidden secrets and answer mysteries that we want demystified—or at least that we are told that we want demystified. In the immortal words of Al Pacino in *The Devil's Advocate*, we're after "the final hiding place, the final fig leaf."[4] We want secret information that allows us to control our lives, to take different courses, and we are frustrated by our finiteness and lack of omniscience. We're after the missing puzzle piece that dampens our own claim to deity. Aren't we curious because we deeply believe that we deserve that missing piece?

Authorial Reinterpretation & Guerrilla Warfare

In Edward O. Wilson's fine book *Consilience*, he describes our culture's artistic climate as one that is more willing to interpret data and symbols experientially and personally, rather than connecting them with "facts," reason, or a structured, methodical interpretation (hermeneutics). He writes that "the tradition of Homer, Dante, Leonardo, Shakespeare, Beethoven and Goethe is not dead. It is growing up in the cracks of the postmodern concrete."[5] *The Da Vinci Code* sinks its roots firmly into those same said cracks while it sprawls out over the concrete. *Voila!* We have the ideal cultural climate for such a blockbuster book and movie, a climate that doesn't gravitate toward realism and truth in its "edutainment"[6] as much as what we might call "fictional reality."

This is the world that great movie directors like Oliver

Stone inhabit, one constructed to fit what they want us to believe as opposed to the more obvious "surface" reality. Their films are, as Michael Moore once quipped, a "version of the Op-Ed page."[7] In other words, even though they might be producing a documentary or "historical fiction," the material is presented both as "fact" and, in a lesser fashion, as opinion and perspective. Oliver Stone is a master of this style, as demonstrated in fantastic movies like *Platoon* and *JFK*. In an address to the University of California at Berkeley, Stone lamented the lack of spirituality and storytelling in the United States, saying that film is "drama as catharsis, as release, as reaffirmation of the power of the spirit."[8] He went on to say,

> I think with movies we can begin to strengthen people's immune systems, because people go into the movies with their defenses down. It's not real, therefore not threatening. When they least expect it, that might be the best time for the guerrillas of art to get in there and move the head and the heart.[9]

I really enjoy guerrilla art. But is it wise to passively enjoy it? Wouldn't it be much better to engage art and culture with a formidable mind and a full set of hermeneutical lenses that can interpret the many signs and symbols such artists foist upon us? Avoiding such engagement for the sake of a "pure" truth does nothing more than pollute the truth and muddy our own story.

Dan Brown, by contrast, is quite comfortable paradoxically extolling the power of symbols with the zeal of the most wooden literalist. As we will discuss more fully later, Langdon perhaps channels one of Dan Brown's key presuppositions: "Every faith in the world is based on fabrication. That is the definition of faith... Every religion describes God through metaphor, allegory and exaggeration."[10] Does Langdon have his definition of faith right? Digging into the significance of this claim is important in order for us to fully enjoy *The Da Vinci Code*—and discern the supposed secrets of the code. What part of that definition is true, and what part is false? Does it matter what we think about this, or should we be content to simply let Langdon steer our convictions?

Interpretive Reading

There are many symbols all around us, and in some way all of language is symbolic and culturally constructed; but we are equipped with a rational capacity to interpret and communicate. While absolute understanding still eludes our grasp, interpretation doesn't. Certain perspectives on symbols will doubtless be determined by our cultural, religious and tribal points of view, but that does not negate the underlying reality of the symbol or the truth it symbolizes. Robert Langdon and I agree on this point.

If I were to bring forth an American flag, for instance, I'm sure it would not only symbolize different things for an American than for an Iraqi insurgent, but it may also have vastly different connotations for a Berkeley student from Marin County than it has for a truck driver out of Memphis, Tennessee. Still, none of these diverse interpretations of a single symbol can mitigate the fact that the flag has survived over the years as the government's central symbol—or set of symbols—of our Republic and the Revolutionary War that secured its status.

Symbols indeed abound, and they are powerful indicators of our belief systems and the stories they tell. Symbols, like mythology, are not false or untrue, but a representational attempt to connect our hearts to the data that surround us. Modernism tried to reduce everything to mathematical equations, but as we emerge into the twenty-first century, it appears that the Enlightenment failed to purge western art of neo-classicism and romanticism. Humanity still demands more than a soulless hermeneutic. The rational mind desires to make order out of everything, revealing the patterned and orderly creatures we are, while the existential, affective self listens to the soul, desiring eternity and something transcending the senses.

Christianity, at least, explains Dan Brown and his

imitators, Christian or otherwise: it claims that we are made to be creative, and to create; so we do, and sometimes truth lies in the balance. We continue to waffle between two halves of the same truth—our cognitive and affective desires—while we argue with one another for hermeneutical rights, and sometimes our hearts' affections feel the need to set truth aside for the perceived sake of our souls. This is part of the human condition of angst, and part of what I believe it means to be human.

Personally, as a believer in a Creator who is both creative/artistic and rational/mathematical, I do believe we pursue both of these mediums of expression for the sake of God's glory because that's what He's made us to do. After all, Christian Scripture says we are called to love Him with all of our heart, mind, and soul.[11] As rational beings, we don't need to shun symbols and their tendency to encourage relativistic interpretations because symbols and metaphor allow us to create language—the very means by which we interpret and communicate data and concrete ideas. At the same time, those of us embroiled in the arts need to recognize that there is ultimately no lasting art without an underlying concrete meaning, a specific purposeful story transmitted from the author to the reader/hearer/observer.

I should note at this point that, although I don't resonate entirely with postmodern philosopher Michel Foucault's claim that "everything is an interpretation,"[12] I do think that we all come to any data or symbol with our own perspectives, and that we need to do some cultural reconnaissance to interpret the "truth" of the culture's narrative. And this is as true for readers of *The Da Vinci Code* as it is for the scientific rationalist who often jumps the gun by assuming godlike cognition and personal objectivity before arriving at conclusions "inductively"—and it is just as true for readers of *Left Behind*, but more on that later.

The Interpretive Stranglehold

Ultimately we are all artists in need of articulating our individual stories within the larger story of our culture (the "metanarrative," deconstructed as merely the traditions of the powerful). On this point, I do agree with Foucault: "What strikes me is the fact that in our society, art has become something which is related only to objects and not to individuals, or to life."[13]

This may be no truer than in the case of *The Da Vinci Code*. Dan Brown has given us a fictional story that is meant to be enjoyed, one that does not hold up well to surface scrutiny. He has loaded it with symbols, and even offers interpretations of those symbols only to fail—perhaps deliberately?—in the end. But we shouldn't worry whether Brown has interpreted those symbols correctly; rather, we ought to ask why they continue to be important, and why the tales behind them are being retold again in the twenty-first century. What is it that Dan Brown wants to reveal? Does he merely want us to discover the evil of Christianity?

I'm not really sure. First of all, in most of his interviews about the book and the movie, he has been clear to answer that he just wanted to write a story and had no intention to deceive or offend. And in an ABC Television documentary on the book, he told Elizabeth Vargas that during his research on the subject he went from skeptic to "believer" in the Grail story.[14] But what did he mean by that, exactly—that he became a believer that these ancient allegations about the Grail were in fact an authentic alternate myth, or that they were not only authentic, but the One True Myth?

Every artist, of course, creates from a particular perspective, but we need to see it as just that, a "perspective"— even one we might be projecting onto the artist. The subtitle of the ABC presentation suggests Dan Brown's possible intent to "Discover the Truth Behind the Mystery." But was that Brown's intent, or ABC's?

Don't we all want that kind of knowledge, hidden knowledge? I remember as a kid wanting to discover an unknown band that no one knew about and then introduce my friends into my hidden yet pleasurable world. That was pretty hard back then in a world without Napster, and that made it even cooler. But discovering that hidden band didn't really make that band "the best." Just possibly, Dan Brown may simply be trying to encourage that sense of discovery rather than suggesting that his alternate story is "better."

That's a tough nut to crack. Symbols and myths, after all, generally aren't created to allow for alternate stories. They are created to explain the truths as the user of the symbol or myth sees them, much like Oliver Stone does in his movies. They are an integral part of the story that is being told. The ancients used myths and symbols to help tell a story (a true story, by the way) instead of merely analyzing all of the data and presenting it in sterile, objective reportage. Jack Finnegan, in his book *Myth and Mystery*, defines myth as "a form of symbolic thought in which intellect, imagination, and emotion combine to communicate a perceived truth. A myth is not. . . a fanciful tale, but a symbolic or poetic expression of that which is incapable of direct statement."[15]

Myths and symbols aren't indicators of naïveté or low IQ, then, but poetic and creative means to explain mystery and awe. As C. S. Lewis writes, "For this is the marriage of heaven and earth: Perfect Myth and Perfect Fact: claiming not only our love and our obedience, but also our wonder and delight, addressed to the savage, the child and the poet in each one of us no less than to the moralist, the scholar and the philosopher."[16]

Modern man, by contrast, tends to begin with the presupposition that the ancients were incapable of logical thinking, consequently creating fanciful and untrue stories to explain the unexplainable. This leads to the conclusion that everything in ancient stories is symbolic, without basis in fact, a conclusion which leaves everything up for interpretive grabs.

Robert Langdon exhibits this interpretive condescension when he humorously quips that "a country known for machismo [and] womanizing... could not have chosen a better national emblem than a thousand foot phallus."[17] Yes, I did find that statement about the Eiffel Tower a bit witty and even humorous; but Dan Brown's characters do seem to find a symbol (and a specific—even shallow—interpretation of that symbol) under every institutional rock. They interpret *The Da Vinci Code*'s symbols literally, and accept them at that level; but it doesn't mean that we have to do the same, or even that Brown wants us to.

Robert Langdon (most likely Dan Brown's alter ego, in this case at least) pays lip service to this interpretive freedom. "Telling someone what a symbol 'meant,'" he says, "was like telling them how a song should make them feel—it was different for all people. A white Ku Klux Klan headpiece conjured images of hatred and racism in the United States, and yet the same costume carried a meaning of religious faith in Spain."[18] And Langdon is correct, not only in the context of Brown's fictional world, but in our own. The Nazi symbol of Hitler's evil Third Reich, the swastika, is a symbol of fascism and tyranny. However in India, it has always been a symbol of mystery and spirituality. The confederate flag in the South means pride to some, and death and oppression to others. Religious symbols and stories are no different. Similar symbology does not necessarily equate to identical narrative.

Yet Dan Brown's characters want to have their cake and eat it too. They feel free to deny the uniqueness of the Christian story because its symbol set isn't wholly unique, and they call the Christian meaning of certain symbols "incorrect" merely because other religious traditions use the same symbols for different meanings. Such apparent hypocrisy can be found throughout the book (say, in chapter six, if you really want to have your own adventure and discover that for yourself); but it might be more charitable to say that Brown simply keeps changing the code throughout the book. Half the fun of reading is wading through that maze to find his hidden secrets—or gaffes.

Symbols and *Jesus of Montreal*

Jesus of Montreal, a fantastic French-Canadian film released in 1989, highlights how myth and symbols may change within the religious context, and also how one particular mythic story (the Passion play) has consistently resurrected itself over the last two thousand years, in many different cultures and many different eras.

The film is about five—yes, five!—struggling actors who are asked to bolster a fledgling version of the passion play by an older, unbelieving Catholic priest. When their version is contextualized with artistic freedom and the newest available scholarly information about Jesus, the priest—as well as the Church—is upset. In spite of the play's incredible success, they want to shut it down. This throws the whole cast into its own contemporary version of The Passion. Their predicament includes power struggles, loss, temptation, greed, and a fight against oppression and exploitation. It features the Establishment sticking it to the people and a charismatic young man leading his band of rag tag rejects only to be thwarted and ultimately killed by the powers that want to silence his "blasphemy." (Sound familiar?) Simply put, it is a story about the very human struggles of love, loss, and hope regained. It is the story of the Gospel of Jesus Christ, and in reality the story of practically every religion known to man.

The question ought not to be who owns the truth of this story, or even why director Denys Arcand's version departs from the biblical text; but why does this particular story continue to be so prevalent in the human repertoire of tales? Why do such powerful symbols inspire and lift us beyond this world? Does this film negate the truth of the biblical story by reiteration and revisionist inclusion, or does it bolster the truth by demonstrating its sheer longevity and its pure ontological presence?

Curiously, while *Jesus of Montreal*, like *The Da Vinci Code*, offers an alternate story, I really never got the feeling that I was being duped. *Jesus of Montreal* made me think and contemplate the potential truths of the alternate story while maintaining the integrity of the original.

Arcand doesn't negate the Christian story, as I feel that Brown sometimes does within *The Da Vinci Code*. I never found myself wanting to argue theology while I was watching *Jesus of Montreal*. I could actually even resonate with Arcand's redemptive story, even though it is no doubt one that the institutional church would prefer to edit; but like good art, it allows for tension, begging you to think. Dan Brown's characters, though, often appear as preachy as Jimmy Swaggart on the "Old Time Gospel Hour," leaving as much to my imagination as a game of "hide and seek" with a three year old. (In case you haven't done that lately, they pretty much hide right in front of you.)

Adventuring in Symbols and Significance

I do believe, though, that Dan Brown takes us on an important adventure. It's an adventure that I don't think we need to shun; it doesn't need to affect us like Langdon's fear of elevators, a grating symbol of youth gone awry (we could really have fun interpreting elevator- and well-shafts, couldn't we?). We don't need to fear potential danger, because, like Langdon and his elevator, that would be an unjustified fear caused by poor experiences instead of a dance with the truth.

When it comes to adventures in symbolic significance, we can turn to C. S. Lewis once again, drinking in a wisdom that makes sense out of nonsense and separates the wheat from the chaff while giving us a roadmap to "Holy Grail:"

> Now as myth transcends thought, Incarnation transcends
> myth. The heart of Christianity is a myth which is also a

fact. The old myth of a dying God, without ceasing to be a myth, comes down from the heaven of legend and imagination to the earth of history. It happens—at a particular date, in a particular place, followed by definable historical consequences. We pass from a Balder or an Osiris, dying nobody knows when or where, to a historical person crucified (it is all in order) under Pontius Pilate. By becoming fact it does not cease to become a myth. That's the miracle.[19]

> The elevator jolted to a stop. Langdon stepped quickly out into the hallway; the world into which he stepped, however, was nothing like he expected.

For Further Investigation
The Da Vinci Code, Chapters 1 through 4

Dig a Little Deeper

➤ Which symbols are powerful for you, personally, and why?

➤ Do you think that symbolic equity exists amongst different and often disparate religious traditions? Or does our culture favor one faith's symbols over another?

➤ How does Langdon's definition of faith compare to your own?

➤ Do you agree or disagree with C. S. Lewis' ideas on myth? Why? Why not? Is Jack Finnegan's definition of myth easier to grasp?

➤ What relationships do myth, symbology, and language have?

14

Draw Your Own Conclusions

➤ Resources on Gnosticism:

- *Gnosis and Faith in Early Christianity: An Introduction to Gnosticism*, by Riemer Roukema.
- www.gnostic-church.org
- Also note the language in John 1. Many biblical scholars believe this chapter was written specifically to combat the anti-flesh beliefs of early gnosticism.

➤ Resources on Opus Dei:

- *Opus Dei: An Objective Look Behind the Myths and Reality of the Most Controversial Force in the Catholic Church*, by John L. Allen.
- www.opusdei.org (Official Site)
- www.davincicode-opusdei.com (weblog run by Fr. John Wauk, an Opus Dei priest)

➤ Foucault's Explorations in Philosophy:

- http://foucault.info/
- *Madness and Civilization: A History of Insanity in the Age of Reason*, by Michel Foucault.

➤ C. S. Lewis' Life and Thoughts

- http://www.cslewisclassics.com/
- For starters, try *Mere Christianity* or *Surprised by Joy*.

➤ Jesus' Use of Symbolic Language:

- Mark 4:1–20.

➤ Apocalyptic Symbolic Language:

- Revelation 21.

> **"In times of turmoil,"**
> **Langdon continued, "a**
> **newly emerging power will**
> **take over the existing**
> **symbols and degrade them**
> **over time in an attempt to**
> **erase their meaning."**

Newly Emerging Power

Mike Gunn, Lead Investigator

I'm not sure that a description of a man can tell us anything about him unless that description is written by the man himself. Now of course, according to the postmodern "hermeneutic of suspicion," we should be utterly suspicious of anything written by men in power, or of any history written by the victors. Naturally, only the oppressed can be objective and write meaningful things.

Very early in *The Da Vinci Code*, we are treated to a description of Mr. Robert Langdon that I find amusing:

> His usually sharp blue eyes looked hazy and drawn tonight. A dark stubble was shrouding his strong jaw and dimpled chin. Around his temples, the gray highlights were advancing... His female colleagues insisted the gray only accentuated his bookish appeal. ... "Although Professor Langdon might not be considered hunk-handsome like some of our younger awardees, this forty-something academic has more than his share of scholarly allure. His captivating presence is punctuated by an unusually low, baritone speaking voice, which his female students describe as 'Chocolate

for the ears.'" ... Harrison Ford in Harris tweed.[1]

My own hermeneutic of suspicion can only lead me to surmise that this is Dan Brown's *Mona Lisa*-like description of himself.

Now, I also write as a forty-something, and I would say that every guy in his forties still sees himself as the "hunk-handsome" cool guy who just might be whisked off to exciting world adventures while winning the "dame." Even ol' Indiana (of *Raiders* fame) was a bit of a womanizer, and definitely a chauvinist. (Heck, Harrison Ford is even coming back for a fourth film—and he's well over sixty!) This just makes Langdon an even better version of Ford, since he is a champion of the "sacred feminine." But is he, really?

Men, on the Trail of Women

If I were to deconstruct this literary character just a bit, I think I could pretty easily unearth an author who is still writing under the intoxicating influence of a male-dominated power base. After all, isn't Langdon a bit of a James Bond? Doesn't he exude a machismo that dominates the intellectual landscape of both *The Da Vinci Code* and *Angels and Demons*? How many leading ladies is he going to go through before this series is over? How many Langdon Women will Brown write out of the script? Didn't Langdon bed Vittoria Vetra in *Angels and Demons*, and isn't she waiting for him, somewhere, for their twice-yearly tryst?[2]

The romantic cur. He is at least wistful about not keeping that appointment as he rides in the cab to the Louvre. When he gets there, Captain Bezu Fache shows him Jacques Saunière's carefully laid-out murdered corpse, surrounded and covered in pentacles, circles, and messages in blood and fluorescent ink. And pretty soon, he naturally forgets all about Vittoria when, in the pitch darkness, cryptologist Sophie Neveu arrives—she of the burgundy hair and olive green eyes. My, Robert—what keen eyesight you have in the dark. I thought Sophie had the head for figures...

At this point in the story, we're also introduced to Bishop Aringarosa's female-suppressing Opus Dei, and get the scoop on how the monk Silas came to be tied up with such goombahs. Over at Saint-Sulpice, Sister Sandrine gets the call that lets her know that one of Opus Dei's operatives will be paying a late-night visit to the church. Not to worry, Sister—Silas is only there to kill you, not rough you up.

Because of their vows, of course, neither Aringarosa nor Silas have anything like the prospects of Langdon—and given the inevitability of striking out, why not do something wacky like, I don't know, steal the Grail? I'm pretty sure I know why Robert Langdon's so interested in the sacred feminine, though. After all, doesn't he end up in Sophie's arms at the end of the *Code*? Sounds like James Bond to me.

Now Bond, as the *Austin Powers* spoofs remind us, is archaic, misogynist, and chauvinistic. Didn't the Bond franchise even try to make its hero a bit of a metrosexual after Roger Moore and before Pierce Brosnan? You know, sensitive—less of a womanizer? (He even got married, if I recall correctly.) It seems as though they did, but apparently it didn't sell and everyone wanted to see Brosnan naked. So I guess that pendulum just bounced back instead of really swinging, and some sexism is still okay these days as long as the women being womanized are perceived to be "manizers." So the franchise went back to womanizing tough but sensual women like Halle Berry; and heaven knows she doesn't feel like she's being taken advantage of. But maybe my revisionist mind is just making something out of nothing?

Now, I'm sure Langdon would object to such nonsense. After all, we are a free society, and jettisoning our Puritan roots for a more rational, liberated, sex-ritual-loving culture has got to be far more fun. Until, of course, sexually transmitted diseases reach epic proportions, I suppose. How possible is it that the women's-movement desire to subsume male roles is playing into the hands of guys like Langdon who aren't interested in commitment, only the act of commitment? I mean, if women don't want commitment either, à la men, doesn't that just make men happier?

What if the "new power" that emerges within a postmodern deconstruction of old powers is simply a hyper version of older ones? If institutions like Christianity have truly thwarted the feminine side of our spirituality—which, according to *The Da Vinci Code*, it has—then what if the Older Power, the one that Christianity itself thwarted, was worse? Is it possible that the goddess-worshipping pagan religions simply used women as biological ovens to cook us up some more males to propagate the race, and nothing else? We'll explore that line of thought more thoroughly in a later chapter, but I want us to chew on that a bit until then. The question is relevant to the discussion at hand, and is maybe even something that Langdon (or Dan Brown) can relate to.

What Goes Up Must Be Torn Down

In Dan Brown's storyline, Robert Langdon is certainly expressing something that is often true about emerging power bases. We see the same inner workings in our own political structure: in order to gain and hold on to power, one very often must discredit one's opponent. In the field of debate, this approach is called *ad hominem*. Whether one's own stand is true or right is immaterial; what matters is that the opponent is discredited, and his or her ideology subsequently discredited as well. We witnessed that approach in the 1990s when the Republican Party spent more money trying to discredit President Clinton and his wife Hillary than it did promoting its own agenda. The opposite is now happening with the Democrats' often ridiculous assault on the Bush Administration. During elections we seem to be more concerned with "Did they inhale?" or "Did he ingest cocaine when he was a sophomore in college?" than with candidates' domestic, foreign, and financial policies.

Doubtless, certain seasons of Church history have indeed witnessed wicked acts in the name of God; but Church history is not a monolith. Often times the collateral damage that the Church did was to its own—not that that's any better. But the Church is a diverse and sometimes disagreeable body of believers that most often is at war with itself in one way or another. Not every Christian has burned supposed witches or sided with Hitler, and Christians have always been quite instrumental in speaking out and re-righting the sinking ship.

Skeptics might have us believe that Christianity invented slavery, and that humanists saved the day. In fact, both humanists and Christians owned slaves and justified their wicked actions by the same culture-marrying arguments: they convinced themselves that Africans were subhuman, and that the European races were superior. Later, both secular humanists and Christians worked together to lift that blinding veil off of British—and then American—soil, helping purge the west of (at least some of) its wickedness. Can't we just stop the mutual degradation and work toward an understanding of one another, while constructing a mutually beneficial culture?

A few years ago, our church congregation hosted a screening of *The Two Towers* (the second in Peter Jackson's *The Lord of the Rings* trilogy). We held the event in a public high school auditorium and invited the public to attend. Afterward, Greg Wright delivered a brief talk on, yes, the power of symbols in the movie and their relation to war.[3] Afterward, a discussion with Greg and fellow film critic Jeffrey Overstreet was opened up for Q & A. One older woman stood up (an apparent survivor of the holocaust) and levied a venomous attack against men and the harm they have caused this world. When she was done, in all honesty and with due respect, I wanted to undress her self-righteous and misdirected comments.

But her position has its supporters within much of this

country's academic power base. It is articulated in the theses of such books as Dale Peterson's and Richard Wrangham's *Demonic Males: Apes and the Origins of Human Violence*, which promulgates the notion that males are the reason for all wars and violence perpetrated by human beings.[4] That sentiment has been concocted by an academia which has denigrated the male role in the family, suggesting that apes wage war because they don't have a primary role in nurturing babies: in their boredom, they create wars to fight.

My reading of *Demonic Males* once again demonstrated to me that deconstructing histories and texts with skeptical eyes yields pretty predictable results. If we're always looking for meaning-manipulating power structures we will always find them, because they are presupposed to exist. And I can't help but think that the interpreter is quite possibly blinded by the same set of power-hungry mechanisms that he is deconstructing. If our stated goal is to "lift the dominant ideological veil,"[5] to borrow a phrase from Fabienne André Worth, then aren't we interpreting with the same jadedness that we are trying unveil? Yet this is the hermeneutic by which Langdon seems to live his life.

The Willing Suspension of Credulity

Both Dan Brown and his nominal alter ego Robert Langdon are deconstructionists. Deconstruction is a postmodern interpretive tool used to determine the meaning of the text, its goal being the revelation of implicit and hidden underlying assumptions that shaped the author and subsequently the text itself. The basic idea is that language is a collection of symbols formed by a writer's historic sociological context—one usually subjugated by the dominant power structures or "host" culture. The goal of the exegete is to see beyond the words to the supposedly real meaning behind the text.

Langdon himself says that such *"connections may be invisible... but they are always there, buried just beneath the surface.*"[6] The connections Langdon speaks of are life's coincidences and the "web of profoundly intertwined histories and events."[7] According to Langdon, life and its complexities are a series of symbols and events that are connected to one another through archetypes and mythologies that tell a rational story about life here on earth.

A hermeneutic of suspicion guides Langdon, and he reaches for symbols and stories that help him critically deconstruct the dominant narratives of our culture. Langdon's approach is deconstructionist in that it presupposes suspicion, since the victor always writes the history; and it is Hegelian in that it always pits opposites or contradictions against one another in order to yield a third option. Langdon only believes in the sacred feminine to the extent that it opposes the dominant power in need of deconstruction. The opposition of the two can then lead to a Hegelian Other. I even doubt that Langdon is ultimately a believer in any mythology outside of his preconceived notion that mythology and religion is mankind's "quest to understand the Divine."[8]

This is interesting because it appears that Dan Brown has purposefully placed many opposing clues and contradictory symbols throughout his book, to help guide us to a new synthesis of truth. For instance: why does a male writer who seems to be championing women author a book with a woman named Sophie (*wisdom* in the Greek) who is so obviously lacking in that area? Why is she so reliant on men like Langdon and Teabing to discover the truth? There's not even a hint of opposition from the apparently naïve subordinate. She drinks it in like a two-year-old looking up to her daddy. Over the space of five pages, "Sophie nodded, her eyes riveted on [Langdon]. ... Sophie looked uncertain. ... Sophie glanced up with a surprised look of recognition. ... Sophie already looked troubled. ... Sophie looked confused. ... Sophie looked uneasy. ... Sophie looked skeptical."[9] Sophie is not wise at all. She is the *tabula rasa* from

The Sound of Music, an open book just waiting to be written upon. As Langdon himself observes, "Replication. Repeating a symbol is the simplest way to strengthen its meaning."[10] Dan Brown wants to ensure that we know Sophie is a simp.

Another interesting foible that I dug out of *Angels and Demons* was Brown's usage of an "ancient 'god-making' rite of Euhemerus," which (according to Langdon) is where the "ritual of Christian canonization is taken from."[11] Is canonization a ritual in the Christian tradition? Hmm... Maybe Langdon has some secret information that we don't know? Well, from the only historical reference to Euhemerus I could find, he appears to have been a fourth-century Greek mythographer who developed a theory of mythological interpretation.

> He is chiefly known for a rationalizing method of interpretation, known as Euhemerism, that treats mythological accounts as a reflection of actual historical events shaped by retelling and traditional mores. In the skeptic philosophical tradition of the Cyrenaics, Euhemerism forged a new method of interpretation for contemporary religious beliefs. The reputation of Euhemerus was that he believed that much of Greek mythology could be interpreted as natural events given supernatural characteristics.[12]

It seems that old Euhemerus was a rationalist some twelve hundred years before Descartes. What's interesting is Dan Brown's insertion of this guy into his novel, and using him as the source of the "ritual of canonization." Could Dan Brown actually be a rationalist in postmodern disguise? Is Brown using a postmodern hermeneutic to promulgate a rationalist worldview which demands that everything be interconnected by the one constant—human reason?

The Last Temptation & the Emerging Power of Fools

Years ago, another film came out that roused the ire of

many Christians. It also was a film based on a book about Jesus that dealt with similar subject matter. Martin Scorsese adapted Nikos Kazantzakis' novel *The Last Temptation of Christ* into a movie about Jesus the Christ, a man who, though the Messiah, was tempted like all of us are. Although the movie didn't really explore anything other than the author's speculations about the temptations that Christ must have faced as a man,[13] it became the focus of a huge controversy headed up by evangelical and fundamentalist leaders who attempted to raise enough money to buy the movie and burn it.

Great plan! It turned the otherwise plodding three-hour film into the critical hit of the year! The now metaphysically-challenged Gene Siskel made it his top movie of the decade! Scorsese was well pleased, and has allegedly been heard trying to get James Dobson to promote his next movie...

The problem with many religious leaders in our country is that they still feel that they own that voice of authority—yet shout out into a vacuum of disinterest. The Christian metalanguage is archaic and often demeaning; thankfully, through its own efforts, the Church's message has once again become "foolishness" to the Greeks.[14] I regret to say that Christians have largely forgotten how to have conversations without returning to the language of power, trying our best to hold on to a faint memory of a mythical Christendom that once dominated the landscape.

The assumption is that the "Christian" voice is the one that brought this great country to where it once was, and that only that voice can bring it back to greatness. The problem here is that the deconstructionist misguidedly agrees with the first premise—and wants no more of a voice that supposedly brought only slavery, oppression of the poor, and first-strike imperialism.

But what part of the Christian voice created that kind of power? Only the segment that was married to power. We could hardly blame those ills on the Amish, the Quakers, or the Bruderhof.

In defense of Christian power paranoids, yes—it is very true that the Bible has been banned from certain countries (perhaps even our own) from time to time; but more often than not—say, for several hundred years—it was the Church itself that was on the power end of such bans. The Church itself has fueled conspiracy theories like that found in *The Da Vinci Code* because the Church has most certainly jockeyed for power by suppressing its enemies. This cannot be denied. This is what people in power do. Only people who are attached to material things on this earth feel the need to protect themselves.

I was in South Africa in early 2006, and I was struck by how many of the homes in wealthy Johannesburg and Pretoria neighborhoods are individually gated, with personal security teams watching out for the bad guys. Michael Moore lied to me, man; he said in *Bowling for Columbine* that America was the most violent nation, and that Americans were the most xenophobic people. Well, it seems as though we are at least one-upped by the South Africans.

The fact is, fear is not only endemic to the West; it is pandemic to the sinful, broken human community. Even the Church is fearful. We fear because of our inability to trust the sovereign grace and providence of our Father who is in heaven. Any time we have gained power, we have jettisoned our trust in God and have become sold on keeping our power—because that's what people in power do.

Jesus certainly attacked Roman values and power structures, and the early Church was quite subversive—but its provocateurs did its revolutionary work as ambassadors, not as senators. The early Church saw itself as separate from this world, and subsequently didn't care about losing anything. Its power came not through partnering with the world, but through questioning the ethic of a world that saw no universal value in God's own image-created humanity. The Apostles lived by a strange ethic: "Now as always Christ will be exalted in my body, whether by life or by death. For to me, to live is Christ and to die is gain. If I am to go on living in the body, this will mean fruitful labor for me."[15] And by this sentiment expressed by the Apostle Paul, they were able to operate powerfully and boldly from the political margins. They had only Christ to live for, and everything to die for.

Only when we accumulate stuff and power do we begin to live for the moment and relegate Christ and our Christian life to an impotent, irrelevant, listless mythology. As Nietzsche rightly observed, it is "we who have killed God."[16]

Instead of engaging the art community and using *The Last Temptation of Christ* to enter into dialogue with a culture that doesn't speak Christianese—seizing a great opportunity to talk about Jesus as a god who came to earth in the form of a man, who did no wrong yet took all wrongs upon himself through his love for his creation—the Church became fearful and moralized the situation, losing another chance to tell God's story.

Maybe Christians could have used the Bible's assertion that Jesus was "tempted in every way, just as we are"[17] in a real conversation with real people, instead of leaving it in the pages of the Bible as an abstract, if fuzzily personal, thought. The Church could have presented Christ as Scorsese did—as a man who was beset with temptations just like us, but who didn't succumb to a very natural but counter-purposeful temptation to sex and marriage. Unlike in *The Da Vinci Code*'s theory, Scorsese's Jesus doesn't get married—He doesn't even have sex, contrary to Leigh Teabing's bogus claim[18]—but goes on to the cross to do His Father's will, abandoning his dream of a very normal marital relationship with the woman he loved.

Sorry, Leigh. Jesus wasn't into ritual orgies in service of the sacred feminine; and He wasn't a misogynist. He was a normal guy who liked women. He just loved His Father and His Father's will greater, which is a phenomenal lesson that *The Last Temptation* could have taught us.

Scorsese's film may not have been the best film of the 1980s; in fact, I'm pretty sure it wasn't. But it was a great lost opportunity for the Church to tell its story, and to honor a Christian filmmaker for making that story visible—but like the authorities in *Jesus of Montreal*, Church leaders tried to ban it because their false sense of power and authority seemed to be under attack.

Right now, we should go see Ron Howard's film version of *The Da Vinci Code*, and use it to the glory of God. If Christians are actually right, God's purposes will ultimately be brought about through Dan Brown, Ron Howard, and Tom Hanks! Can the authority and power of the Gospel and the Lord Jesus Christ be undone by the ideologies and philosophy of man?

Writing a New, "Improved" History

Movie burning, book burning, and heretic burning are nothing new to mankind, nor to the Church. We do it well and we do it often. Censorship is part of the power-monger's scheme to hold on to power. It is the dominator's methodology to remain dominant. For that, even Leigh Teabing has good reason to be suspicious. Even Christians would do well to take lessons from their Savior and question the dominant and oppressive cultural ideologies—but from the margins, allowing God to sovereignly work in any given culture.

Many skeptics assume, as in John Lennon's imagined utopia, that religion has a monopoly on grand metanarratives that assault our sensibilities and devastate mankind. But there are other power structures dominating the philosophical and linguistic landscape of our culture.

When I was in South Africa, our ministry group was invited into the public schools to tell them about Jesus and talk to them about the AIDS epidemic that is killing 40% of their male population. Now, right away, if you are a skeptic, let's face it— this news makes you seethe. Christians have no right to talk about faith and AIDS in public schools with these poor unassuming kids. Right?

Let's get the censorship dogma on the table: "Separation of Church and State." Isn't that the sermon preached to us on a consistent basis? Isn't that just a convenient way of keeping some voices out of the marketplace while allowing others in?

I was also invited to speak about faith in Russian schools soon after the Berlin Wall came down. What amazed me in both situations was that the students and principals asked us the same question: "How often do you speak in the schools in your country?" When I informed them that such proselytizing is illegal in my country, both cultures were shocked and asked the inevitable: "Don't you live in a free country?" I guess that all depends on how one defines "freedom."

I recently read an interesting article in our local alternative newspaper, the *Seattle Weekly*. The column was entitled, "The Plot to Kill Darwin: How Seattle's Discovery Institute Orchestrated a Plan to Take Down Evolution—And Almost Succeeded." It was the usual lobbying against the philosophical concept of "Intelligent Design," a model that challenges Darwinian evolution. The article indicated that the scientific establishment had billions of dollars at their disposal, while the Institute barely has a four million dollar budget annually. Certainly a "David and Goliath" type situation, and certainly a battle between a marginalized view and the dominant view of the host culture.

So why don't skeptics and deconstructionists apply the hermeneutic of suspicion to our own culture's dominant stories? Well, scientific materialists not only tend to assume they are right, they also assume the reasonably moral high ground. And they make these leaps of faith based on a set of presuppositions and hermeneutical, *a priori* assumptions. And from this standpoint, all must pass by the gate of materialistic truth to be real. Nothing exists outside the material world, because we haven't experienced it, nor have we been able to rationalize it in our own very small brains. Right? Isn't that a pretty closed system of thinking?

Yes, Robert Langdon is right. "A newly emerging power will take over the existing symbols and degrade them over time in an attempt to erase their meaning."[19] Scientific rationalism comes equipped with its own dogma, its own set of gate-keeping rules. The *Seattle Weekly* article goes on to describe some of those rules, such as the need for "peer reviews" before "legitimate" researchers can be accepted into the club. All of the Intelligent Design proponents have written extensively on the subject, but they aren't accepted into the Priory of Science because they do not believe in the presuppositions of the club's founders. It is, by definition, impossible for their research to be academically reviewed; therefore, Intelligent Design must remain wholly outside the Academy.

The article also notes that the executive director of the Institute is a "Fundamentalist Christian"—a play of the *ad hominem* trump card that automatically squelches (and wins) the debate. Apparently, only those who discount belief in God are able to be objective, and have no temptation to be dominated by cultural metanarratives.

Yes, a newly emerging power has arisen, and the "rotting corpse of Christianity"[20] has been exorcised and successfully set in the margins—made irrelevant by the new power's propaganda machine. Ooh, a new conspiracy! Maybe even a new book! Of course, only loonies would believe in such scandalous conspiracy theories. Only the power-mongers' conspiracies can be credible, because they debunk what's already discredited. Wouldn't that be a little bit like Ben Roethlisberger dissing Terry Bradshaw?

Actually, I for one am excited about Christianity's dying power base. I continue to pray for the demise of secular Christendom. Then, from the margins, Christianity will shine, as it gets back to its core story—free from the reins of power, yet empowered by those who love God and love others, those not afraid to speak the truth in love because they are no longer chasing the carrots that motivate the world.

We live in a messed-up culture with a secular gospel that tends toward power instead of truth—that fosters and promotes misunderstanding so that it may conquer, that values self-preservation to the exclusion of all else. But only the flower that dies can go to seed and grow anew. "Whoever loses his life will preserve it."[21]

> **Da Vinci had always been an awkward subject. *Misunderstanding breeds mistrust,* Langdon thought.**

For Further Investigation
The Da Vinci Code, Chapters 5 through 9

Dig a Little Deeper

➤ Presuming God's existence, in what ways have you mistrusted God, instead seeking to be personally in control?

➤ What are some common methods we use to individually seek after power?

➤ How and why do you think the Church has often been at the forefront of tyranny?

➤ How do you think the dominant culture's values, both historically and presently, have shaped the Church's presentation of the Gospel?

➤ What do you think are the current dominant cultural values and ideals?

➤ How can you embrace those values and still live a spiritually rewarding life?

Draw Your Own Conclusions

➤ Church History:

- *Church History In Plain Language*, Updated 2nd Edition, by Bruce L. Shelley.

➤ Nietzsche and the Will to Power:

- *The Will to Power*, by Friedrich Nietzsche.
- http://plato.stanford.edu/entries/nietzsche/

➤ Deconstructionism:

- http://en.wikipedia.org/wiki/Deconstructionism

➤ On the "Hegelian Dialectic":

- marxists.org/reference/subject/philosophy/works/it/croce.htm

➤ Christ and the Problem of Temptation:

- Chapters 6–8 of Paul's letter to the Romans lays out the problem of human desires conflicting with what we know to be right—and proposes the spiritual solution. Hebrews 4 describes where Jesus stood with relation to temptation and sin.

Powerful Motivators

Mike Gunn, Lead Investigator

I played twelve years of football and had the really strange idea that I was one day going to play in the NFL, even play in the Super Bowl. I suppose many kids grow up with that kind of dream tucked away in the recesses of their minds, but I actually believed it and did everything in my power to try to make it happen—before I was brought back to earth and reality with a number of injuries and the ensuing toll they took on my body.

Motivation is one of the most important things in the world of sports, and I was an athlete who was best motivated by fear. Right before big games, my coaches would often threaten me with losing my starting spot in order to watch me take it out on the poor sap in front of me. After all, football revels in that type of barbarism, which makes it the ultimate machismo sport.

If there ever were evidence for social biology's major tenets, it would have to exist in football. I certainly began playing the game for the fun of it, but as I got into college and drew near to my dream of doing it for a living, it became all the more appealing—not because I would play only for money, but because I was so close to making money, big money, playing a kids' game and loving every minute of it. As I got closer to "The Show," as we often referred to the NFL, and as I talked with friends who had

33

"made it," I began to realize that the pay was the only thing motivating some of us to play. Some were even playing in spite of injuries that would come back to haunt them sooner than later.

Dan Brown is right in his assessment that money and power have often been the carrot dangling in front of some of the most heinous acts in human history. On a simpler level, they can steal the love and life right out of the reason you started enjoying something in the first place. They can become an end in themselves rather than the reward.

But Bishop Aringarosa merely remarks that faith and money are both powerful motivators, as if they are on an equal plane with one another. By contrast, I suggest that they are actually mutually exclusive motivators. Those who are truly motivated by money would be so motivated regardless of issues related to faith; those who are truly motivated by faith would be so motivated regardless of circumstance:

> Through glory and dishonor, bad report and good report; genuine, yet regarded as impostors; known, yet regarded as unknown; dying, and yet we live on; beaten, and yet not killed; sorrowful, yet always rejoicing; poor, yet making many rich; having nothing, and yet possessing everything.[1]

Yet the love of money can shove faith right out of the picture.

Meanwhile, Back in the Audi...

As Silas arrives at Saint-Sulpice, we come to understand the connections between Aringarosa, "the Teacher," and the albino monk. We begin to understand how tenuous and self-serving is the trust between the three of them—and we get some sense of how disastrous that misplaced trust will become for them all.

Back in the john at the Louvre, Langdon also finds that Agent Sophie Neveu is demanding a boatload of trust. Sure, she's got a head for figures, and so does he—particularly the kind with burgundy hair and olive-green eyes. But her claims about Bezu

Fache and Saunière's murder are so far-fetched... Still, she's got that photo of Saunière's full, original message, plus the bombshell that the dead guy is her grandpa. And then she forces the issue by tossing the micro-GPS unit out the window and into the street. Innocent or not, appearances will be pretty damning—and the chase is on. Aringarosa's power play has set the dominos to falling.

In our previous chapter, we discussed the motivating—even intoxicating—influence of power, and how the human heart, left unchecked, disintegrates in the crucible of absolute power. In this chapter we will discuss power's very close cousin, money—or better yet, the greed that motivates us to do most anything for it.

We too often assume that the wealthy are corrupt while the poor are innocent and pure. Of course, this view is usually held by people like me who have no money. But in reality, I have known some of the most gracious and generous wealthy people; I have also met greedy and self-centered poor people. And, of course, the reverse is also true. But while money is most certainly a powerful motivator, and can most certainly corrupt, it does so because of our greedy desire to have more—not because money is a problem in and of itself.

The Bible is often misquoted here as indicating that money is the root of all evil; but it actually says that "the love of money is a root of all kinds of evil,"[2] which is another way of saying that the problem lies within ourselves and not with the money. Jesus also said, "No one can serve two masters. Either he will hate the one and love the other, or he will be devoted to the one and despise the other. You cannot serve both God and Money."[3]

A Problem of Hearts, not Wallets or Systems

So the issue once again resides in our hearts. But cultural watchdogs like Michael Moore seem to want to blame large wealthy institutions instead of seeing that the problem lies with the individuals who make up the system—as well as, perhaps, the individuals who attack the system.

On the flip side, conservatives often deny the reality of evil systems when their Bibles are quite clear that systems themselves may often be the agency of evil (see, for instance, Ephesians 6:12–20). As a consequence, hardly any progress is made between social liberals and social conservatives because both groups fail to understand that a new system is not the answer to the problem—only new hearts can curb millennia of human greed.

The assumption in some circles is that civilization itself is evil, and everyone whom civilizations oppress is innocent. The French Romantic philosopher Rousseau popularized the notion of the "noble savage," an unfortunate caricature that remains with us today. In short, the concept of the wholly innocent native is a naïve fantasy that even *The Lord of the Flies* couldn't deconstruct.

One of my favorite movies is *The Gods Must Be Crazy*, a 1980 South African film (yes, South African—even though it was passed off as a Botswanan film due to strict embargoes against apartheid). It tells the humorous tale of N!xau, a Kalahari bushman who discovers a Coke bottle thrown out of a plane (no doubt by a right-wing Christian Republican Exxon employee, right?) and believes it is a gift from the gods. The problem begins when N!xau brings the bottle back to his otherwise peaceful village, transforming it into a literally bush-league WWF Smack-Down because of everyone's burning desire to own the bottle—which gets misused in myriad ways by the tribesmen.

Now, the movie is a great example of how technology can destroy a culture, and even how contextualization of a message is as important as the message itself. But for our purposes here, it clearly depicts the heart of man. Though anthropologists may posit that perfect indigenous cultures exist, and that we westerners, corrupted by technology and capitalism, can learn from their supposed innocence, this movie depicts the reality of man's true nature when adversity and temptation come upon us.

Once again, neither the Coke bottle itself, technological corruption, issues of possession, nor distinctions based on ownership are the problem—at the core of the destructive dynamic are greed, pride, and desire for power. Anthropological or romantic wishful thinking about man's innocence is simply warped. Human hearts give traction to oppressive circumstantial responses.

Those Darn Christians?

In our particular situation in *The Da Vinci Code*, Aringarosa—the nominally Catholic Opus Dei bishop and co-conspirator with the Teacher—has negotiated to exchange vast quantities of Vatican bearer bonds for possession of the Grail. The Teacher gets the loot, and Aringarosa gets... well, whatever mega-powerful thing the Holy Grail really is. The first step is to silence the four top members of the Brotherhood of the Priory of Sion, the secret society formed to protect the Grail from getting into the wrong hands.

Now, this is an interesting part of this story. We learn that the Priory of Sion intends to ultimately reveal the "powerful secret"[4] of the Grail. (This is a speculation, by the way, which is debunked later in the book. The Priory actually has no real plans for revealing the truth, just for protecting it—which is pretty weird, if you ask me. What good is truth if you hide it under a bushel, so to speak? Better to light a candle than to stumble and curse the darkness, as they say.)

Aringarosa is a caricature of the greedy and ignorant religious zealot, protecting an impotent mythology and an appearance of power—even though he is actually being used as a puppet by the megalomaniac skeptic Teacher, Leigh Teabing, who wants to get his greedy hands on the proof of the Grail legend to manipulate its power to his own nefarious ends.

Teabing actually wants Jacques Saunière and his *senechaux* dead because he feels they've betrayed the Priory's

Aquarian pact to reveal the truth of the Grail. He merely uses Bishop Aringarosa and Silas to get the Sangreal documents for his own selfish reasons, and only cares about the Vatican bonds as a means of blackmailing or smearing the Church. Aringarosa, for his part, cares about the Grail only to the extent that its possession will be the bargaining chip he needs to restore his status with the Vatican. He appears not to care one bit about what it actually is, or about its ultimate fate.

Caricatures like Aringarosa have long been a popular motif in movies and books, which often depict those who are religious in a less than flattering light—precisely the kind of propagandist campaign against which Robert Langdon rails in a later chapter. With such caricatures, Dan Brown does to Christianity what he points out was done to other myths by ancient Christians. Such characterizations unfairly depict the religious as greedy, inept, superstitious, and power-mongering, while enlightened souls like Langdon and Sophie virtuously search for truth, freedom and the American way! Brown's sap of a bishop represents an archetype that's been around at least since Chaucer, one now used by western materialism to degrade and deconstruct the dominant worldview.

"Misunderstanding breeds distrust,"[5] thinks Langdon. Oh, so right he is; misunderstanding breeds fear, which breeds disunity, which results in mistrust. And many of us are well-educated in misunderstanding and the resultant fear. Just as I was motivated by the fear of losing my position as a starter on the football team, many of us are motivated by the fear that we might lose our influence in the culture. How easily are we bought by the culture's lure of success? It pains me to acknowledge that Christians have so often exchanged the pure water of God's "river of life"[6] for the modern allure of power and money. It would behoove us all to consider the advice of St. Francis of Assisi, written over eight hundred years ago: "Oh Divine Master, grant that I may not so much seek to be consoled as to console, to be

understood as to understand, to be loved as to love."[7]

But many of us are not only familiar with being misunderstood. Many of us are also quite adept at promoting misunderstanding. Isn't that what Langdon is doing? He and Teabing both set up a straw-man Christianity in order to easily and disingenuously knock it down, simply to elevate the competing message to a higher, or at least equal, place.

But seriously—if individuals within the Catholic Church can be so easily motivated by money, can't we assume that Dan Brown is also motivated by money? Can't we also assume that his publisher, Doubleday, might be motivated by the same cash enterprise?

How about the dogmatic authority of our western culture, the scientific community? Aren't they motivated by fellowships and grants? Isn't it possible that they, too, might slant or even hide the truth for the sake of fame and grant money? How many times will cold fusion be discovered? How many scientists will make bogus claims to cloning firsts? One author put it this way:

> Fraud is what scientists tell each other is fraud. This raises the question, why are certain things called fraud and others not? My general answer is that the social definition of fraud is one which is convenient to most of the powerful groups associated with science. This includes government and corporate sponsors of scientific research, and the scientific community itself, especially scientific elites.[8]

Those who live in white linen houses shouldn't sling mud too freely. There's more than enough to go around, once you get started.

Jesus' Passion Finally Reaps Big Bucks

Can we assume that Hollywood is also motivated by money? After all, even Jesus has become quite popular in Hollywood after Mel Gibson raked in $300-plus million by filming *The Passion of the Christ* in Aramaic. We make what sells, and Jesus seems to be selling right now. Disney even banked on the Jesus trend and took a chance on financing and distributing the big-screen version of C. S. Lewis' *The Chronicles of Narnia: The Lion, the Witch and the Wardrobe*. Even before the DVD was released in April 2006, and prior to its tour of China, it had done pretty well at the boxoffice, becoming Disney's highest-grossing live-action film. So, yeah, money motivates.

But Gibson's *Passion* depicted a different type of motivation, and presented quite a different Jesus from that of *The Da Vinci Code*. This Jesus was motivated by something greater than money, power, or sex. He was motivated by faith in His Father.

Certainly, unrestrained faith married to poor dogma and the desire for money can, and usually will, end in disaster—as with the westernized Christian theology of the self, which demands to score "a word of blessing"[9] or an "enlarged territory"[10] from God while denying God His own right of command. But the Jesus of *The Passion* presents such a different God from the one we construct here on earth. His motivation and His passion are found elsewhere. His values aren't the values of this fallen world.

The Passion startled Hollywood and the arts community because the project seemed like professional suicide for Gibson—and quite possibly, for his acting career, it may have been. But he took a chance with his own money because he believed in the project, and the rest is history. I really don't think he was motivated at all by the potential payday, since there was hardly anyone alive who thought that he wasn't throwing his money down a rathole. Just like Dan Brown, Gibson believed in his project. Jesus' bigger-than-life story tells and sells well and is one that still intrigues people after two thousand years of telling and retelling. Even Roger Ebert, an avowed agnostic, wrote the following respectful commentary with regard to Mel Gibson's *Passion*:

It is a film about an idea. An idea that it is necessary to fully comprehend the Passion if Christianity is to make any sense. Gibson has communicated his idea with a single minded urgency. Many will disagree. Some will agree, but be horrified by the graphic treatment. I myself am no longer religious in the sense that a long-ago altar boy thought he should be, but I can respond to the power of belief whether I agree or not, and when I find it in a film, I must respect it.[11]

This is a story that doesn't seem to go away, even after stories like Dan Brown's appear to be so damaging. Brown's isn't the first epic story to depict an alternative version of the faith. Writers like Voltaire, Russell, Camus, Sartre, and Paine have all written eloquently over the years, trying their best to dismantle the story of Jesus' death and suffering, but their efforts haven't had much effect. The skeptic might reply that millions of people are merely ignorant, looking to religion because of their fear of the unknown; but such dismissive thinking is naïve and simplistic. Disdain can effectively end arguments, but it can't win them.

Gibson's movie definitely made him richer, but there was more to the film's success than great boxoffice numbers. *The Passion* is a tragic story told well—a compelling story about a man who claimed to be God and took on His culture's power structures without an army or a desire for earthly power. His story is about a king from a strange land claiming authority over the current kingdom's power base and being executed as a result.

This is the story that is left out in the *Code*. Jesus was not motivated by power or by money, and He calls His followers to the same motivation as His: love. It is an ethic so different from that of this world, which can only see power, money, and other materialistic pursuits as authentic motivators.

Naturally, a caricature like Aringarosa would think of money and faith as co-equal motivators because he can't see the motivation of Jesus' love—because Dan Brown's narrative has written it out of existence. And if there is no loving God, then why should any of us be motivated by anything other than money and the will to power?

As long as we try to rid the world of God and religion, we will struggle to find a worthwhile reason to do anything at all. No wonder books like this take root in a culture that's bored with tired earthly religions that don't motivate, that don't deliver the earthly promises the preacher said they would. As long as we chase a god who gives us what we want, we will always be substituting power and money for the joy we were meant to experience in Christ. The chase is a dead-end run toward the mystery religions of the ancient past, a desperate trail in pursuit of the transcendent.

Beyond Boxoffice, Beyond Power

Love is simply a more worthwhile motivator than money. The Puritan preacher Henry Scougal put it best when he wrote in the eighteenth century, "The worth and excellency of a soul is measured by the object of its love."[12] Langdon might be right when he looks into the Church from the outside, but he is wrong about Jesus, who went to the cross for no other motivation than love. It might make sense to die for someone who loved Him, but according to Paul's letter to the Romans, "God demonstrates his own love for us in this: While we were still sinners, Christ died for us."[13]

What we love is what motivates us. The object of our affections is ultimately what motivates anything we do, and the problem is that the object for which we settle is too often second-rate. If we love money, we will be motivated by money, but that love will never fully satisfy. And this is true of the churched as well as the unchurched. Our culture almost wholly buys into the materialist presupposition that there is really nothing outside of the physical, phenomenal world—so the only hope we have to be happy is to get all that we can. Over fifty years ago, C. S. Lewis wrote,

> We are half-hearted creatures, fooling about with drink
> and sex and ambition when infinite joy is offered us, like
> an ignorant child who wants to go making mud pies in a
> slum because he cannot imagine what is meant by the
> offer of a holiday at the sea. We are far too easily
> pleased.[14]

Yes, we are far too happy to chase the American dream instead of the God who created us to find our joy in Him. When we don't love as Christ taught us, we become mere clanging symbols.

French mathematician, Christian, and philosopher Blaise Pascal said, "Men never do evil so completely and cheerfully as when they do it from a religious conviction."[15] Though I agree in principle, and though Pascal's position appears to side with Aringarosa's thoughts that opened this chapter, I would say that Pascal is particularly right when religious convictions are tied up in notions of temporal power—as is the case with the fictional Opus Dei bishop—rather than devotion to the teachings of Christ Himself.

"For me to live is Christ, and to die is gain,"[16] wrote the Apostle Paul. A call to martyrdom? Perhaps. But to die for what? Money? Power? Some vague future reward? No. Paul, like Jesus, was willing to die for the same thing for which he lived. Love.

"And now these three remain: faith, hope and love. But the greatest of these is love. Follow the way of love."[17] If we could begin to understand the depths of Paul's words, we would no longer be satisfied with "making mud pies in a slum."

> Sister Sandrine nodded.
> "You obviously have
> powerful friends." You
> have no idea, Silas thought.

For Further Investigation
The Da Vinci Code, Chapters 10 through 19

Dig a Little Deeper

➤ What motivates you to keep living?

➤ How are Bishop Aringarosa's thoughts quoted at the head of this chapter true? Are money and faith powerful motivators for you? Which is more powerful?

➤ What presuppositions are you starting to recognize in Aringarosa's thinking? How much of Dan Brown do you think is in there? How much of that is realistic for a priest?

➤ Is faith itself a powerful motivator, or does the object of our faith affect our motivation?

➤ What do you think about Henry Scougal's thoughts, a couple of pages back? How much thought do we give to the object of whatever faith we have?

Draw Your Own Conclusions

➤ Rousseau's Ideas of the Noble Savage:
  • *Rousseau: The Discourses and Other Early Political Writings*, by Jean-Jacques Rousseau. Edited by Victor Gourevitch, Raymond Geuss, and Quentin Skinner.

➤ Hermeticism and *The Da Vinci Code*:
  • http://altreligion.about.com/library/texts/bl_differentdvc.htm Another interesting conspiracy theory about Leonardo's art.

➤ Jesus' Ideas on Earthly Treasures:
  • Matthew 6:19–24.

➤ Biblical Faith as Motivation:
  • Genesis 22:1–18 tells the story of Abraham and his son Isaac. New Testament writers call the type of faith demonstrated by Abraham in this story "saving faith."

44

Part Two:
Everyone Loves a Conspiracy

> Sophie stamped her foot.
> "I don't like secrets!"
> "Princess," Saunière smiled.
> "Life is filled with
> secrets. You can't learn
> them all at once."

A Gnomon

Mike Gunn, Lead Investigator

Many moons ago when I was a kid, probably about five or six years old, there was a murder in my neighborhood.

Now this wasn't an everyday occurrence, so it caused quite the stir—especially when the police couldn't find the guy who did it, and some even suspected it was a serial killing. The neighborhood was in fear, and investigators were going door to door to get statements about the girl who was killed, and trying to find anyone who saw any "suspicious" activity leading up to the murder.

Tension ran thick, but a couple of my buddies and I were determined to crack the case, to find evidence of this murderer's dirty little secrets. It became our mission, our search for the "smoking gun!" Of course, we couldn't drive, so our search was carried out in the context of our small neighborhood. Since we had no idea what we were doing and had to be in by 5:00 PM, we didn't have as much time as the real cops; but we were determined to uncover the "truth." This was going to be our *Mona Lisa!* The thrill of it was in the hunt, and the chance that secret knowledge was really out there—and we were going to be the ones who "discovered" it. We wanted to do something adventurous.

One day, we were walking in the woods "looking for evidence" and came upon an old broken down shack. We became convinced that this must be where the "bad guy" was hanging out, so we went inside with all of the fear and exhilaration that comes from adventure—even when every bit of that adventure is created in the mind of a six-year-old. As we walked in and began to look around, we couldn't believe our eyes. There it was in front of us—the hidden clue that would crack the case. There were gun shell boxes and gun shells on the floor of the cabin! We had almost literally found the smoking gun. We were elated, and couldn't wait to tell our parents.

Our joy soon turned to melancholy, though, because in reality all we discovered was the cabin of a neighbor who went up there to shoot skeet. Details, details. Who cares that the murder wasn't done with a shotgun? We were still convinced that we were on to something, and feel to this day that the police just couldn't handle the truth!

The Need to Know

Aren't we all looking for the smoking gun, or the set of truths that will set us free? Aren't we a people just dying to be "in the know"? Our tabloids and rabid media are sure counting on it! Yes, we are vultures looking for that elusive knowledge that will shoot us to fame, or ease our pain. Life is indeed full of secrets, as Jacques Saunière told his granddaughter—and we all want to know them, at once! It is one of the fundamental rights of the western world.

As I write this chapter, Dick Cheney has given his critics, uh, plenty of ammunition by mistakenly shooting his friend during a quail hunt in Texas. Brilliant! This guy is leading our nation? But the media frenzy really hasn't been about the shooting (after all, is that even a crime anymore?). The controversy is about the four-day "cover up," during which the press wasn't briefed so that the Vice President could get his story right. Yes, the media were upset because Dick didn't get on his cell phone while attending to his wounded friend in the field and provide a full disclosure about what happened—replete with pictures and interviews with his bleeding friend and others on the hunt. We don't merely want a statement, we want it from Dick *and* George, and we want it yesterday. We have earned that right!

We are almost crazed by our demand to know the whole truth and nothing but the truth—and this from a nation that has little or no desire to actually tell the truth. We expect everyone else to do what we don't feel the need to do. I sort of agree with the title of Robert Fulghum's *All I Really Need to Know I Learned in Kindergarten*—in the sense that half of what America wants to know is spurious at best.

Fifty years ago, books like *The Da Vinci Code* would have been discarded by scholars—along with books like Gary Allen's *None Dare Call it Conspiracy*—as a bunch of nonsense. Now our supposed scholars are actually writing this type of story, passing it off as "fact" because checkout-line "inquiring minds want to know." And in the face of such pseudo-scholarly quackery, figuring out the truth and the little secrets of life can be quite a task.

Figuring out what secrets we actually need to know can be even more daunting. Discernment is a necessary, if dying, discipline in an information age that has more opinions than people, and more useless garbage than Mexico City's refuse heap! Where's the call to listen wisely? Even Jesus, when preaching in parables, called those with discerning ears to listen carefully to the message He was teaching—most likely because He was trying to keep the nut jobs away. I guess it didn't work? Discernment might well be the next lost art.

Meanwhile, Back in the Louvre...

While Sophie and Langdon head for the exits, we get a lesson on Fibonacci, the pentacle, the Divine Proportion—and anagrams. The two realize that Saunière's dying message was about the *Mona Lisa*—and also, Langdon suspects, about the apocryphal Priory of Sion. Foregoing a prompt escape, they return to the gallery, where Langdon confirms his own suspicions and Sophie's most nauseating fears. And they find Saunière's next clue scrawled across the glass of the *Mona Lisa*'s frame.

In Saint-Sulpice, Silas follows a brass line across the floor of the church—an embedded strip that runs to the base of an obelisk, up its side and to the very top. The Rose Line was "a gnomon, Silas had been told, a pagan astronomical device" used as the basis for terrestrial navigation—a device connected to the Compass Rose, and "guiding souls in the proper direction."[1] The Rose Line brings Silas to what he thinks will be the end of his murderous but righteous quest.

Aringarosa's flight lands in Rome—and, mystifyingly, the Bishop soon expects to be "in possession of something that would make him the most powerful man in Christendom."[2]

Hmm... As it turns out, Silas, Aringarosa, Sophie, and Langdon are all about the get the same lesson as Bezu Fache. They are all about to set out on a quest to chase down and arrest a bar of soap.

Like that nutty quintet, we have also lost our way! We have become lazy listeners and our compasses are out of whack. So often, we follow gnomons of the sort that Silas runs into at Saint-Sulpice—ones that ultimately prove to be dead ends, as with the thrilling secret-cabin discovery that proved so empty for me and my boys.

Very Telling Stories

Our choice of compass is vital, especially when it comes to deciphering information that doubles or triples in volume every year. Anyone can write a book claiming that the Christ story is a rip-off of mystery religions like Mithraism, but is the claim true? Have we any means of verifying or repudiating these alternate stories? Are there any ancient manuscripts that verify Leigh Teabing's claim that Mithras died, was placed in a cave, and was resurrected to new life after three days?[3] The only documents that actually support these claims come from biased "researchers" like Timothy Freke and Peter Gandy,[4] who merely quote from other contemporary writers who tell the same story. The same might be said for the authors of *Holy Blood, Holy Grail*. If the origin of Christianity is so suspect, why trade it in for an alternate myth even more dubious?

Is Dan Brown's narrative soliloquy about compasses even accurate? How about his claim that "long before the establishment of Greenwich as the prime meridian, the zero longitude of the entire world passed directly through Paris, and through the church of Saint-Sulpice"?[5] Is Brown's compass right, or is he smoking crack? What if Dan is quoting from guys who are wrong? What if he isn't even interested in being right? What if he knows darn well that the gnomon in Saint-Sulpice doesn't align with the Rose Line that runs through the Louvre—or Rosslyn Chapel, for that matter? What if the web of connections is all just symbolic, and not real at all?

Life is certainly filled with much mystery and many

different secrets, and we most certainly can't "learn them at once." But can we learn them at all if our interpretive compass is askew? As an avid climber I have learned that lesson myriad times.

About ten years ago, I was leading a team of nine guys up the side of Mount Hood in Oregon. I had a bunch of newbies in the group, so I chose a particularly easy route for their first alpine ascent. What began as a virtual stroll in the park, though, almost ended in disaster.

We began the climb at 2:00 AM in order to ensure hard ice on the mountain—so our crampons could sink well into the glacier, and so that we would be protected from loose rocks and potential avalanche danger. We set out from lower altitudes in rain, but the weather was still safe enough to carry on. As we reached higher altitudes, the rain turned to sleet, and then to snow; by the time we came to the most difficult and dangerous part of the climb, we were in a whiteout and unable to see more than twenty feet. While some of my very inexperienced team wanted to carry on, I could see that others were not doing well. I decided that we would turn around and head back home.

On Mount Hood, that would normally be easy, but in whiteout conditions the retreat turned ugly. It would have been no trouble at all to stray off course, get lost, or even stumble off the side of the mountain to a most certain death. I'm trained in compass use, of course, but successfully navigating through a whiteout takes a certain expertise and grace—especially much of the latter. I had earlier back-shot an azimuth and followed those settings as well as watching my altimeter, while at the same time checking my topo maps (simply following altitude contour lines since there was no topography for visual confirmation) to determine my approximate place on the mountain.

I followed my readings religiously while sight-reading what was an arm's length in front of me, and incredibly I dead-headed our party right on the top of a ski lift that helped guide us down to safety. We could have passed a few yards to the wrong side of the pylon without even knowing it. That was one literally incredible day. In spite of chaotic and often confusing conditions, we were brought to safety by trusting a $20 compass, a $5 map, and a $150 altimeter.

The compass we used mattered. It was what helped steer us in the right direction, in spite of not being able to see very well with our eyes.

Bad Compasses

The compass that leads us through the quagmire of information that exists in this world is our set of presuppositions. We all would love access to secret knowledge, but in reality, whatever knowledge we acquire comes to us as a result of the suppositions through which we filter symbols, data, or text. Langdon's filters are predominantly materialist and gnostic.

Gnosticism is a historical term encompassing various religious sects and schools of knowledge. Among other doctrines of gnostic sects is a dualistic understanding of the spirit and the flesh; the pursuit of hidden or secret knowledge (gnosis) can ostensibly make us wiser or spiritually enlightened. The movement (if one could even call it that) is so variegated, unfocused, and antiquated, however, that a thorough understanding of it is impossible. Nonetheless, we do know that gnosticism was not an exclusively Christian movement, nor did it originate within Christianity.

In recent years, a number of studies (even pseudo-studies) have been published concerning gnosticism and its place in Christian history. The impetus was a cache of gnostic literature discovered by Muhammad Ali[6] in a cave near Nag Hammadi, Egypt in 1945. The gnostic philosophy was plain to see amongst the alternate "lost" gospels found at Nag Hammadi—such as the Gospel of Thomas and the Gospel of Philip.[7]

Now, if truth is to be found in secrets (*gnosis*, again), then only the initiated or specially gifted can be in the know. And maybe this is true in some way. Maybe without revelation it is impossible to know who God is, and what He requires of us. The real issue here is, "What compass are we willing to use to interpret the world around us?"

Consider how Langdon solves the anagram Saunière left regarding the *Mona Lisa*: *O, Draconian devil! Oh, lame saint!* Inspired by the scrambled Fibonacci sequence (oddly missing the numeral 0), he correctly interprets the curator's message to really mean, "Leonardo da Vinci! The Mona Lisa!"[8] Now, he could have as easily interpreted it, *"Oh man! Anti-social and evildoer!"* which I think is more biblical; or even *"Oh! Innovate, cordial ladies' man!"* which appears more appropriate for Langdon's character. But he correctly interprets the message because he knows who wrote it. If he didn't know Saunière, he wouldn't have a clue. But his knowledge is his compass, and in this case it works.

But the incident illustrates the fact that Langdon is constantly interpreting symbols in ways that (not surprisingly) dovetail with the preconceived notions of the alternate story he promulgates in his book in progress. Consider his analysis of the Divine Proportion, for instance. Because the pentacle is "the *ultimate* expression of the Divine Proportion," it follows that it has always been "associated with the goddess and the sacred feminine."[9] Really? In the first place, Langdon's assessment of the pentacle's ultimacy is entirely subjective; and in the second place, the presumption hardly dictates that the symbol be read as feminine. But that's what Langdon's book is about; we shouldn't be too surprised. As he tells his publisher, he and Leigh Teabing, among others, are "believers."[10] We also shouldn't be too surprised that believers of other stripes find affirmation of the sacred Father in the Divine Proportion. Symbols tend to be mirrors that reflect compasses.

So Langdon's and Sophie's adventure begins with a biased

compass, as would mine or anyone else's; but Langdon's bias soon yields to outright misinformation, and that leads to further misinformation. In our next chapter, for instance, we will see that Langdon bases his guesses regarding the *Mona Lisa* on an intriguing hypothesis that is, nonetheless, misinformed. Perhaps the "courtesan with a gauze veil,"[11] to use David Shugarts' description, gets the last grin after all.

Course Correction Required

This is what often passes for knowledge in the age of information—oracles that are secret for good reason, knowledge that only the initiated can perceive and appreciate. As Langdon and Sophie move through the pages of this book solving one secret code after another, we must begin to wonder if they aren't chasing a shadow cast by a warped gnomon. Ultimately, Dan Brown appears to lead his heroes on a wild, misinformed goose chase—only to let his readers down with a clunker of a finish. As Dan Burstein remarks, Leigh Teabing's story

> falls apart. His motives for setting this whole plot in motion prove irrational and implausible. The Priory of Sion appears to wimp out on the legacy that has occupied much of this book. And the fearsome Opus Dei seems humbled and unlikely to launch new conspiracies and intrigues. The strong allusion that is made to the ultimate resting place of the Holy Grail seems silly to many readers.[12]

Can Dan Brown possibly be unaware how many times Sophie, Langdon, and the Teacher are just flat out wrong? Or is Brown dropping just enough "clues in his art"[13] to suggest that he doesn't want us to merely discover what is obvious in his text— that he quite possibly wants us to dig a bit deeper and exercise our atrophied minds enough to open them and wade through the mass amounts of conflicting stories that dominate the airwaves? If this is true, we can, with Dan Brown, cry out, WAKE UP!

The Church can certainly use this exhortation, and begin to train the ears of those who have become "dull of hearing,"[14] as one biblical writer says, to learn to listen to the world's pulpits with a better compass than personal likes and dislikes. How many of us are closed to the truth because we are following false, culturally-constructed gnomons? How many of us can honestly say that we are on a quest for knowledge and truth? And how many Christians can honestly declare that they are actively purifying truth claims through the crucible of the Gospel?

And how about unbelievers and skeptics? How many are truly exercising their minds by examining their own presuppositions? Or are they equally adopting a closed-minded, predetermined lens through which to see the world? Might it even be that a quest for secret, hidden knowledge is a smokescreen for an emptiness that can only be filled with the latest scoop?

Many skeptics, for instance, claim that all religions are the same. This is reflective of a seemingly reasonable, rational bias in that direction; but such a position can only be taken as factual if one presumes that any given religion is just as useful or senseless as the next. Others believe that religion is the source of mankind's problems, and never or rarely a cure; but once again, the facts cannot matter in such thinking. University of Washington professor of Sociology and Comparative Religion Rodney Stark writes,

> Religion has played a leading role in directing the course of history. Unfortunately in today's intellectual environment, that simple and obvious statement is widely regarded as both unfortunate and false. Proponents of this revisionist claim overcome its inherent contradiction by assigning many of the most unfortunate aspects of history to religious causes, while flatly denying even the most obvious and overwhelming evidence that religion was the basis of the 'good' things that have come to pass.[15]

Such thinking, Stark goes on to point out, leads to such ludicrous ideas as the notion that "Christianity played no significant role in sustaining the abolitionist cause, but was instead a major factor in justifying slavery."[16]

It is easy to get on a bandwagon of popular beliefs and hidden secrets, only to find that what we believe is false. Books like *The Da Vinci Code* and *The Prayer of Jabez* are written because the climate is ripe. I just hope we all read, watch, and listen with thinking minds and well-researched opinions. Books like professor Stark's *For the Glory of God* are admirable in that they attempt to examine the truth even when the truth hurts. Honest truth-seekers, Christian or skeptic, must be willing to admit when their worldviews come up short.

The Search for the Grail and Monty Python

Way back in 1975 when Dan Brown was playing Little League baseball, there were other, more critically-acclaimed men doing Grail research: John Cleese, Terry Gilliam, Terry Jones, Graham Chapman, and Michael Palin—better known to geeks as "Monty Python." Actually, in all (or partial) seriousness, Terry Jones is something of a historian, having directed a four-part History Channel series on the Crusades. (Of course, the series does have its bias, not to mention a certain comedic edge.)

Naturally, it's hard to accuse the Pythons of complete objectivity. *Monty Python and The Holy Grail* is a work of comedic and satirical art. A host of Python geeks have turned the odd British film into a cult classic, mainly because of its bold and strange sense of humor. The film surely strikes a nerve resonant with many people's experiences with the institutional church—as does *The Da Vinci Code*. But the movie is obviously a satire, and a really funny one at that. It doesn't even take itself very seriously, merely sending barbs at the Church that are well-deserved (if surely exaggerated) and comically, intelligently crafted.

While the Pythons are indeed creatively satirical, they are

also fully jaded by their own set of biases against the Church. But their piece of satire doesn't stop at attacking the Church and its many follies; it also takes its shots at the silly folk who believed in the Grail. In Python's vision, the Grail hunters were a bumbling batch of blithering idiots who honestly weren't concerned with the truth, but only with fulfilling their "divine" calling. Right away we see Arthur riding up—er, hopping up—to his first castle, where he is comically confronted by a French sentry about the fact that he isn't really riding a horse. He is galloping on foot, with a servant hitting coconut shells together to make the sound of hoofbeats. Arthur's response? "I'm not interested."[17]

Don't confuse me with the facts; I am on an important mission! Don't we all fall into that trap from time to time? Of course, the Pythons later skewer the denial of truth and reality in one of the more humorous slapstick pieces I have ever seen on film: King Arthur's sword duel with the Black Knight. After slicing off one of the Black Knight's arms, the following dialogue ensues:

> King Arthur: Now stand aside, worthy adversary.
> Black Knight: 'Tis but a scratch.
> King Arthur: A scratch? Your arm's off.
> Black Knight: No it isn't.
> King Arthur: What's that, then?
> Black Knight: [after a pause] I've had worse.
> King Arthur: You liar.
> Black Knight: Come on ya pansy.[18]

Arthur continues by cutting off the knight's remaining three limbs, and then walks away to the Black Knight's insane denial, "Okay, we'll call it a draw….Oh! Had enough, eh? Come back and take what's coming to you, you yellow bastards! Come back here and take what's coming to you! I'll bite your legs off!!"[19]

Humorous to be sure; but it's tragic when our pride demands that we obey our delusions, that we follow warped gnomons—especially when we chase "divine callings" that most often have more to do with our own desires than anything very divine.

And here we come to the two choices in front of us: Either we must accept that we all create our own gnomons, in which case the state of the world truly is "every man for himself," and it's just as silly to criticize Leigh Teabing or Saunière as it is to criticize Constantine, Silas, or Aringarosa. Or, we can choose to believe that there really is One True Rose Line, an accurate Gnomon that is greater than ourselves—one in which we can actually trust.

Those who choose the latter, and also choose to believe that Christ is that Gnomon, would do well to stay close to His Word rather than to our culturally layered, warped interpretations of that Word. That may seem impossible, but it isn't if we remain diligent in our pursuit of truth. We are given a Gnomon that unlocks some of the mystery of who God is and what He requires of us. If we refuse to become lazy in our pursuit of knowing God, we will find Him.

Much of the craziness that movies like *Monty Python and the Holy Grail* depict exists because the Church stopped following the truth of Scripture (as it always does) and chased after other less capable ideologies, namely reason and tradition. The fact remains that the "Dark Ages" of western civilization were exacerbated not by people who were reading their Bibles but by powerful institutions that forbade the Bible and forced their people to believe superstitious religiosity and conjecture.

An Empty Quest?

Dan Brown, like Monty Python, recognizes the folly of following superstition. While the Pythons use satire to uncover such silliness, Brown uses mystery and intrigue. His plot reeks of the suggestion that he doesn't believe in the Grail story or the Priory's mumbo-jumbo any more than he believes in the "historical Jesus." Langdon sums up Dan Brown's presuppositions well when he says that "every faith in the world is based on fabrication. That is the definition of *faith*." He goes on to say that "those who truly understand their faiths understand the stories are metaphorical. ... And living in that reality helps millions of people cope and be better people."[20]

We'll examine those claims more fully in a later chapter; but we may say that Dan Brown's gnomon is set. His course is directed by his presuppositions, and there isn't much that can drive him off that course. That is true of many reading these words. Whether you are a believing Christian, a Muslim, or a radical skeptic proud of your freedom from "irrationality," you are being led by your presuppositions and the environment that helped create them—and that, my friends, is an act of faith. I just hope that as you read this book you begin to get rigorously honest with yourself, and with your prejudices. Can we extricate ourselves from our prejudices and biases, or are we all doomed to continue with campaigns of propaganda?

> **Langdon chuckled. "No. Da Vinci didn't 'screw it up.' Actually, this is a little trick Da Vinci played."**

For Further Investigation
The Da Vinci Code, Chapters 20 through 27

Dig a Little Deeper

➤ What compass (set of presuppositions) do you use to make sense out of life? Is that even a relevant question?

➤ What secrets, if you could discover their truths, would you want to know, and why?

➢ Why, do you think, does God seem to remain hidden?

➢ What do you think of the Christian claim that God wants us to know Him by faith?

➢ Of what consequence is the pursuit of "knowing" God?

➢ What would change if you discovered that everything you believed about reality were untrue?

Draw Your Own Conclusions

➢ On the Council of Nicaea:

- *The First Seven Ecumenical Councils (325-787): Their History and Theology*, by Leo Donald Davis.

- *The Catholic Encyclopedia* at www.newadvent.org also provides a wealth of information on the ecumenical councils.

➢ Concerning Mithraism:

- http://www.mithraism.org/

➢ The Divine Proportion, Phi, and the Golden Ratio:

- http://en.wikipedia.org/wiki/Golden_ratio

- http://www.summum.us/philosophy/phi.shtml

➢ Arthurian Legends of the Holy Grail:

- www.timelessmyths.com/arthurian/grail.html

➢ A New Testament Definition of Faith:

- Hebrews 11:1–12:2.

> Langdon stared in astonishment. "The early Christian church 'conned' the world by waging a campaign of propaganda that demonized the sacred feminine..."

A Campaign of Propaganda

Mike Gunn, Lead Investigator

Imagine that—powerful men trying to cover up something that might incriminate them or even remove them from power! It seems as though this is what men do in one form or another. Aren't we all inclined to suppress the truth of counter-claims to make our own points seem more plausible, ourselves more intellectual, or our causes more righteous?

Now, Robert Langdon doesn't personally seem to have much at stake in the power struggle over the purported mystery of the Grail. As he and Sophie bolt from police supervision at the Louvre, secure in the knowledge that he is Bezu Fache's prime suspect in Saunière's murder, he's genuinely intent on sharing what he's learned. But the story's villains— including Silas, who finds that his murderous quest has come to a dead end at the Rose Line in Saint-Sulpice, and Aringarosa, who's about to have his prelature cut off from the Vatican—are all about suppressing or controlling such knowledge. And the Teacher, of course, to whom Langdon and Sophie are unwittingly running, expects to wholly wrest the secrets of the Grail from both the Priory and the Church to further his own puzzling and ill-defined ends.

61

Curiously, Brown's novel tantalizingly suggests that the Vatican is behind Aringarosa's chicanery. As we come to see, though, it's not! All the Vatican is preparing to do is cut its public relations losses by severing financial ties with Opus Dei. So much for conspiratorial continuity over the millennia.

But let's just grant, for a moment, that Langdon's assertion about the early Church is correct—that it really did wage a campaign of propaganda against the sacred feminine. So what? What does that ultimately prove? Isn't it possible that goddess worship, as it was practiced in the fourth century, actually needed to be suppressed? Don't all societies try to suppress things they believe are evil? Wouldn't the Teacher, even Langdon, love to suppress the Catholic Church? Aren't the practices of Opus Dei, as illustrated by Dan Brown through Silas and Aringarosa, worthy of suppression by exposure, even slanderous fictionalizations? Hmm?

Freedom and Speeches

We all cry for freedom of speech when our own voices are being quelled, but no one really advocates universal freedoms, do they? After all, voices and ideas are being silenced on a regular basis right here in the good ol' free country of America.

I was in Africa in early 2006 and went into the public schools to talk about God. They recited the Lord's Prayer, and were shocked to find out that it was illegal to do so in the United States. One student asked, "Isn't America a 'free' country?" I had to answer, "No." The situation and my response echoed a similar circumstance when I was in Russia fifteen years ago. Yes, even America sees fit to repress dangerous ideologies. Isn't that what freedom is all about?

So maybe Langdon doesn't have all the details. What if goddess worship, while benign in its precepts, was, in practice, a heinous blight that needed to be done away with, and Christianity actually did society a phenomenal favor once upon a time? What if Langdon just parrots someone else's twisted propaganda? What if one of Langdon's primary sources of information turns out to be the story's primary villain? Or am I giving too much away? And when that turns out to be the case, doesn't that tend to destroy most of Langdon's credibility?

Why should I trust a fictional Robert Langdon, a very real Dan Brown, or anyone else who presents such ancient "facts" to me? After all, if I believe, as I am told in *The Da Vinci Code*, that the Bible has been ruthlessly doctored, why shouldn't I be equally skeptical of opposing, equally biased opinions written in the same very old and superstitious time-frame? How can we know whether most of this information is a matter of speculation instead of based on "fact?"

Langdon, for instance—based on conclusions drawn from highly suspect, biased, villainous authorities—"enlightens" his students regarding Da Vinci's use of anagrams. He is convinced that the name *Mona Lisa* is a "secret" anagram really meaning AMON L'ISA, representative of the androgynous union of Egyptian fertility gods Amon and Isis.[1]

Now, that's very interesting; but I got to thinking, was *Mona Lisa* the original name that Da Vinci used for the painting? After all, wasn't he Italian? "L'isa" is French. Da Vinci must have been a grand master indeed, because only he could have known that the name that the Italians used for the painting, *La Gioconda*, would be long after transformed into *Mona Lisa* so his "code" could be revealed.

Da Vinci publicly wrote that the painting was of Lisa, the wife of a silk merchant named Francesco di Bartolemeo di Zanobi del Giaocondo.

Whew! That must make for some incredible anagrams. There must be all kinds of conspiracies hidden in that name!

Over the centuries, art historians have speculated that the subject of the *Mona Lisa* was everything from Lisa Francesco di Bartolemeo di Zanobi del Giaocondo, as Da Vinci claimed, to

Leonardo's mother (this was Freud's theory, having to do with Leonardo's Oedipal urges, I guess) to even a self-portrait confirming his alleged androgyny and homosexual tendencies. I guess when truth and reality are left to personal interpretation, anything can be true. In many ways, that's the beauty and irony of art.

My wife is an artist, and my college apartment was once graced with a painting she did when she was sixteen. A group of wannabe art critics, fresh from their "Freud and Art" class, tried to get into the head of the artist at a party we threw, and interpreted her as a moody, depressed person because of the painting's cloud patterns, the very lonely landscape probably exposing her lonely inner child. It was quite humorous knowing that my wife's painting was an exact Xerox-like duplication of a photograph she had taken—reflective of a physical reality, not at all a psychological one. So much for lame interpretations.

But the question of a painting's name is not the same as the wide-open question of its meaning. The original English name of Da Vinci's masterpiece was *Monna* (a further contraction of the contraction Madonna, from Mia Donna, "My Lady") *Lisa*, and a spelling error finally morphed the name to *Mona Lisa*. Presuming these details to be true, how plausible is Langdon's AMON L'ISA theory? But all that really doesn't matter, does it, since it might unravel such a cool conspiracy theory? Maybe the reason for *Mona Lisa*'s "knowing smile"[2] is that she had read Dan Brown's book.

How are such theories any different from the "Bible Code" nonsense that closed the twentieth century? Yet Bible Code enthusiasts are likely to be incensed at Dan Brown's heretical theories; and, interestingly, many who would buy into Dan Brown's conspiracies would mock those who buy into Bible Code conspiracies—and rightly they should! I once had a friend who was enthralled with the Bible Code's numerology and divine secrets until I informed him that chapter and verse markers weren't even added to the Bible until the thirteenth century. So much for the basis of another "hidden code" conspiracy.

But Langdon briefs Sophie on an insidious plot by "powerful" men to deconstruct the sacred feminine in order to pump the world with male testosterone and rid this place of anything feminine, since goddess-worshippers would most likely force the world to drink light beer and replace Monday Night Football with reruns of *Oprah*.

All sarcasm aside, Langdon's claim warrants further investigation because there is some truth to it. But opposition to the sacred feminine did not always arise from questions of temporal power; often, it arose from concern over doctrinal purity.

On the Trail of the Christian Deity

We should first consider the question, "Is God male or female?" The answer to this question, from a Christian perspective, is really only relevant if you're a Christian—or if you're willing to listen to what Christians actually have to say for themselves instead of biased propaganda. And it's a question, naturally, that also brings out the disdain of gender-sensitive theologians.

The Bible teaches that when God created mankind, He created them "in his own image, in the image of God he created him; male and female he created them."[3] But Scripture also teaches that God is Spirit;[4] unlike human beings, He does not have concrete physical attributes and isn't made in the image and likeness of mankind. Therefore we can deduce that God isn't male or female, precisely; rather, there is an essence of both masculinity and femininity in the "image" of God.

At the heart of both God's identity and creation, then, we find both distinctiveness and unity—at the same time. Couldn't any religious observation of such truth be the basis for fertility cults and rites of the sacred feminine? Is it philosophically necessary that femininity issue from a deity other than the Christian God? And are the distinctive pairings that God ordained (light/dark, male/female, physical/spiritual, animal/human) a good thing for us, or a bad thing? Many religious systems find value in such symbolic pairings.

When God created, He said that it was "good." After God created male and female, He said that all of creation was "very good."[5] Quite possibly, worship of the sacred feminine was an early, legitimate attempt to balance human notions of God's identity; and then—as with later doctrinal error that overemphasized God's masculinity—it created a "koyanisquatsi,"[6] an imbalance of its own, even falling into the error of creating a separate feminine god. That seems plausible enough, unless we presume that reverence for the sacred feminine could never become unbalanced. After all, the Bible itself describes how the Israelites were influenced by the male, female, and animalistic Egyptian gods; and once in Palestine, it wasn't unusual for them to worship Asherah (the mother goddess often associated with Baal in the Old Testament) as the wife of Yahweh. This, of course, is one of the reasons they were warned by God to stay away from her and burn the "high places" and idols that honored her.[7] It wasn't Asherah's distinctive femininity that was evil; it was her absence of masculinity and her worshipper's disruption of deific unity. As much as the godhead has its own feminine side, worshipping a separate deity was an abomination to the Lord. Very likely, the early Church felt the same way with regard to the sacred feminine.

While God saw that these male/female distinctions were good, philosophers like the postmodern theorist Michel Foucault disdained such distinctions, believing them to be artificially constructed by man as a means of creating and maintaining a basis of power; as such, they needed to be deconstructed for the sake of harmony and oneness. There is no doubt that Foucault was stung by the abuse of sexual distinctions during his life, as he himself was a gay male. Naturally, this influenced his own ideas on gender, and may have been the cause of his personal agony and philosophical presumptions. Foucault advocated a sort of androgynous, egalitarian culture that sees no distinctions; but that simply is not realistic (given the way that humans reproduce), nor is it a plausible solution to the human condition.

Too often has the human race fought to form power bases; but these struggles are not borne of gender distinctions, rather of greed and pride—sins practiced in all societies: patriarchal, matriarchal, or otherwise. Foucault and Langdon may wish to deconstruct existing power structures and replace them with harmonious, egalitarian solutions; but no matter how hard we try to create power bases for the powerless, greed and pride always lead us to revert to improper, disunified distinctions which lead to further tyranny—no matter who the progenitor.

God lovingly and artfully created the distinctions as a reflection of His own image, and our desire to destroy them is a desire to destroy the image of God in His human creation, which is mankind's underlying problem. Christians, of course, believe that the solution isn't dissolving the distinctions, but redeeming the distinctions under the Lordship of Jesus Christ and in harmony with His will. So it is that the Apostle Paul could very precisely and seemingly paradoxically describe the God-ordained roles of men, women, slaves, and masters in Ephesians 5 and 6, yet write in Galatians 3:28 that "there is neither Jew nor Greek, slave nor free, male nor female, for you are all one in Christ Jesus." Distinctions remain, yet all have the same standing with God through being clothed "with Christ."[8]

Pursuing Alternatives

Man, left to his own devices, creates disharmony. We continue to devolve into chaos in spite of our desire to create unity. As Scott Stapp once aptly sang, "The world is heading for mutiny, when all we want is unity,"[9] and the answer doesn't appear to be more women in politics. Utopia was not achieved by Indira Gandhi or Golda Meir; and we all remember Margaret Thatcher, don't we? Politics and the pursuit of power do as funny things to women as they do to men. We might as well believe, à la Carl Sagan, that our hope is in alien beings.

Whether through politics or religion, or through ideals like communism, capitalism, and atheism, man keeps reaching for answers only to realize that there is no system that is going to "save" man from himself. The distinctions of our culture are not themselves the problem, and bringing back an ancient sacred feminine complete with its Priory of Sion sex rites is not going to magically bring change and harmony to this chaotic world. If what Sophie Neveu witnessed at Saunière's château is any indicator, it won't even eliminate supposedly destructive distinctions. It'll just dictate who comes out on top.

Now, if we accept that God created these distinctions as a good thing, we can accept with little difficulty that Langdon is indeed advocating an element of God's essence that in some way we may be missing: His "feminine" side.

Here's where the whole issue of God's community within His perfect unity matters. God is one, yet exists in plurality (three "persons," the Father, the Son, and the Holy Spirit) within that whole. He is truly a foundational example of unity in diversity. This is the mystery of the Christian orthodox teaching of the Trinity (Tri-unity). Mankind seems to want unity, while at the same time wanting diverse expressions of the self, but we constantly struggle to keep a balance. The Church has been no different in that respect, composed as it is of human beings. But in the Godhead (the Trinity) is perfect community and balance—and that is how we were created: balanced, male and female.

The Apostle Paul describes how this perfect and equal unity nonetheless had a form of chain of command within its structure.[10] This might give us some insight as to why biblical authors refer to God in the masculine—not because He is a

"Father" or a "man" in the sense of physical masculinity, but because our created gender distinctions are useful metaphors for understanding the unity of the Godhead. God created man with the role of "headship," and that symbolically represents how the person we know as "the Father" functions within the Godhead. He created man first, and gave him the job to name all the animals, and ultimately name his own wife, which is a symbol of authority. Paul elsewhere affirms this original intent of God's creation.[11] The power of symbols, indeed.

So much for God's intent. The problem with such role distinction is that the fall of man created confusion and power struggles over role behavior that God never intended. Headship is about responsibility, not entitlement—as it is usually played out in our human pride. Someone is always determined to be on top, to be the sole King, Queen, or Knave of the Hill. Consequently, mankind has tended to live under the domination of unscrupulous men, in spite of the fact that men were created "to protect and to serve." The authorities in our lives, whoever they are, take advantage of their positions by lording it over those over whom they have authority, creating a hierarchical pecking order of pain that unfortunately has played its way into every relationship known to mankind, and most certainly in the male-female relationship.

Making the Feminine Sacred

Maybe Langdon would like to counter-adjust a societal and moral wrong; but it seems he proposes doing so through another wrong, one that seems benign compared to the nightmare that men have caused this world. But is there really any reason to believe that women in power would be more benevolent, that we'd thereby live in a kinder, gentler world? I don't think so. This is merely one of the popular ideas of the western world, a theory promulgated and left largely unchecked by thirty years of feminist ideology, often cemented in pop culture's pulpits.

But let's examine history. Even though the Greco-Roman world, for instance, was a matriarchal society, were the women in that society equal to men? According to writer Sharan Newman,

> Both Greek and Roman law and custom relegated women to the home. They could not own property in their own right, but only through a male "tutor." Both men and women were subject to the rule of their father, but boys were free of this when they reached the age of fourteen. Girls remained children under the law all their lives.[12]

Another writer, Eva Cantarella, says, "A dominant female deity cannot be considered proof of women's social and political power. The most that can be assumed is that this is a sign of the dignity that society ascribed to the maternal function" of child-rearing.[13] Even the guru of mythology Joseph Campbell writes that physical gender differences and roles simply will not go away: we still "have the problem of the woman and the man in relation to mythological experience. In spite of what the 'unisex' movement states, the differences are radical from the very beginning to the end. This is not a culturally conditioned situation."[14]

It just doesn't seem like the sacred feminine has historically had the type of influence and harmonizing power that Langdon idealizes. The question, then, remains as to why Rome or the Church would want the goddess silenced, especially since it appears that she really didn't have any legally sanctioned power beyond her ability to bear and nurture children.

Now, there is little doubt that the Church has nonetheless had a less than consistently chivalrous attitude toward women, and little doubt that the Church (especially the Protestant Church) has at times misogynistically oppressed women—as is brought out in Langdon's reminder of the witch burnings in the fifteenth through eighteenth centuries.[15]

But none of that is reflective of the truth of Jesus' life,

which brought an amazing honor and status to women in His world. The sacred feminine certainly did nothing for the status of women in His day; the dominant Hellenized Roman culture even included the practice of infanticide for female babies. But Jesus raised the cultural status of women, meeting with women of ill repute in the heat of the day, including women as part of His rabbinic group, and allowing them to ask questions of Him and learn—which was unheard of in both the Greek philosophical and Jewish Rabbinical schools. Jesus came to the aid of a woman caught in adultery, and He chose a woman to be the first human to see Him after His resurrection.

Jesus changed the status of women in His time, and His disciples protected that status. The Samaritan woman at the well evangelized an entire town. Priscilla worked and preached in equality alongside her husband, Aquila. Phoebe was a noted deacon in Cenchrea. And Paul, again, while affirming God-ordained gender distinctions, also emphasized sacred gender unity by reminding the Galatians that there is neither "male nor female; for you are all one in Christ."[16] This was revolutionary in His time—and, lest we forget, this formed the moral basis of modern universal suffrage movements! A good thing, indeed.

Faith and Temporal Power

The teachings of Jesus championed—and, after two long, painful millennia, finally brought about—women's rights more consistently and effectively than any goddess religion ever did; but unlike Jesus, the people in His Church are still pretty sinful, and there is no reason to believe that they would create anything other than a den of iniquity from time to time. An unwarranted, even judgmental, expectation is often placed upon the Church, an expectation that it should never become corrupt. But corruption is what we humans do best, especially as we begin to build our power-starved and self-perpetuating institutions, which are merely larger versions of the sinners who created them. Anyone who believes that the Church shouldn't be or isn't corrupt has a false understanding of the nature of humanity.

Unfortunately, this misunderstanding is partly the fault of a Church that piously places itself far above humanity, and hypocritically puts on an air of perfection. Pride and greed are deadly, and are corrupting influences in the primordial soup of institutional power. The Church indeed married its culture through Constantine and has been reeling ever since. But the Church has always done well and offered correction from the margins, and I believe it was created to mostly dwell there. If the Church is living according to its ethic, it will always be as strangers in a foreign land—ambassadors, as the Bible says, or "resident aliens" as Wil Willimon and Stanley Hauerwas call them in their book of the same title.

But the Church continues to fight for the supposed power center it once had in its own warped imagination. It fights for the right to pray in public—but it lavishes God with prayers for personal comfort. It demands legislated "Christian" morality—yet it can barely keep the marriages of its own people together. Even though it can't even come to consensus on the practice of its own beliefs, it wants those beliefs enforced. Christian activism is often unreasonably and contradictorily focused on political processes and temporal power struggles.

Now, Jesus was an activist, yes—but He advocated for the oppressed, and He did so from a place of divine authority and human weakness, ultimately sacrificing Himself on the cross. The Church is not called to fight for temporal political power that goes as fast as it comes. It is called as ambassadors for God's kingdom in an alien land. We should all, Christian or otherwise, without reservation, be outraged at injustice—but we should never revert to equal and opposite injustice, oppression, and propaganda in order to combat its evil.

Conspiracy theorists like Langdon have plenty of cannon fodder to misinterpret the motives and actions of the Church over the ages, but history has told us that conspiracies are usually in the eye and mind of the beholder, and usually devoid of factual basis. When it came to "stamping out heresy"—whether it acted rightly or not—the Church no doubt acted out of pride, but not solely or malevolently so; it also acted out of an honest desire to keep theology pure. Much as Dan Brown's fictional hero Robert Langdon, it believed that truth was on the line, that a sacred story was being corrupted—in this case, by a third-century gnosticism incongruent with eyewitness accounts and the testimony of early Church fathers such as Irenaeus and Polycarp.

Propaganda and the Quest for Relevancy in *Dogma*

Kevin Smith's *Dogma* did a masterful job of depicting the Church's preoccupation with relevancy in a time of ebbing power and influence. Smith's "Buddy Jesus" is the perfect satirical mirror of the Church's attempts to make itself look good cosmetically. When it does this, it usually looks pretty cheesy— even uglier than it does without the makeup on. The conspiratorial ramblings that Dan Brown's book parrots are a bit more insidious than a Fonzie-esque Boomer Jesus giving us the thumbs up, but *The Da Vinci Code* does indeed describe a more violent version of the same thing in a time of turmoil and failing ratings. Langdon's claim is that the Church needed a boost, so it bought that boost by killing its competition, creating an Uber-Jesus from the crusty old failed formulas of the Greek, Roman, and Egyptian divinity myths.

There is no doubt that Christianity borrowed metaphors from its neighbors' stories to properly communicate its own story. We see this clearly in Acts 17 when Paul used pagan religious symbols, and the poetry of Epimenides and others, to preach Christ—but claiming that he reconstructed Christ after these strange deities is nothing more than an unprovable theory. Sure, the Church fashioned some of its festivals after pagan celebrations. But that doesn't prove that the early Christian writers stole their stories and concocted a Jesus who was never born.

Curiously, *Dogma* doesn't question the Christian story as much as it questions the institution built around the story, highlighting the Church's modern desire to appeal to a public disenchanted with the institutions that Christians have created. The Church, especially the institutionalized Church, has had a falling out with a new generation of westerners who have been raised to see it as wholly irrelevant, superstitious, and even downright criminal. The Church, in fact, deserves critiques like *Dogma* and those underpinning *The Da Vinci Code* because much of the criticism is accurate. The Church is in dire need of a new reformation and revitalization of its story.

But the Church still tends to interpret books and movies like Dan Brown's and Kevin Smith's as tools of the devil and "untrue." So instead of taking notice of what more than half of our population thinks and believes, the Church continues to shape itself after Constantinian power structures, creating more idols like "Buddy Jesus" so people will like us—instead of telling a counter-cultural story, an alternarrative that makes sense of life, connects people to both physical and spiritual reality, and whisks them off to a transcendent place while their feet remain firmly planted in the grass roots of their everyday adventure.

Christianity offers such a story, but we seem to be more easily enthralled with the world's version than we are with Jesus' vision. We have at our disposal the blueprint to live alternatively—as Switchfoot describes it, "a new way to be human"[17]—yet we are stuck creating cheesy slogans and self-centered programs that usually fall on very deaf ears. The Church, right along with mainstream culture, has become more enthralled with enlarging its own territory instead of proclaiming and living God's kingdom in the midst of a world hungry for real community.

Is Kevin Smith's dogma any worse or more offensive than

the Church's own twisted version? Smith acknowledges the power of God in *Dogma*, but shows how the Church has done a masterful job of hiding it by its poor theology and the equally poor quality of life that poor theology produces. Christians have become more concerned with Wall Street, Capitol Hill, and the influence of Hollywood boxoffice figures than about becoming the presence of God in our communities, showing God's love to those in need spiritually and physically. In true ends-justifies-the-means fashion, preparation for the upcoming political season—or the next Narnia or *Passion*-like picture—has become more important to the Church than equipping or training its people to be a hands-on transformational part of a God-glorifying community.

Can you imagine a church dropping its multi-million dollar building campaign for the sake of the poor in the community? Can you imagine a church opening up an AIDS hospice, instead of protesting gay marriages? Now that might be some propaganda that looks a little more like Christ—more like *Jesus of Montreal* and less like "Buddy Jesus." Would books like *The Da Vinci Code* then become less compelling? Well, maybe.

The Real Politics of Faith

It might be best for the Church to take a ten year hiatus from politics and spend its time serving those in need, actually listening to and caring for the community—instead of planning more crusades and campaigns promoting bold claims of what God is going to do in the world while most of the world laughs in the face of such anemic attempts to "reach the lost." The Church has a grand opportunity to stem the tide of conspiracy theories by reaching out in real and authentic ways to its communities, showing them the love of God with no strings attached, no propaganda designed to intimidate, cajole or convert—just acting out the Gospel incarnationally to those who badly want to see righteousness lived and not merely preached.

Instead of yelling at Dan Brown, the Church should thank

him for a wake-up call; it should become the missional outpost it was meant to be. In reality, Christianity has an incredible message that no amount of propaganda could possibly touch or subvert. The Church should stick by that, preach it well, and as St. Francis of Assisi said, "If necessary, use words!"[18]

> Sophie frowned. She could think of far less scandalous routes than the Bois de Boulogne, but tonight she was not going to be picky.

For Further Investigation
The Da Vinci Code, Chapters 28 through 35

Dig a Little Deeper

➤ What can you find in the movie or the book that speaks truth to the Church?

➤ What kind of propaganda does Langdon himself use?

➤ Does this novel bother us at all? If so, why? Is it because it is actually destroying the truth of the Gospel, or because it hits too close to home in other ways?

➤ What baggage from our western Christian heritage does this book force us each to think through?

➤ What possible difference is there between a "Traditional" rather than a "Biblical" Christianity? Which sounds more appealing? Have you possibly been seduced by what merely sounds appealing, rather than what is right?

Draw Your Own Conclusions

➤ Da Vinci's Art and Theories Behind It:
  - *Math and the Mona Lisa: The Art and Science of Leonardo Da Vinci*, by Bulent Atalay.

➤ Bible Code Theory:
  - http://en.wikipedia.org/wiki/Bible_code
  - *The Bible Code*, by Michael Drosnin.
  - *Bible Code II: The Countdown*, by Michael Drosnin.

➤ Nag Hammadi Texts:
  - www.nag-hammadi.com
  - www.webcom.com/gnosis/naghamm/nhlcodex.html

➤ The Dead Sea Scrolls:
  - *Hidden Scrolls: Christianity, Judaism, and the War for the Dead Sea Scrolls*, by Neil A. Silberman.

➤ Matriarchal societies
  - www.reference.com/browse/wiki/Matriarchy

➤ Irenaeus, Polycarp, and Other Church Fathers:
  - www.ccel.org/fathers2/ANF-01/TOC.htm

➤ Jesus on Traditions:
  - Matthew 15:1–11.

> Langdon paused. The
> Templars' history was a
> precarious world
> where fact, lore, and
> misinformation had become
> so intertwined that
> exacting a pristine truth
> was almost impossible.

A Pristine Truth

Greg Wright, Lead Investigator

To this point in the story, Dan Brown has played things pretty straight. Though many of the details of the story are outlandish, and though some of Robert Langdon's ideas may strike us as rather strange, Brown hasn't yet thrown any out-and-out curveballs. Real places are real places, and Brown's landmarks root his story in what seems to be a very real geography.

That's about to change. The story now takes us to places that are invented out of whole cloth, and into corners of Paris we'd maybe rather not visit. There's the signpost up ahead. No, it's not Bois de Boulogne—we're about to enter the Da Vinci Zone.

On the Trail of... Well, the Trail

After our heroes ditch Sophie's car at Gare Saint-Lazare, they catch a cab to the outskirts of town, following the clue left by Saunière on the back a of a mysterious key. That clue? An address: 24 Rue Haxo. The cabbie knows where that is. It's out "near the tennis stadium on the western outskirts of Paris."[1] And the quickest way to get there is through Bois de Boulogne. As they continue their adventure, and before they end up kicking out their uncooperative driver, Sophie and Langdon talk about the Knights Templar—and the legend of their connection to the Holy Grail.

Meanwhile, Silas learns that he's been deceived by the *senechaux* he murdered. The Keystone is not at Saint-Sulpice. And down in Italy, Bishop Aringarosa arrives at Castel Gandolfo for a meeting with Roman Catholic mucky-mucks. Because they're Catholic, because they're well-placed in the Church, and because we're just naturally predisposed to think ill of pious people, we just *know* they've got to be up to no good. Oh, that clever, clever Dan Brown. Plays us like a banjo, or maybe like a kazoo. Whatever will he think of next?

With Sophie finally behind the wheel of the cab, and with the—ahem!—magic forest left behind, she and Langdon arrive at their destination on Rue Haxo: the Depository Bank of Zurich.

As you'd find out if you went to Paris, it's at this point that we really can no longer follow the adventure of Sophie and her tutor. We can go to Rue Haxo, sure. And we can go out to the tennis stadium to the west of Bois de Boulogne, too. But we'd have to go to two different places to do that. Rue Haxo is actually to the east of Paris, not to the west. And there's no Bank of Zurich either on the real Rue Haxo or out by the tennis stadium.

Darn that cabbie! He really did deserve to get ditched.

Dan Brown has deliberately staged the geographical background of Langdon's Templar yarn against the lurid Bois de Boulogne. Not only has he gone to great lengths to get us there just at this point in the narrative, but he has also out-and-out invented a geography for Paris in which east is west and west is east. And it's within this context of reversed reality that Langdon tells Sophie about the Templars, a history which is, in the narrator's words, "a precarious world where fact, lore, and misinformation had become so intertwined that exacting a pristine truth was almost impossible."[2]

Gosh, Dan. Thanks for helping straighten things out for us.

What does this very episode present but its own impossible intermingling of fact and misinformation? If I were predisposed toward conspiracy theories, I might almost think that Dan Brown were sending a message. But what could he possible be trying to tell us? Perhaps something about the precarious nature of taking even serious history too seriously?

A Pristine Historical Jesus

One of the great projects of the nineteenth century was a concerted attempt by German theologians to determine, with some measure of precision, precisely who was the man known in Scripture as Jesus. Was He in fact real at all? If He was real, how much do we really know about Him?

The great mind who summarized this project was the humanitarian, scientist, and theologian Albert Schweitzer. In 1906 he published *The Quest of the Historical Jesus* (translated into English in 1910). In this volume, he presented a thorough analysis of the project to date, identifying as its basis a high-minded and honestly-motivated effort to purify the dogma of the Church. The theory, according to Schweitzer, was that the Christian faith could be revitalized by stripping away the dross of religious dogma and revealing the pristine truth of the man who really lived in history by the name of Jesus. For the project to proceed, one key dogma needed to be overcome: that of Jesus as both human and divine. (Curiously, Schweitzer pegs the codification of this dogma as the Council of Chalcedon in 451, rather than at Nicaea in 325; who's got it wrong, Schweitzer, Teabing, or both?) Naturally, the element that must go, if one is searching for the Historical Jesus, is the issue of divinity. So the two major problems in getting at the real Jesus, according to Schweitzer, are His reported miracles and His purported self-awareness as Messiah. The miracles, naturally, have to be wholly discounted. The problem of eschatology was not so easy to resolve.

Oddly enough, though Schweitzer concluded that the project completely destroyed the historicity of the biblical Jesus, he found that the project had two unexpected results. First, this purified Jesus did nothing to revitalize the Christian faith of the scholars involved. In fact, once the Historical Jesus became known, He promptly left the scene and returned to His own time, having little (if anything at all) to offer contemporary scholars. The second surprise was that the deconstruction of Jesus turned out to have virtually no impact on the power of Christianity itself, which, Schweitzer conceded, really lies in its ideas, not in its historicity. The person of Jesus may have disappeared, but His ideas and the things he lived for turned out to be pretty indestructible.

In response to his disillusionment with western culture and the institutional church, Schweitzer moved to equatorial Africa to practice medicine among indigenous peoples, devoted to the ideals of Christianity if not its gospels or its Jesus. Other scholars, like Barthes, continued the project along the lines that Schweitzer laid out.

In the latter part of the twentieth century, the Jesus Seminar took up where the pursuit of the Historical Jesus left off. It asked the next really important question: if, in fact, we cannot trust the history of the gospels, how much do we really know about what Jesus actually said? Launched under the auspices of the Westar Institute in 1985, the Seminar determined to compare five gospels (those in the Christian Bible plus the gnostic Gospel of Thomas found near Nag Hammadi in 1945) and reach conclusions as to the reliability of the text. Robert W. Funk, the Seminar's leader, worked with John Dominic Crossan, Marcus Borg, and several dozen other academics, to publish *The Five Gospels: The Search for the Authentic Words of Jesus* in 1993. The project presented translations of the five gospels, color-coded according to the probability of authenticity. Not too surprisingly, the Seminar concluded that no better than twenty percent of the words attributed to Jesus were actually spoken by Him. Another blow struck against historicity. But orthodox Christianity still wouldn't go away.

In 2000, I participated in CNN's online message boards regarding the paperback release of *The Jesus Mysteries* by Timothy Freke and Peter Gandy. Freke is a devotee of what he calls "lucid living," a contemporary updating of the ancient philosophy of gnosis. The path of the Historical Jesus, and a devotion to gnosis, took their project one step further: not only does the Bible bear little relation to the truth of the Historical Jesus, the authors claim, He in fact never existed. On one thread of the CNN message board, *The Jesus Puzzle* author Earl Doherty and I debated about his own disingenuous attempts to discount the authenticity of biblical texts out of hand. Then Tim Freke himself weighed in. "As an Englishman I have been following these discussions with a mixture of fascination and horror," Freke wrote. "What makes American Christians so unpleasant and irrational? English Christians are generally not like this at all. What's going on? There seems to be a great deal of fear and division at work. How can we overcome this and meet as human beings exploring together this remarkable mystery called life?"[3]

Good question.

Between the Truth and a Hard Place

What's at work is not, as Freke concluded, a general tendency of American Christians to be unpleasant and irrational. It's the tendency of Americans to be unpleasant and irrational. In fact, Americans not only take a certain pride in being unpleasant and irrational, we find unpleasantness and irrationality to be pretty entertaining.

Take, for instance, the lawsuit brought against Dan Brown's publisher by *Holy Blood, Holy Grail* co-authors Richard

Leigh and Michael Baigent. The claimants sued in British courts for damages associated with copyright infringement. Why? Because they felt that Dan Brown had not credited them properly as the source of his novel's information about the supposed history of the Holy Grail. To no one's real surprise, the judge in the case found the suit to be utterly without merit.

What I found really interesting was how perfectly ordinary the event seemed to the British press. In the United States, however, not one peep about the story was printed until the very day Dan Brown showed up for court. At that point, the story became a feeding frenzy, with nary a lick of hard analysis regarding the actual claims of the suit. All flash. All personality. Can we catch Dan Brown saying something titillating? Can we catch Leigh and Baigent spouting something really silly? Of course we can, and we'll print it. Meanwhile, British papers were actually printing the contents of court documents. So very dull, if factual.

American tastes do not run to the pleasant and the factual, really, and that's a trait which is not limited to conservatives or Christians. When it comes to American film, in fact, we can find examples from the full range of ideological commitment. On the one hand, for instance, we have Mel Gibson, whose *The Passion of the Christ* (which we discuss elsewhere in this text), was purposefully unpleasant and more than willing to embroider historical details. On the other hand, we have filmmakers like Oliver Stone and Michael Moore.

Personally, I enjoy Stone's body of work, though I don't agree with his politics. Unlike many filmmakers, he has been very up front about the intent of his films. His project has been to illuminate the history of the Viet Nam War era. We always know where Stone stands; consequently, we can readily determine where we stand in relation to him, and appreciate his films for their craft without some lingering suspicion that he's trying to pull a fast one on us. We *know* he's trying to pull a fast one.

Stone's most controversial film (though not the most unpleasant—*Natural Born Killers* takes that honor) has thus far been *JFK*, his refictionalization of Louisiana Attorney General Jim Garrison's assassination conspiracy theory. In what amounts to a *tour de force* of cinematic technique, Stone literally tampers with history, recreating the Zapruder film, restaging the assassination of JFK, and through cinematic technique making it appear as if he were using the actual Zapruder film and newsreel footage—which he wasn't. The film might lead us to ask ourselves—and Stone would be pretty pleased if we did—why to this day the public can't see the real Zapruder film; but I won't digress, because the politics of the assassination investigation are not relevant to our discussion here (though the appeal of conspiracy theories is).

What Stone achieved, however, most definitely did incur the wrath of the journalistic establishment, which has long had a vested interest in the conclusions of the Warren Commission's report. Stone did this deliberately, because, as he put it, he wanted to propose "a countermyth to the myth of the Warren Commission."[4] And he knew he could count on the American public to respond to his film viscerally, not intellectually. After all, we're exceedingly free to consider the Warren Commission's report a myth; which one of us has ever read it? Which one of us could afford the months necessary to track down and digest its volumes? Stone's three-hour polemic can indeed compete with the Warren Commission's report as an alternative myth, due to our own ignorance. We're more fascinated by conspiracies than we are by history.

Filmmaker Michael Moore explains why the cinema is such a potent force for shaping ideas and perceptions. "All art," he says, and "every piece of journalism manipulates sequence and things. Just the fact that you edit, that certain things get taken out or put back in. ... We are not talking about objectivity. We're talking about a *style*."[5] Even though the public may consume his films as factual, objective, and informative, Moore is able to somewhat coyly refer to any one of his movies as "a documentary told with a narrative style."[6]

This "narrative style" allows Moore to portray events that may or may not have actually occurred. The *Bowling for Columbine* sequence in which Charlton Heston walks away from Michael Moore's camera, for instance, is as much a cinematic trick as Oliver Stone's synthetic Zapruder film in *JFK*—we must ask ourselves: How did Moore edit reverse-angle one-shots when he only had one camera on site for the interview? What was Heston really walking away from? What was Moore really saying to Heston, if anything at all? The sequence shapes a new Heston myth to compete in the public's mind with Cecil B. DeMille's Moses-Heston myth.

George Bernard Shaw, the British playwright and essayist, rather presciently foretold that the cinema would one day help to determine what the public would think—not only in terms of politics, but also in terms of morality. "The cinema is going to form the mind of England," Shaw wrote. "The national conscience, the national ideals and tests of conduct, will be those of the film."[7] In essence, he was correct, and not just about England. The films that we see—and the way that we see them, especially if we consume them without reflection—have the ability to shape what we think about morality and about our role in the world.

The problem is not really about what's history and what's fiction. The problem is not really about truth. The problem is that we really just don't have much of an appetite for truth. We don't have the time for it.

The Hard Truths of Historicism

So what about the Templars? Does Langdon have his story straight here? To the extent that he documents what can only be described as a historical muddle, he is correct. I've read several different histories of the Templars, including contemporary accounts such as that found in *The Forgotten Monarchy of Scotland* and dustier accounts such as that recounted in Sir Walter Scott's *Tales of Grandfather*. From what I can gather, Langdon is indeed correct in asserting, "The one thing on which all academics agree is this: The knights discovered *something* down there in the ruins... something that made them wealthy and powerful beyond anyone's wildest imagination."[8]

Now, if we talk about sheer history and leave speculation aside, all evidence suggests that they either found material wealth itself, which they somehow managed to husband and parlay into further wealth and consequent power; or they discovered principles of banking—which allowed them to husband and parlay whatever wealth they already had into further influence. The latter seems the most likely. How could a physically vast treasure have been successfully and secretly spirited out of the Holy Land? How could mere secrets of masonry result in such wealth and influence? How on earth could a stack of genealogical documents and a sack of sacred bones translate into such material power? Yes, there's that blackmail theory; but clearly, the Templars were up to a lot more than just sitting on a guarded chest.

In the context of Dan Brown's story, even more perplexing problems present themselves. If the Sangreal documents bring with them such power and riches, why do Saunière, Marie Chauvel, and the *senechaux* live in such obscurity, while conspiracy theorists like Teabing enjoy actual wealth and privilege? Seriously, what would Teabing possibly stand to gain by procuring the Grail? Would he give up knighthood and become a museum curator, or maybe the caretaker of a Scottish park? That's moving up in the world!

The hard truth of historicity is not that history is written by the winners. It's not even that we, like Teabing, ultimately see what we want to see. The hard truth about history is that we'll eventually have to take somebody's word for something.

Why not believe the winners? Was there never a winner who was on the moral side of an issue? Would Langdon and Teabing argue alongside Holocaust deniers that the Allies faked the historical record? Typically, the losers usually leave behind plenty of their own records of activity, and often enough they're just as incriminating as the actions of the winners.

So if we choose to believe the losers simply because we don't trust winners, that says more about us than it does about any truth of the matter. And if we blindly accept the stories of the winners simply because of the weight of "authority," we have no one but ourselves to blame when we find out we've been "lied to," as when my mother was finally forced to admit to me that Santa Claus wasn't real. Wow. Bummer. How could I possibly have trusted my mother? What a dummy.

I wrote the following on the CNN forums in response to Freke and Doherty:

> Is it problematic that Herodotus makes no mention of the nation of Israel? Certainly. It is also problematic that Herodotus asserts that there were ants in India as big as dogs, ants that mined gold; and that he had personally seen them in the courts of Persia. Does this completely discredit Herodotus? Are we to say, then, that there was no historical Darius? No historical Xerxes? No historical Croesus? That would be rather silly, wouldn't it?[9]

Ultimately, we are probably best off concluding that what makes truth pristine is that it simply exists—somewhere, covered with dust in some remote cave, or perhaps as close as the bookshelf in our hallway or the church down the street. And we can diligently apply ourselves to the adventure of its discovery, knowing that discernment will be required.

But one thing I know: I'm a lot more likely to trust a book that actually advocates discernment, as does the Bible, than I am to trust one that says, "Take my word for it. I've got this thing figured out." As André Gide observed, "Believe those who are seeking the truth; doubt those who find it."[10]

Should we trust Teabing and his theories about the bloodline of Jesus? After all, his is a conspiracy hiding right in plain sight, there on the pages of Dan Brown's novel. This is one knight I know I won't trust.

Should we trust Langdon's ideas about the sacred feminine? He's wrong enough, often enough. Even in this section of the novel, he's certain of "two important facts": First, that "Leonardo knew where the Grail resided during his lifetime." Second, that the "hiding place had probably not changed to this day."[11] The first fact is not a fact at all; its a presumption based on the premise that the most reliable history is written by losers. The second fact is not only speculative, it also proves completely wrong, in the context of the novel. Dan Brown even goes so far as to establish that Langdon is in the habit of telling himself consoling lies.[12]

I would trust Dan Brown just a little, though. He, at least, goes out of his way to tell us that we should question the truth of what his characters say.

How is that so different from what the Church has told us?

Church History and *The Barbarian Invasions*

Early in the twentieth century, dramatist and novelist Booth Tarkington observed that the then-new "frankness" on Broadway amounted to little more than artistic laziness. How much better, Tarkington asked, to rather be goaded into creativity by acknowledging and accepting social constraints? Necessity, as they say, is the mother of invention.

Denys Arcand's *The Barbarian Invasions* is a frank movie. It makes no attempt to portray its primary protagonists as "heroic" or "noble" people—and true to the ways of the world, *Invasions* is populated by imperfect, earthy, passionate people. As a consequence, they tend to be crass, irritable, and petty. They are materialists, philanderers, opportunists, and heroin addicts. They kind of remind me of Dan Brown's characters; and because of the film's frankness, we are treated to the full-throated color and bleakness of the world they inhabit.

Interestingly, Arcand seems to suggest that the less attractive colors—and darkness—of our present world may be traced to the singular developments that came out of Rome in the 1960s. For in Arcand's frankness, we also find an open admission of what many other films rather blandly and blindly deny: that religion plays an enormous role in the lives of most people, though not necessarily the role that religion itself thinks it should play.

The movie revolves around the circle of friends and relatives which reunites when a French Canadian man named Rémy—yes, Rémy—falls ill with a terminal illness. In Montreal, as in the France about which Dan Brown writes, "Christianity was not a religion ... so much as a birthright."[13] In one pivotal scene, we discover the extensive connections individuals in this group once had to the Catholic Church. Yet over the years, they have all gone searching elsewhere for what the Church never managed to give their lives—meaning. Sadly, the philosophical and metaphysical phantoms they chase also prove empty, and the hero's final physical release comes only through the ministrations of an addict who is herself not long for the world.

Arcand's film seems to imply that the spiritual vacuum which gobbled up the end of the twentieth century was the result of an event—one with as much cultural import as the destruction of the World Trade Center in 2001—referred to only cryptically in the film. It seems likely that Arcand points to the landmark Vatican II conferences in Rome, which concluded in 1966 and led to monumental reforms in Roman Catholic theology and liturgy.

Traditionalist Catholics, such as Mel Gibson, openly claim that the Church's reforms have not only broken with the heritage of the Church, they have also broken the faith. Arcand's film seems to agree, though not so openly. In a second pivotal scene, a Catholic priest meets an art dealer in the catacombs of mothballed iconography—only to discover that the Church's symbols have lost not only their spiritual significance but their monetary value as well.

The value of the Church, Arcand seems to say, is not in its ability to change and adapt to the culture. Its value is in its constancy—literally, for the priest represents not only a bridge to the Church's past, but a bridge to Arcand's cinematic past as well: he portrayed Father leClerc in Arcand's *Jesus of Montreal*, which we discussed in our first chapter. Not insignificantly, the two films share another key character: Constance, a fallen woman who finds her redemption as a disciple of Arcand's Canadian Jesus. She is Arcand's Mary Magdelene. In *Invasions*, hers are the hands that carry the body of Christ to the hospital's dying souls, and hers is the voice that urges Rémy's son to declare love for his father.

And of course, therein lies the heart of this film. For while the physical solution of Rémy's pain is heroin, the spiritual solution is what Sister Constance knows is still the greatest asset of the Church: love, forgiveness, and reconciliation. And this is a frank admission—one that cannot necessarily be made without equal frankness about the shortcomings of the options.

Arcand's frankness is an inventive frankness, one of which even Tarkington may have approved, though many audiences may not.

The Garden of Earthly Delights

So to what extent does the Catholic Church represent "the winners" when it comes to writing history? The Protestant Reformation certainly continues to style itself as the winner in its successful rebellion against theocratic monopoly. And who knows but that the fruit of the Reformation's iconoclasm isn't the kind of impotent symbolism that Arcand postulates? Did the winner's success persuade the loser to adopt the enemy's own tactics, leading to a further destruction from the inside? That would be the ultimate victory, wouldn't it? Desperate times call for desperate measures, maybe even a conspiracy or two.

So what is the Catholic Church up to? Are they sending robed monks around to assassinate museum curators? Is Leigh Teabing correct in attributing Silas' actions to the machinations of the Pope? Of course not. Silas is in fact doing what Teabing tells him to do. But if Teabing wins, he'll surely be able to pin Silas' crimes on Aringarosa and, through him and a stack of bearer bonds, on the Church. "Real historians"[14] like Teabing—ha!— sure bank on the premise that the winners get to write the history. And he banks on the public's willingness to think poorly of Catholics and charitably of historians.

But the Catholic Church is neither dead nor irrelevant—far from it—and the Reformation's iconoclasm has neutered its own Protestant symbols as much as it has neutered the symbols of Roman Catholicism. The real fruit of iconoclasm is, in fact, right here in the text of *The Da Vinci Code*. One hundred and fifty-plus weeks on the best sellers list attest to the fact that people still do find symbols terribly powerful; but what they're offered in church is self-help and dry exegesis. They're looking for beauty and spiritual significance, and they're coming up empty.

And what do they find in *The Da Vinci Code*? If they're not careful, they'll find only what they want to see. If they're attentive, though, they'll see that Dan Brown is sending pretty strong messages.

"*Everyone loves a conspiracy*,"[15] thinks Langdon. Indeed. And, as Langdon himself observes, "Repeating a symbol is the simplest way to strengthen its meaning."[16] To that end, Dan Brown makes sure we get his point about conspiracies. The next time through the book, count the number of different characters who repeat the refrain. Even the librarian gets to chime in.

So what is Langdon up to? Sure, he's written a book about

the historic symbology of the sacred feminine; but does he really buy into his tales of the Templars, the Grail and the bloodline? Later on, he tells Sophie that "There's an enormous difference between hypothetically discussing an alternate history of the Christ, and ... presenting to the world thousands of ancient documents as scientific evidence that the New Testament is false testimony." Conveniently, he tries to ride the fence, telling her that he makes "no judgment either way."[17]

And what is Dan Brown up to? The clues are probably right there in the text—in flag-waving choices like Rue Haxo and Bois de Boulogne, a forest known to "Parisian cognoscenti" as "the 'Garden of Earthly Delights'... dark and twisted, a purgatory for freaks and fetishists." As Langdon launches into his Templar tale, Brown tells us that the symbologist is "unable to imagine a less congruous backdrop for the legend he was about to tell... an astonishing chronicle of secrets, blackmail, betrayal, and even brutal torture."[18] Hmm. Actually, it sounds pretty congruous, to me. But there it is. And the lurid tale continues as the cab proceeds past "topless teenage girls," past "well-oiled black men in G-strings," past hookers and the "underbelly of Paris leering in the shadows."[19]

And then Langdon's tale is done. The nightmare is over. Langdon is behind the wheel. Sophie asks, "I trust you've seen enough of our magic forest?" With Langdon we nod, "*Plenty.*"[20]

Perhaps we can say of Dan Brown (as Brown similarly says of Leonardo), "His artwork seems bursting to tell a secret, and yet whatever it is remains hidden, perhaps beneath a layer of metaphor, perhaps enciphered in plain view, perhaps nowhere at all. Maybe Brown's plethora of tantalizing clues is nothing but an empty promise left behind to frustrate the curious and bring a smirk to those in the know."[21] There are clues in his art, to be sure. But what do they mean? At the very least, as with history, we would be mistaken to presume that Langdon's tale in this episode represents pristine truth. As Brown himself points out, "A career hazard of symbologists was a tendency to extract hidden meaning from situations that had none."[22]

I guess that means I could be wrong, too, doesn't it? Perhaps Dan Brown is, when all is read and done, just a "pop schlockmeister looking for a quick buck,"[23] to use Faukman's words—an idiot who can't read a map.

> Langdon felt his imagination starting to run wild as he fantasized about what they might find. Everyone loves a conspiracy.

For Further Investigation
The Da Vinci Code, Chapters 36 through 41

Dig a Little Deeper

➢ Is it possible to take history too seriously?

➢ What do you make of Schweitzer's conclusions about the historicity of Jesus and Christianity?

➢ How do objectives such as Oliver Stone's influence us, his audience? Or society in general?

➢ "The films that we see—and the way that we see them, especially if we consume them without reflection—have the ability to shape what we think about morality and about our role in the world." Based on this statement, what changes could you make in your own film-watching in order to be less influenced by what you see?

➢ Is history always written by the winners? Can you think of examples where such is not the case?

➢ How do we choose whom to trust?

➢ Is it possible that, like symbologists, we try to "extract hidden meaning" from situations that have none? How can we know the difference?

Draw Your Own Conclusions

➢ The Westar Institute and the Jesus Seminar:

- www.westarinstitute.org

- www.religioustolerance.org/chr_jsem.htm

➢ The Knights Templar:

- www.templarhistory.com

- *The Knights Templar: The History and Myths of the Legendary Order*, by Sean Martin.

➢ Vatican II:

- www.vatican.va/archive/hist_councils/ii_vatican_council/

- www.vatican2voice.org/index.asp

➢ The Historical Jesus:

- *The Quest of the Historical Jesus*, by Albert Schweitzer (full text online at www.earlychristianwritings.com/schweitzer/).

➢ Examples of Iconoclasm in the Old Testament:

- Judges 6:25–32 and 1 Samuel 5–6.

Part Three:
Clues in His Art

> Langdon spied the
> building's main entrance.
> *Talk about mixed messages,*
> he thought. *Welcome and*
> *keep out.*

Welcome and Keep Out

Greg Wright, Lead Investigator

The earliest recurring dream I remember was a nightmare. In the dream, I am an infant. I'm cradled in a bassinet on the front seat of a '56 Oldsmobile. My mother is at my right, in the passenger seat, and my father is at my left. My brother and sister are in the back seat.

Because this is the early 1960s, and we're a driving in a 1950s-model car, the bassinet is, of course, not buckled in. It just rests on the front seat, rocking a bit with the motion of the car as it rolls down the road. In those days, parents had also not gotten wise to putting bassinets in seats backward, to provide better protection in case of accidents. So I'm able to look out over the dashboard from my precarious seat.

Actually, no one in the car wears a seat belt. The car doesn't seem to have any. And that's a pretty crucial issue, because my dad soon leaves the paved road and starts following a country rut. It's a farming road of some sort, and soon we're well out into the backwoods, along a river. Before long, even the ruts disappear, though it's still obvious we're on a road.

We come to an old bridge across the river. My dad turns right on the rickety structure, merely a wooden span across the water, with no covering, no rails, hardly even a surface to drive on. Why are we crossing? I'm not sure. It's obvious the road ends just the other side.

Halfway across the bridge, right in the middle of the river, the boards collapse under the weight of our tires. The frame of the car lurches down onto the bridge's superstructure, and the jolt causes all the doors of the car to pop open. My parents and my siblings all tumble out of the car and into the river, leaving me bobbing in my bassinet, perched in the front seat, the car hopelessly stranded.

When, as an adult, I told my mom about this recurring dream, she told me that it was, in fact, a recollection of an actual drive we had taken when I was an infant—accurate in all details except, of course, for the collapse of the bridge and the loss of my family.

Ever since, I've had a moderate fear of driving down blind country roads, not knowing where they lead. Maybe that's why I've never much cared for *The Wizard of Oz*. I can sense from the very start that Dorothy and Toto are on a wild goose chase, that the Wizard has no clothes, so to speak—that the yellow brick peters out, goes nowhere, is a dead end.

Just as Dan Brown used the lurid background of a Bosch painting for Langdon's tale of the Knights Templar, in the next section of the book he employs consistently conflicting imagery of welcoming paths and locked doors. *Welcome and keep out.*

Codes Within Codes

Sophie Neveu and Robert Langdon arrive at 24 Rue Haxo and find themselves in front of an odd architectural anomaly. The Depository Bank of Zurich is a "squat citadel,"[1] a "windowless rectangle that seemed to be forged entirely of dull steel." They stop their stolen cab in front of the "enormous metal brick," bringing the car to an "imposing gate"[2] that leads to an underground parking garage. It's here that Saunière's odd key comes in handy. They use it to open the first gate, then come to a second. It also opens to their key. It's nice to have keys.

The garage is "small and dim, with spaces for about a dozen cars. ... A red carpet stretched across the cement floor, welcoming visitors to a huge door that appeared to be forged of solid metal." Once again the key will be required. *"Talk about mixed messages,"*[3] indeed.

But who was actually talking about mixed messages? Oh, yes—I guess we were, in our last chapter. We were discussing how Bois de Boulogne is actually a fitting background for Langdon's Templar tale, rather than incongruous, as Langdon found it.

Langdon must have been reading our minds. Or did Dan Brown plant that thought? Wow. That whole "reader-response" school of criticism really pays dividends.

Sophie and Langdon again use Saunière's parting gift, easily foiling the giant metal citadel's defenses. (Get it? *Foiling*?) They've been given the key to the city, it seems. Keep out? I think not. Yes, it's nice to have keys.

Once inside, the two manage to neatly weave their way through the cryptic practices of Swiss banks, having been led to a reception room somewhere far underground. There they discover that the key provides access to Saunière's safe deposit box.

Welcome!

Oh—but they'll also need to enter a ten-digit security code into the computer in order to retrieve the box. Keep out!

I guess keys only get you so far.

Meanwhile, Silas phones the Teacher to let him know that the trail to Saint-Sulpice was a dead end. Welcome, and keep out. The Teacher tells Silas not to fret—he's just got wind via the TV that Sophie and Langdon are on the run, and wanted by Interpol. The game's not over yet!

At this point, the bank manager comes in to inform Sophie and Langdon that the police are on the way, thanks to the security guard in the bank's lobby. It turns out that the manager, Vernet, is an old chum of Saunière's. And in one of the book's more dumbfounding unexplained red herrings, it's apparent that Vernet is particularly attached to the rosewood box in Saunière's account. Why? We never find out. Welcome, and keep out.

After Vernet goes to placate the police, our heroes discover that Saunière's anagrammatic Fibonacci sequence provides the ten digits necessary for access to the safe deposit box. So that's why the zero is missing from Saunière's sequence! Who'd want an eleven digit passcode?

Alas! my analysis is too simple-minded. This book is much deeper than that. Saunière was "the master of double-entendres," Sophie tells Langdon. "He loved anything with multiple layers of meaning. Codes within codes."[4]

> When Sophie had first seen the scrambled Fibonacci sequence... she had assumed its sole purpose was... to get [her] involved. Later, she realized the numbers were also a clue as to how to decipher the other lines—*a sequence out of order ... a numeric anagram.* Now, utterly amazed, she saw the numbers had a more important meaning still. They were almost certainly the final key to opening her grandfather's mysterious safe-deposit box.[5]

Okay, well, maybe not the final key. But it is certainly nice to have keys. Are we clear on that yet?

They grab Saunière's rosewood mystery package, and Vernet returns to spirit them out the bank in the back of an armored car. As Vernet speeds them away from the scene of the crime, they eagerly examine the contents of the box: it's not the Grail itself, as they had somewhat rashly hoped, but a cryptex—a keyed cylinder of five stone discs which, when properly aligned, yield access to the cylinder's contents. Stumped again.

Yes, it's nice to have keys.

The Welcome: Establishing Trust

Yes, Dan Brown has laid the red carpet down for us. He's handed us all the keys to the mystery, and in many cases, if we're used to moderately demanding puzzle-books, we are so well-equipped by Brown that we can stay a page or two ahead of both Langdon and Sophie. If Brown keeps up the pattern of this section of the story, we can be fairly confident that he is not merely leading us along the garden path. Maybe he'll take us to Oz and beyond, holding our hand all along the way. What a nice, gentle mystery.

A church I used to attend as a child had an interesting custom when inviting regular attenders to become members. During the altar call, the preacher would talk about extending "the right hand of fellowship." In my overactive and paranoid imagination, I always envisioned that hand as a right uppercut to the jaw, following by a quick left jab for the knockout. It was during the period when the hippie-gospel song "Put Your Hand in the Hand" was popular on the radio, and I wasn't having any of that, either, thank you very much. Who knew where those hippies' hands had been?

But giving someone a hand up (or even a handout, often) can be a great means of establishing trust. The extended hand does indeed say, "Welcome. You can trust me." Consider how

Silas comes to trust Aringarosa. The nascent monk has been miraculously freed from prison by an earthquake, and, in a confused blind stumble, tumbles into a boxcar. After a sleep, he is dragged from the train and beaten. He looks in vain for food, and finally throws himself in a ditch to die.

Aringarosa, however, like the Good Samaritan of the parable, doesn't just pass by the beaten man. He takes the bloodied, hulking albino back to his home, cleans him, nurtures him, and cares for him. Three days later, it seems to Silas, "the stone has been rolled aside" and he is "born again."[6] In his haze, Silas mistakes the voice of Aringarosa for Jesus himself. And apparently, the priest doesn't correct him. Silas repays the kindness by saving the priest from a violent robber.

Now, years later, when the bishop recruits Silas as "a soldier of God," the monk is only too eager to acquiesce. He falls "to his knees before Bishop Aringarosa—the man who had given him a new life." He tells the bishop, "I am a lamb of God. Shepherd me as your heart commands."[7] Sounds a little sycophantic, and more than a tad like blind loyalty. Yet to date, the bishop has only done right by Silas. Long years of faithfulness and trust lie behind the monk's loyalty. We can almost imagine Aringarosa intoning, "There are no locked doors between us, Silas."

The bishop equally imagines that there are no secrets between him and the Teacher—whom he trusts implicitly and misguidedly, and into whose hands he places the trusting Silas.

Saunière establishes the same kind of bond with Sophie. When Langdon explains the significance of the five-petal rose to her, she recounts how her grandfather had used the symbol as a means of establishing trust. "He used to hang a rose on his office door at home when he was having a confidential phone call and didn't want me to disturb him." The significance? "*Sweetie*, her grandfather had said, *rather than lock each other out, we can each hang a rose—la fleur des secrets—on our door when we need privacy. This way we learn to respect and trust each other.*"[8]

One of the most common uses of trust, of course, is the entrusting of secrets. And keeping secrets is the worst way of breaking trust. Saunière keeps the most scandalous things secret from Sophie. The Teacher wholly misrepresents himself to Aringarosa. Silas' trust is violently and destructively abused. And Dan Brown keeps the worst kind of secret from his readers.

A red carpet, yes—and a locked steel door, too.

The Lockout

More than any other passage in Dan Brown's text, the episode at Rue Haxo stresses the symbolism of enforced, exclusive boundaries. Consider that when Langdon and Sophie read the address from the back of the key, and ask the cabbie to take them there, they venture for the first time into the territory of the "Parisian cognoscenti"[9]—those "in the know." Who represents this class any better than the "president of the Paris branch of the Depository Bank of Zurich," Andre Vernet, who has always wanted to "rub shoulders with the true *cognoscenti*"[10]—though even he has been denied the privilege?

This episode is indeed all about locks, keys, barriers, and boundaries—vaults, codes, and cryptecies. Red carpets? Ha! There's always some new barrier to block your way. Says Dan Brown,

> Many great minds in history had invented cryptologic solutions to the challenge of data protection: Julius Caesar devised a code-writing scheme called the Caesar Box; Mary, Queen of Scots created a substitution cipher and sent secret communiqués from prison; and the brilliant Arab scientist Abu Yusuf Ismail al-Kindi protected his secrets with an ingeniously conceived polyalphabetic substitution cipher. Da Vinci, however, eschewed mathematics and cryptology for a mechanical

solution. The cryptex. A portable container that could safeguard letters, maps, diagrams, anything at all.[11]

And Dan Brown invented the Da Vinci code.

Just what is the Da Vinci code, anyway? Of all the ciphers, anagrams and other doodads discussed in Dan Brown's book, nowhere is anything ever identified as "the Da Vinci code." Ever. The closest we come are the passwords that open up Saunière's cryptecies, "sofia" and "rose." But these are Saunière's codes, and they are only based on Leonardo's ideas. And Da Vinci's alleged fascination with imagery of the sacred feminine unlocks nothing beyond the frame of *The Last Supper*. Sure, a semiotician might refer to such symbols as "codes," and say that Da Vinci's meaning has been "encoded." But you and I aren't semioticians, are we? When we see "Da Vinci Code," we think "I'm gonna decode ancient messages!" But that's not really what Dan Brown gives us. And art historians would likely categorize such symbolism as Leonardo's idiosyncrasies, anyway, not as codes or conventions found throughout art.

Let's digress for a moment, and examine one of the passages that describes Leonardo's methods:

> Da Vinci painted Christian themes not as an expression of his own beliefs but rather as a commercial venture—a means of funding a lavish lifestyle. Unfortunately Da Vinci was a prankster who often amused himself by quietly gnawing at the hand that fed him. He incorporated in many of his Christian paintings hidden symbolism that was anything but Christian—tributes to his own beliefs and a subtle thumbing of his nose at the Church.[12]

Presuming that Langdon is right, shouldn't such an assertion lead us somewhere concrete? Shouldn't we be allowed in on the secret that led Leonardo to such lengths? If he deliberately left clues to radical beliefs, and Langdon is hip to them, too, why can't we also be allowed access to the truth of the Grail? But all

Langdon does is offer very narrow interpretations based on his own symbol set. Oh, that's right: welcome, and keep out.

Like it or not, Dan Brown ultimately shuts down every avenue of inquiry that he opens in this novel. He consistently and repeatedly leads us down the red carpet, only to bring us to another closed door. Again, what is the Da Vinci code? Where is the Holy Grail? Is it documents? Is it a collection of relics? Some combination of the two? Is it even real? Is it all just a dream?

Maybe, just maybe, "Dan Brown" is a substitutionary cipher for "Da Vinci." Maybe the text is merely self-referential. Maybe Dan Brown writes goddess-worship themes not as an expression of his own beliefs but rather as a commercial venture—a means of funding a lavish lifestyle. Maybe Brown is a prankster who often amuses himself by quietly gnawing at the hand that feeds him: his secular audience. Perhaps he incorporates hidden symbols in his mainstream novels that are anything but goddess-centric—tributes to his own Christian beliefs and a subtle thumbing of his nose at disdainful skeptics like Baigent, Leigh, and Lincoln.

Why, exactly, does Brown open such an enormous Pandora's Box yet provide no concrete answers to the questions he raises? Not that there's anything wrong with that—but remember, the other major thread of *The Da Vinci Code* is gnosticism, which is all about secret answers, not questions. And *The Da Vinci Code* only offers questions. Is that a dig against gnosticism, too?

This leads to a second option, and perhaps an even more insidious one. If there really is secret knowledge behind *The Da Vinci Code*, real Gnostic treasure, Dan Brown's not letting us in on it. Perhaps, like Vernet, Brown ponders his readers and tells us, "*You obviously have no business here!*"[13] What would be the purpose of such an approach? Well, in the words of Robert Langdon, it "keeps out the slow learners."[14] Despite professing the Christian faith, Brown might really be a closet Gnostic.

Or maybe, just maybe, Dan Brown is like the Coen brothers' Barton Fink, lugging around a mysterious box; and when someone asks what's in it, all he can do is mumble, "I don't know."[15] To which agent Collet might reply, "You're telling me you don't have keys to your own truck?"[16]

Now, this third option is not a criticism. Many films, like *Apocalypse Now!* and even *Barton Fink*, are about the creative process: about struggling with creative blocks, overcoming them, getting caught up in the generative dynamic that is art—and yet finding, at the end of it all, that the creation itself has overcome the creator, and the artist has no idea what has been wrought. As Madman Mundt bellows in the climactic scene from *Barton Fink*, "I'll show you the life of the mind!"[17] It's often a hellish sight.

Cognoscenti, indeed.

So, succinctly put, if we accept the premise from our last chapter that Dan Brown is not an idiot, at least three options remain to us: first, Dan Brown is really an artistic Christian prankster, gently thumbing his nose at goddess-worshipers and Gnostics; second, he is a closet Gnostic who smugly refuses to let us in on his secrets; or third, he is merely an artist who, like all artists, is not entirely in control of what he has created.

Regardless of which of these three options is correct, one thing is certain: whatever the answer is, we don't get it. *The Da Vinci Code* is ultimately as impenetrable as the steel brick that is the Depository Bank of Zurich. We've been locked out, baby, and Dan Brown wants to make sure we know it.

What are the Odds?

Never mind that Brown either can't or won't trust us enough to reveal his novel's secret; never mind that the gates are securely barred against us. There are three factors that *The Da Vinci Code* brings to bear in its refusal to give up its sacred relics.

First is the element of improbability—and Sophie is right there to do our math for us.

Clues in His Art: Welcome and Keep Out

To start with, consider the chain of coincidences that puts this plot in motion. One: Bishop Aringarosa jumps the gun on the Vatican's timetable by nearly a month. Two: Robert Langdon happens to be lecturing in Paris the very night that Silas gets put into play. Three: Silas shoots Saunière so poorly that the old curator has time to write on the key, plant it on the *Madonna of the Rocks*, scrawl on the *Mona Lisa*'s glass, struggle back to the scene of the crime, inscribe a circle on the floor, dream up and write out the Fibonacci/Da Vinci/Langdon clue, undress, scrawl a pentacle on his stomach, and so on. (Whew! Maybe if he'd just stayed put and conserved his energy and blood, he would have lived.) Four: Sophie happens to be working the night shift in the crypto lab. Five: Bezu Fache has the nerve to (quite surprisingly) destroy evidence at the scene of the crime. Five coincidences. What are the odds of all those happening? If we conservatively estimate that perhaps twenty-five alternate events could have occurred for each one that did, the odds would be precisely the same as that of randomly selecting the right code to open the first cryptex: "that's twenty-six to the fifth power... approximately twelve million"[18] to one.

And if we could stack on just a few more coincidences—such as Vernet's spent shell happening to land where Langdon could wedge it in the armored-car door, Langdon choosing to flee directly into the Teacher's arms at Château Villette, and so on—we could easily reach ten coincidences, and postulate at least nine other possibilities for these. Ten plot points with ten options at each juncture. The odds then? The same as the odds of randomly guessing the correct code for Saunière's safe-deposit box: ten to the tenth power. "Ten billion possible"[19] scenarios against Brown's one. The improbability of the plot rises in inverse proportion to our chances of determining its significance. It's just not probable that we can figure out what Brown is getting at.

If only Doctor McCoy were around to grouse at Sophie's odds-making as he did with the infernal logic of Mr. Spock.

The second element working against us is impossibility. How many times can unavoidable truths turn out to be avoidable? How many times can "facts" which mesh "too perfectly"[20] become instantly muddy? How often will Robert Langdon and Sophie simply be flat-out wrong? In this section of the story alone, Langdon is wrong about the ten-digit code, is also wrong about the Grail being hidden in the rosewood box, and naïvely allows himself to be locked in the back of an armored car. When certainty is so constantly disproved, either everything is possible or nothing is.

The third element is outright deception. The characters in Brown's story not only deceive themselves and each other, they deceive us as well. Eventually, we lose track of what's true and what isn't. When Brown tells us, for instance, that "Langdon had harbored several fantasies about what they might find" in Saunière's rosewood box, and that "clearly he had been wrong on every count,"[21] it's easy for us to forget that Langdon had precisely one brief fantasy, not several, and that he hardly had time to ponder that one possibility, much less "harbor" it.

Dan Brown not only leads us directly into a brick wall, he stacks the deck with improbability, impossibility, and deception. And still we feel like we know what's going on. That red carpet is so inviting.

A Lawsuit in the Wings: *The Omega Code*

The key content of Dan Brown's book, the biggest red carpet of them all, is his fictionalization of the speculative non-fiction work *Holy Blood, Holy Grail*. As we discussed in the last chapter, two of the book's three authors, Richard Leigh and Michael Baigent, recently lost a copyright infringement case against Brown's UK publisher, Random House. Even Leigh's and Baigent's former publisher testified against them, referring to their work as a book which "purports to be non-fiction."[22] How's that for damning with faint praise?

Clues in His Art: Welcome and Keep Out

What the publishing world has really lost track of in all the furor over copyrights and Christology is *The Da Vinci Code*'s similarity to *The Omega Code*, a theatrical release produced by Trinity Broadcasting Network co-founder Paul Crouch, and directed by Robert Marcarelli.

Leaving the very titular similarities aside, consider the film's plot. The story concerns the fulfillment of various supposedly obscure biblical prophecies. The key to deciphering them is an ancient secret code. The film opens with the assassination of an old man who is the guardian of great secrets. The killer, who is in the employ of a shadowy international power-monger, thinks he has the secret key, but it has in fact been hidden. The actual code then falls into the hands of a male academic celebrity and a female professional who happens to have the ability to spirit the hero away from immediate danger. After some narrow brushes with capture, they escape from mainland Europe on a jet... Sound a little familiar?

Of course, *The Omega Code* has very different concerns. It's a specifically apocalyptic thriller, and the villain turns out to be the anti-Christ himself, not merely a power-hungry conspiracy nutjob like Teabing. Yet the similarity of the plot and many of its twists are uncanny.

What's even more uncanny is how *The Omega Code*, in spite of its fairly decent special effects and production values, mirrors the simple-minded cryptography of *The Da Vinci Code*. Marcarelli's decoding scheme is computer-based, built on the rather fanciful *Bible Code* craze of the early 1990s. As the film would have it, the discoverer of the Omega Code managed to construct a three-dimensional model of biblical texts, and this 3-D Bible would occasionally spit out "secret" messages of hidden biblical prophecy. The problem is, all those messages are hiding right in plain sight in the Bible. No code necessary, thank you very much, just a pair of eyes and a lexicon. The consultant on the film was Hal Lindsey. I guess that explains a lot.

Another similarity is that Marcarelli gets his theology as wrong as anything one can find in *The Da Vinci Code*. Now, the film's pre-tribulation, premillennial eschatology is clearly an arguable interpretation; but it's hardly definitive either, and questionable as the basis for a film that purports to preach the truth. But get this: *Omega*'s anti-Christ has never actually read the book of Revelation, and has no idea that he loses in the end or any clue as to the signs of his demise. The reason he loses is that he's the only one in the cast or the audience who doesn't know how the story ends! What an impotent villain. What an empty, anti-scriptural anti-Christ. What a waste of a pretty decent performance by Peter York.

The upshot is that Dan Brown appears to steal an awful lot from a really mediocre Christian thriller, and that Christians who want to criticize the theology of Dan Brown's novel need look no further than the inspiration of his book for the origin of such wacky ramblings.

On the Trail of Meaningless Pulp

No, neither *The Omega Code* nor *The Da Vinci Code* are the "guiding star" that leads to "secret truth."[23] At the very best, each work "speaks of"[24] such truths, dancing around them, inviting us down the red carpet to find them, only to dash our hopes in front of a closed door.

When an element does work, like the triangular key that Saunière leaves Sophie, it is comfortable and snug; when we see where it goes, we say, like Langdon, "Something tells me it will fit."[25]

Sometimes, we even end up feeling like Silas, convinced that we have simply discovered the Wizard of Oz, that the red carpet has led us down "a devious dead end."[26]

More often than not, though, Brown's deceptions and improbabilities lock us out. They leave us feeling like Vernet, muttering, "I never know what the hell I'm lugging."[27]

> *Vinegar and papyrus,*
> *Sophie thought. By the*
> *time anyone extracted*
> *the secret message,*
> *it would be a glob of*
> *meaningless pulp.*

For Further Investigation
The Da Vinci Code, Chapters 42 through 47

Dig a Little Deeper

➤ On what basis do you tend to establish trust? How can a person exercise discernment and still be trusting?

➤ How is "keeping secrets" the "worst way of breaking trust"? Is there an appropriate time to keep secrets?

➤ When we come across something we don't understand, we often leap to the conclusion that it is either wrong or uninformed. Why is that?

➤ Do you generally feel that other people are more intelligent or less intelligent than you?

➤ What motivations do you attribute to people who are more "successful" or more powerful than you? How often do you think you are correct?

➤ Do you think it is possible to determine what Dan Brown is "getting at"? What are some other possibilities for his intentions through his novel?

Draw Your Own Conclusions

➤ "End Times" Theories and Eschatological Doctrine:

- www.religioustolerance.org/millenni.htm
- *Encyclopedia of Millennialism and Millennial Movements*, by Richard Landes.

➤ Baigent's and Leigh's Lawsuit Against Dan Brown's Publisher:

- http://news.bbc.co.uk/1/hi/entertainment/4754308.stm
- www.timesonline.co.uk/article/0,,200-2123600,00.html

➤ Probability and God:

- *Intelligent Design: The Bridge Between Science and Theology*, by William A. Dembski.
- *Unintelligent Design*, by Mark Perakh.

➤ Really Bad Thinking in Biblical Stories:

- The story of Samson: Judges 14–16.
- The story of David and Bathsheba: 2 Samuel 11–12.

> Sophie looked unsettled.
> "In cryptology, that's
> called a 'self-authorizing
> language.' That is, if you're
> smart enough to read it,
> you're permitted to know
> what's being said."

If You're Smart Enough

Greg Wright, Lead Investigator

My paternal grandfather was mostly raised in sod houses in South Dakota and the plains of Alberta. When the first of the dust-bowl drought years struck, the boom in high-plains grain farming came to an end. Irvine's father J. E. was forced to sell the Excel, Alberta, homestead and send his family to live with relatives in Oregon. Their first stay was in a woodcutter's shed on Mason Road just outside Jefferson.

After soloing through one last winter on the plains, John Edwin Wright also pulled up stakes and followed his wife and children. I wrote of that event in my grandfather's biography, *Strange Things Done*.

> In the spring of 1924, J. E. Wright packed up what remained of the farm and headed south. In order to take a homestead in Alberta, J. E. had become a naturalized Canadian citizen; as such, he was allowed to emigrate, but only carrying personal belongings. Knowing he might have to leave all behind him, he headed for the Canadian border with the full team of horses and wagon loaded down with farm equipment. According to family

legend, the customs official at the border noticed that J. E. wore a Mason's insignia; himself a Mason, he elected to help his Brother and let J. E. pass, citizenship or no.[1]

Masons will tell you, of course, that such tales are merely apocryphal—that Masons cut each other no more slack than would golfing buddies. It's nonetheless difficult to otherwise account for how my grandfather managed to arrive in Oregon with his farm's complete outfit in tow. Besides, such brotherly blind eyes turn up in other tales as well, as in Rudyard Kipling's *The Man Who Would Be King*—and, of course, in *The Da Vinci Code*.

On the Trail of Masonic Secrets

Neither Robert Langdon nor Leigh Teabing are Masons, of course. But they do treat each other as if they were.

As Langdon and Sophie huddle with the rosewood box in the back of Vernet's armored car, Langdon regales his young initiate with the history of the Freemasons, a "secret society" devoted to safeguarding the ancient mysteries of Masonic principles. One of their primary secrets, Langdon tells Sophie, is the design of keystones, the center blocks in vaulted arches over doorways.

Yes, that's right. The Masons protect their mysteries by installing them right over doorways—the last place in the world anyone would ever think of looking for something secret.

So how do secret societies like the Masons work? How do they pass on their secrets (aside from putting them in places where any child of four could observe them)? Through "*preuves de mérite*," as our French heroine calls them. Dan Brown explains:

> Tests like this were extremely common in secret societies. The best known was the Masons', wherein members ascended to higher degrees by proving they

could keep a secret and by performing rituals and various tests of merit over many years. The tasks became progressively harder until they culminated in a successful candidate's induction as thirty-second-degree Mason.[2]

And then what? Well, no one really knows, because it's all a secret.

But Langdon is pretty sure of this: recent rumors about the Priory of Sion indicate that the secret hiding place of the Holy Grail is tied up with a Masonic keystone—and he concludes that the cryptex in Saunière's rosewood box must be a figurative keystone, rather than the literal one that Grail enthusiasts (like Sir Leigh) have been seeking for the last decade.

Vernet interrupts the storytelling at this point. Guns have a way of ruining the flow of thought. He attempts to wrest the rosewood box from our heroes, claiming that he intends to return it to Saunière's account at the bank, before reporting the fugitives. Clever, clever Langdon foils Vernet's plan, however, and the banker is left bloodily and dustily surprised as the armored car speeds off without him. He quickly calls the bank and has a staffer activate the transponder in the armored car, so its location can be tracked. Oh, for another bar of soap.

Down in Italy, Aringarosa wends away from Castel Gandolfo, smugly clutching his case full of Vatican bearer bonds. He can't wait to swap the loot for the keystone.

Langdon, meantime, misguidedly decides that the best place to lay low is the estate of his good friend Sir Leigh Teabing, with whom he once collaborated on a BBC history special about Grail theories. When Langdon and Sophie arrive at Château Villette, they banter for a bit with Rémy, Teabing's cook/butler/chauffeur. Langdon then asks Teabing, "Any chance you'd open the gate for an old friend?" The good knight replies: "Those who seek the truth are more than friends. They are brothers."

Shades of Rudyard Kipling.

And then Teabing makes Langdon jump through some silly hoops about tea. The Ancient Scottish Rite of the Masons no doubt centers on haggis, hard cider, and shortbread. We can only wonder what the York Rite—whose highest degree is that of Knight Templar—entails.

Having passed the tongue-in-cheek litmus test, Langdon wins safe haven with Teabing. Or so he thinks. He and Sophie venture into Château Villette, perhaps the last place in France they really ought to be.

Men Who Would Be King

Narratively speaking, Leigh Teabing is a stand-in for the authors of *Holy Blood, Holy Grail*, the book that finally put the Priory of Sion on everyone's conspiracy map. Let's listen in on Langdon's thoughts:

> *Jacques Saunière? Grand Master?* . . . Langdon had the eerie sensation it almost made perfect sense. After all, previous Priory Grand Masters had *also* been distinguished public figures with artistic souls. Proof of that fact had been uncovered years ago. . . in papers that became known as *Les Dossiers Secrets*. Every Priory historian and Grail buff had read the *Dossiers*. Cataloged under Number 4° lm[1] 249, the *Dossiers Secrets* had been authenticated by many specialists and incontrovertibly confirmed what historians had suspected for a long time. . .[3]

Actually, the story behind the *Dossiers* is even better known than what Langdon lets on, and is fully documented in *Holy Blood, Holy Grail*, among other places. The *Dossiers* weren't really *discovered* in Paris' Bibliothèque Nationale; they were *deposited* in the library by Pierre Plantard, the Grand Master of the Priory of Sion, a political organization registered with the French government in 1956—and then the existence of the documents was "leaked" to the press. Richard Leigh is not overly complimentary about the *Dossiers*, saying that they "consist for the most part of page after page after page of genealogy. You go through them and you wonder what in the devil is all this in the name of? What is it trying to prove? So bloody what?"[4]

Journalist Jean-Luc Chaumeil, one of the reporters who conducted early interviews with Plantard, explains:

> Plantard developed a myth whereby he was the only one who could save France during the war and after the war, saying that he was part of a secret society. ... These documents try to prove, through a series of stories, that there is indeed a descendant of the Merovingians who is a lost king. In the first interview I did with him, I asked Plantard, "What do you think of this story of the lost king?" And Plantard answered, "The lost king is not as far away as you think."[5]

When he and his collaborators were researching *Holy Blood, Holy Grail*, Leigh says they "were confronted by a group of people in Paris with a seemingly bizarre, bonkers objective— namely to restore a 1600-year-old bloodline."[6] Bonkers, yes. "From the very beginning, and we're talking thirty years ago," says Chaumeil, "everyone in France knew this was a hoax."[7]

So why did Leigh, Baigent and Lincoln further promote the hoax? Because they knew it would serve as the perfect platform to add a new twist to Plantard's tale—tying Merovingian claims to the French throne to Cathar legends of Mary Magdelene's child, a royal bloodline fathered by Jesus.

"Our conclusions," backpedals Leigh, "were simply that, yes, these things are plausible. I can't say, nor will my co-authors say, that we believe them. We will certainly not argue that this was the case."[8]

Men who would be kings—or bestselling authors—will do the strangest things.

Leigh's spin on Plantard's hoax has also found its way into *Bloodline of the Holy Grail: The Hidden Lineage of Jesus* by Laurence Gardner. The Foreword for Gardner's book was written by none other than Prince Michael Stewart of Albany, a French-Belgian man who would also be king.

In a none-too-surprising twist, Gardner wrote the introduction to Prince Michael's book, *The Forgotten Monarchy of Scotland: The True Story of the Royal House of Stewart and the Hidden Lineage of the Kings and Queens of Scots*. It's a fascinating read, and it too—through copious genealogical charts, tales of conspiracies, and ties to the Templars, Masons, and the Holy Land—makes the case that a man raised in relative obscurity is actually the blood heir to a royal throne. In this case, it's not Plantard; it's Prince Michael of Albany himself, direct descendant of Scotland's Bonnie Prince Charlie. Among other fantastic claims, Prince Michael traces his lineage to Israel's royal bloodline through Tamar Tephi, the daughter of Judah's king Zedekiah. According to Celtic traditions, the princess was spirited out of Palestine by the prophet Jeremiah, along with the Stone of Destiny. Their new home? Ireland, naturally. Oh—and this event, which took place about 586 BC, coincided with the concealment of certain documents in the vaults of Solomon's temple in Jerusalem. . .

Also not too surprisingly, Prince Michael claims the titles of Duke of Normandy and Aquitaine; titular Prince of France and Poland; Head of the Celtic Church of the Sacred Kindred of Saint Columba; Grand Master of the Noble Order of the Guard of Saint Germain; and, among a host of other titles, Knight Grand Commander of the Chivalric Military Order of the Temple of Jerusalem.[9]

Yup. Knight Templar.

A secret handshake can take a guy a long way. At least we can have complete confidence that Prince Michael's history is one written by losers.

Plantard and Stewart, however, are not without precedent in using biblical bloodlines to enforce claims to the throne. Charlemagne and his knights employed the same tactic; and my sister has the genealogical data to prove that I, too, am descended from Charlemagne, among many other worthy kings.

Perhaps I also should venture to Europe and claim some lost crown.

Sheesh.

The Name Game

Here's the really odd thing. Dan Brown makes no mention of Pierre Plantard in *The Da Vinci Code*, though he cites the existence of Plantard's forged *Dossiers Secrets* as one of his foundational "facts." What's worse, Robert Langdon and Leigh Teabing appear equally ignorant of both Plantard and his hoax. How can that possibly be? Sir Leigh Teabing even owns a copy of *Holy Blood, Holy Grail*. What's Dan Brown up to?

Before offering an answer for that question, let's take a very brief tour through the names of several key characters.

But first, we should perhaps review the history of the church at Rennes-le-Château, a small village in southern France. As documented in *Holy Blood, Holy Grail*, among other texts, the church was allegedly the scene of the discovery of ancient documents—documents spirited away from a Cathar castle during the Church's medieval crusade against the heretic Albigenses. Their offense? Sir Walter Scott describes them as

> a numerous party of dissenters from the faith of Rome, men professing, in most respects, those doctrines which are now avowed by the Protestant churches... a set of obscure but sensible men, whose minds could not be reconciled to the extravagant tenets of the Roman Church. They did not exactly agree in doctrine amongst themselves, and... had never embraced the faith of Rome, or yielded to its extravagant claims of temporal

authority.[10]

There was the real rub: political power. Struggles between men who would either be Pope or King (or both) led to the slaughter of innocents everywhere, and often in the name of the Church. Certainly that was true in the case of the Cathars.

So events in the south of France, as the theory goes, connect Magdelene's child and the bloodline of Christ through the Cathars to Rennes-le-Château, to the Sangreal documents, Pierre Plantard, and the *Dossiers Secrets*.

So where do Dan Brown's characters come in?

Jacques Saunière, Sophie's grandfather, is named after Berenger Saunière, the priest at Rennes-le-Château. Devotees of Henry Lincoln, co-author of *Holy Blood, Holy Grail*, have organized themselves under the name "The Saunière Society." Berenger Saunière, incidentally, was also a proven fraud.

Marie Chauvel, Sophie's grandmother, gets her name from the first female consecrated as a bishop (literally, a "Sophia") of the contemporary Gnostic Cathar Church (or Assembly of the Paraclete), which was organized in the late nineteenth century during the first wave of esoteric Rennes-le-Château enthusiasm.

Bezu Fache takes his—ahem—Christian name from an ancient Cathar fortress in the south of France.

And Leigh Teabing? His name, of course, is derived from those of the other two authors of *Holy Blood, Holy Grail*: Leigh and Baigent. "Teabing" is an anagram of "Baigent."

So again: what is Dan Brown up to? Clearly, he knows the legends of the Cathars and Rennes-le-Château. Clearly he knows that *Holy Blood, Holy Grail* makes no claim to authenticate Plantard's lunacy. If Dan Brown knows all this, why don't Langdon or Teabing know? Better yet, why don't we, the readers, get clued in?

Parlor Tricks and Riddle Games

I think we've all been at parties at which cryptic games like "hug the potholder," "crossed and uncrossed," or "Chinese knives" have been played. They all work pretty much the same way. Party guests who are "in the know" always play the game correctly, and those who don't know the trick—and especially those who don't catch on quickly—become the brunt of the joke. They're always playing the game wrong and have no hope of playing it correctly.

My favorite example of this type of parlor trick is one which employs a grid of nine magazines laid out in three rows and columns on the floor. Two confederates collaborate on the stunt, one acting as the "pointer" and one acting as the "clairvoyant." When the clairvoyant leaves the room, the pointer asks an uninitiated party guest to select one of the magazines. The clairvoyant is then brought back into the room to guess which magazine has been selected. This is accomplished by the pointer taking a broom handle (or fireplace poker) and pointing in succession to various magazines and asking, "Is this the one?" Invariably, when the correct magazine is pointed to, the clairvoyant identifies it.

The trick lies not in which magazine is first pointed to, nor in the order they are selected. The secret lies in precisely how the first magazine is pointed to: the pointer touches the first magazine in the spot which corresponds to the grid position at which the chosen magazine is located. So, for instance, if the chosen magazine is in the first position of the first row, the pointer's first selection must be touched in the corresponding corner. Regardless of the order in which subsequent magazines are touched, the clairvoyant always knows precisely which magazine has been selected.

The point of such games is that those in the know get a great deal of entertainment value out their secret knowledge. Party guests are either amazed by what seems to be actual clairvoyance, or mightily annoyed at not being able to figure out the "trick."

It's a rare day indeed when anyone who learns the trick

actually takes the game seriously.

Dan Brown's indirect acknowledgment of Pierre Plantard's hoax essentially functions as one such parlor trick. Like Masonic tests of merit, it's "self-authorizing language," to use Sophie's words— "if you're smart enough" to read Brown's clues, "you're permitted to know what's being said."[11] If not? Well, those in the know can just sit back and be amused while you are either amazed by the revelations of the *Dossiers Secrets* or are annoyed because you don't yet see the trick.

Those already familiar with Rennes-le-Château, naturally, are tipped off at the very beginning of the book that Brown's story is some type of in-joke. Plantard's bogus *Dossiers Secrets* lead off the "fact" page, and the name Saunière fairly leaps out of the first line of the Prologue. Dan Brown acts as the pointer, and clairvoyant readers know exactly where he's headed. It's left to the rest of the party guests to be wowed and amazed, or angered.

Surely it's no accident that Brown introduces the details of the *Dossiers Secrets* in the context of revelations about the Masons' secret rites. And what follows at Château Villette amounts to so much wink-wink ritual hazing, Teabing and Langdon joking at length about Sophie's status as a Grail "*virgin*."[12] Oh, what fun they're about to have! Pointer, clairvoyant, and *naïf*.

But where's the pleasure in that? Why would Dan Brown go to such lengths just to play elaborate jokes? Because the fun of parlor tricks, in part, lies in the process of discovery. It's fun to know that you're in possession of a little inside information; and it's even more fun to know that, if you can just pick up a little clue here and there, you can ascend through greater "degrees" of knowledge and join the inner circle.

And as with 33rd degree Masons, we might just find that the bulk of the fun is in getting there, not in actually being part of the inner circle.

My paternal grandfather Irvine, like his father J. E. before him, was also a Mason. He achieved 32nd degree status, mastering all of the official sacred Scottish rites. He was also a member of Eastern Star, an egalitarian sister society replete with its own rituals. Both sets of my grandparents were members of the same Eastern Star lodge, and my maternal grandmother Hazel had the following to say about Irvine's ritualistic obsession:

> He liked to be late. I really felt that he liked to be late, liked to make a late entrance. He seemed to like to be deliberately late, which was odd because his mother and dad were always the first people to Eastern Star. ... If you aren't there when they open, you have to work your way in, and he seemed to like to. There's secret signs and so forth, and to get in you have to go through certain rituals. Irvine liked to make a big production out of every drill we had.[13]

My uncle Rodney, who was a member of Irvine's Masonic lodge, witnessed the same behavior. The rituals, the secret handshakes, the passwords—they're all part of the game. For some, they're a burden; for others, they're almost the whole point. It's the same with riddle games, secret little clues of the type that Saunière often left for Sophie, as he did that one Christmas morning:

> *A treasure hunt!* ... Eagerly she pored over the riddle until she solved it. The solution pointed her to another part of the house, where she found another card and another riddle. She solved this one, too, racing on to the next card. Running wildly, she darted back and forth across the house, from clue to clue...[14]

Riddle Games and *The Last Crusade*

Such riddle games are both the central metaphor of *The Da Vinci Code* and the means by which Dan Brown's plot is driven forward. But, as with Bilbo's and Gollum's encounter in *The Hobbit*, the riddles themselves are not the point of the story. They are merely a highly entertaining means to an end, and are not themselves to be taken seriously.

The point, whether in *The Hobbit*, *The Man Who Would Be King*, or *The Da Vinci Code*, is using riddle games and secret handshakes to get to the treasure—and finding that you're going to have to give up the treasure if you're going to save the day.

The Man Who Would be King, of course, starred Michael Caine and Sean Connery in one of film history's most inspired casting decisions. It was only fitting, then, that Connery should come full circle from monarchy-obsessed Mason to Holy Grail enthusiast, also playing the father of Indiana Jones in the third *Raiders* installment. The narrative follows a familiar thread. . .

An American academic discovers the scene of a crime. Thuggish hoods are looking for clues to a secret treasure, and it appears that a family member is missing or dead. Our rather tweedy hero teams up with a female accomplice in Paris to track down lost secrets. It turns out that the missing relative held a map to the location of the Holy Grail. After a series of cryptic clues and a chase sequence or two through the city's underbelly, the hero must flee by air. The Grail is not in France, but is hidden elsewhere. . .

In the case of *Indiana Jones and the Last Crusade*, however, the hero is not "Harrison Ford in Harris tweed," it's Harrison Ford himself—and the old man who leaves the clues turns out to be not only alive; he also happens to be Sean Connery. I wonder if he was considered for the role of Saunière?

Steven Spielberg's Grail quest, however, leverages none of Dan Brown's contemporary Grail "scholarship," instead focusing squarely on traditionalist Arthurian leanings. We may wonder why. There's no Priory of Sion, after all, no connection to Rosslyn or Leonardo. Neither the Cathars nor Rennes-le-Château enter the narrative. Connery's map leads the elder Jones and his swashbuckling son back, in fact, to the Holy Land, where the Holy Grail is still guarded by an ancient Knight Templar—

perhaps an ancestor of Prince Michael Stewart? Nope.

To gain access to the inner sanctum, however, and to save his father's life, Indiana Jones must first pass the same three-riddle model employed by Teabing at Château Villette. The situation is a little more hazardous, however, than a mere cup of tea. The third riddle, in fact, requires Indiana Jones to take a literal leap of faith, stepping out onto an invisible bridge over a deep chasm. Jones passes the test, gets the Grail, and saves his father, though he still loses the treasure in the end.

Hardy Boys on Steroids?

To be brutally honest, the trail of clues in *The Da Vinci Code* is really no more sophisticated than that of *The Last Crusade*—and it's not meant to be. This is all intended merely as great fun, a sort of grown-up Hardy Boys or Nancy Drew mystery. But where is Dan Brown pointing with all this? Is it all just a glorified literary parlor game, or is there something more at stake?

The primary tension of the plot is provided, of course, between the restrictive conventions of patriarchalism and the supposedly liberating celebration of the sacred feminine. But does Dan Brown really want us to choose between the two? We might use Fabienne André Worth's words to describe the literary function of *The Da Vinci Code*: "The dialogue constantly undermines the oppositions it sets up, and it does not aim at a final reconciliation, that is, the submission of the one or the domination of the other."[15] Robert Langdon, in particular, does not advocate the overthrow of the Church; he just wishes it could rediscover its inner woman.

As we discussed at length in our last chapter, the expositional pattern utilized by Dan Brown is both welcoming and exclusionary. He lays out red carpets that lead to closed doors. Like Saunière's riddle games with the young Sophie, his questions only lead to more questions, not to concrete answers. Like the skewed horizon behind the *Mona Lisa*, the clues that Dan Brown drops let us know clearly that he's playing fast and loose with the facts. He is not make glaring goofs—rather, he is sending loud messages, blaring out from the background. Again to use Worth's words, Dan Brown's book

> seems to have been written to defy the critics' desire for interpretive mastery while at the same time trying 'to engage a carefully designated public into action.' Almost as fluid as the Rorschach test, it affords a favorable ground for exploring the reductive tendencies of interpretation as well as the opportunity for choosing one's own.[16]

That is, if we want to be offended by *The Da Vinci Code*, we may. Or, if we want to believe that Brown is proposing something radically new, we may as well. And if we actually want to believe Plantard's myth—or even the traditional faith of the Roman Catholic Church—there's certainly nothing in *The Da Vinci Code* to prevent us from going down such a path.

But here's one final clue to consider: Fabienne André Worth doesn't actually say these things about *The Da Vinci Code*.

Worth says these things about Diderot's *Rameau's Nephew*, a cryptic eighteenth-century novel about—yes—androgyny. The original title of Diderot's novel, in French, is *Le Neveu de Rameau*.

Sofia—wisdom, feminine.

Neveu—nephew, masculine.

Sophie Neveu, then, represents both the feminine and the masculine. Androgynous. Complementarian.

Worth's comments can be found in an essay titled, "*Rameau's Nephew*, Godard, and *Mona Lisa*: Uncovering the Veil of Gender in the Undergraduate Classroom." The paper was presented at an MLA conference in 1986 and includes a reference to an art historian's conclusion that the *Mona Lisa* was, in fact, an androgynous self portrait. The paper concludes:

Ideology has far-reaching epistemological implications, and texts must be analyzed with an awareness of the framework we bring to them. Godard's film [*Masculin/Féminin*] can help us—teachers and students—to confront the way identity is socially and linguistically constructed in today's world of consumerism and sexism and to understand the ambiguity inherent in the notion of "character" and "subject." Then we can ask why we resist certain elements in Diderot's work. We might discover that by relinquishing the notion of a fixed identity (subject) or of a fixed textual meaning (author), we also dispense with the gender-definition game that polarizes and immobilizes the complexity of life and text into the black-and-white of myth.[17]

Clues in his art, indeed. Did Brown run across Fabienne André Worth's paper on the web while researching the *Mona Lisa*? Was Worth really Dan Brown's muse? Is it possible that Brown is after nothing more sophisticated or devious than an end to polarization and inactivity? Is he perhaps showing us the insanity of pendulum swings, instead proposing a centered, complementarian mode of worship that celebrates God's masculine and feminine traits equally?

Perhaps Dan Brown has written a *Neveu* for the twenty-first century. Maybe he is a Diderot for today.

> **Teabing looked both startled and pleased. "Leonardo was one of the keepers of the Holy Grail. And he hid clues in his art."**

For Further Investigation
The Da Vinci Code, Chapters 48 through 54

Dig a Little Deeper

➤ How does Dan Brown's novel afford "a favorable ground for exploring the reductive tendencies of interpretation as well as the opportunity for choosing one's own," to again use Worth's words?

➤ Is there any way to substantiate any single interpretation of *The Da Vinci Code*?

➤ Do you think Dan Brown is after a single meaning with his novel, or after a range of meanings?

➤ What do you think the "Da Vinci code" refers to?

Draw Your Own Conclusions

➤ Regarding the Albigenses and Cathars:

- www.newadvent.org/cathen/01267e.htm
- www.languedoc-france.info/12_cathars.htm
- www.sociologyesoscience.com/davincicode/catharmyth.html
- *The History of the Crusades Against the Albigenses in the 13th Century (The Extermination of the Cathars),* by J. C. L. Simonde De Sismondi and Robert Weatherburn.

➤ The Significance of Rennes-le-Château:

- www.renneslechateau.com/
- http://priory-of-sion.com/

➤ The Saunière Society and the Search for Truth:

- www.sauniere-society.org/
- www.sauniere.cjb.net/

Clues in His Art: If You're Smart Enough

➤ Putting the Pieces Together:

  • The History Channel's *Beyond the Da Vinci Code* does a fine job of connecting Plantard, Saunière, *Holy Blood, Holy Grail*, and Dan Brown.

  • For a look at how ancient royal bloodlines continue to shape the politics of Europe, and to better understand what drove Plantard, consider finding a copy of *The Forgotten Monarchy of Scotland*. The similarity between Plantard's theories and Stewart's are rather remarkable.

➤ A Biblical Look at the Riddle of Life and Vain Knowledge:

  • Ecclesiastes 1:13–18.

> "And yet," Langdon
> countered, "the Vatican is
> made up of deeply pious
> men who truly believe
> these contrary documents
> could only be false
> testimony."

Deeply Pious Men

Jenn Wright, Lead Investigator

Deeply pious men make the news all the time. Those who are sincerely and utterly devoted to an idea or an ideal, pursuing it with every fiber of their being, are quintessentially pious. We all know pious people—they're the ones who faithfully get up at two dark thirty (without an alarm), read their Bibles with complete attention for an hour (minimum), then spend another hour (at least) in humble, undistracted prayer, all before the children wake up.

Such is the evidence of piety, right?

Well, I'm not so sure. The *American Heritage Dictionary* defines "pious" as "marked by conspicuous devoutness."[1] And while a pious person is often associated with religious fervor, such is not always the case. An earnest devotion to God may look strikingly similar to an equally earnest devotion to animal rights. The person who is devoted to God may choose to express that devotion through proselytizing, participating in peaceful demonstrations, and making drastic changes to his or her lifestyle; and so may the animal rights activist. Piety itself makes no distinction between causes; it is merely the visible response to a

131

personal belief.

So rather than looking at the semblance of piety, perhaps the more relevant questions are where the piety comes from, and what its fruits are. Passionate devotion to something—religion, politics, leaders, virtually anything—neither authenticates nor invalidates it; such is a good thing to keep in mind when reading about conspiracy theorists who are "conspicuously devoted" to their conspiracy theories.

I Say—Teabing and Scones, Anyone?

Now that Langdon and Sophie have safely arrived at Sir Leigh Teabing's Château Villette, the information about the Grail goes from trickle to torrent as Teabing illuminates all the research upon which Langdon has so heavily drawn for his own book. Over tea and scones, the "truth" is revealed about the integrity and authority of the Bible and how it came together, Da Vinci's ostensible personal disdain for Scripture, Jesus' posthumously imposed divinity, and a host of other "facts" that directly oppose religio-historical accounts. As Sophie listens in wonder, Teabing expounds the truth of the oft-misunderstood Grail legend: that the Grail is actually not a cup, but a woman—the wife of Jesus, Mary Magdalene herself. As they examine an enlarged print of *The Last Supper*, the "truths" are revealed: there are thirteen cups, not just one; the Grail, then, *must* be the overtly feminine companion seated at Jesus' right. Further evidence is produced in support of Teabing's claims, which Sophie absorbs with dumbfounded but not dubious fascination. Numerous historical records, including the Gospel of Mary Magdalene herself, add to the snowballing testimony of the Church's major concealment efforts. Teabing goes on to explain the Church's smear campaign—stories of Magdalene's activities as a prostitute, fabricated in order to "cover up her dangerous secret."[2] Sophie finally catches up with her brain when she realizes that "Sangreal" is a double entendre, depending on where you put the space: it means both "Holy Grail" and "Royal Bloodline," referring to both Mary Magdalene and the daughter she bore soon (less than nine months, at least) after Jesus' death. And it is this Mary that the Priory of Sion "still worships... as the Goddess, the Holy Grail, the Rose, and the Divine Mother."[3]

Meanwhile, in the next room, Rémy has just witnessed the news flash about the fugitives. Outside, Silas (under order from the Teacher) lurks in the perimeter, preparing to break in and procure the keystone—with deadly Heckler and Koch force, if necessary. Back at the Depository Bank of Zurich, the Kops de Keystone fumble around waiting for a search warrant, until they finally receive confirmation of Langdon's and Sophie's whereabouts.

Real-Life Piety and its Perpetrators

Piety comes in all flavors and sizes, and is not confined to Christianity in the least. Many non-Christian leaders have demonstrated incredible piety—Gandhi and the Dalai Lama come immediately to mind as very peaceful but intensely devoted men. Yet this deep devotion is not even limited to religious people; those devoted to political or moral causes, apart from religious beliefs, often demonstrate the same harmonious fusion of peace and intensity. Piety can literally be found everywhere; unfortunately, its effects are not always in line with its self-defined intentions.

The Muslim suicide bombers who have used their bodies as extermination devices, for example, are certainly conspicuously devoted men whose beliefs about acting on their faith in this life and rewards in the afterlife have led them to plan and execute countless atrocities all over the globe. While they may be hard to comprehend, their intentions themselves may not be "evil" per se—they simply believe very strongly that Islam is the answer to the world's problems, and ridding the world of infidels will further their cause. Unfortunately, the effects of such singularly destructive actions belie their intents, causing untold damage to the people within the vicinity as well as the reputation of the Islamic faith. Surely they would desire that the effect be a worldwide acknowledgment and adoption of Islam and its tenets, but the results of the myriad suicide bombings to date have not yet seen that intention come to fruition.

In order to be fair, the same could be said of the "war on terror," launched following the 2001 attacks in the United States. Our military action is based on the same certainty of "rightness" as is the Muslim suicide bombers'; though the foundational beliefs may be starkly different, the sense of justification and moral propriety leads us to use violence in the name of peace just as it leads them. As President George W. Bush famously said in a June 18, 2002, speech, "I just want you to know that, when we talk about war, we're really talking about peace."[4]

Yet another example of paradoxical intentions and effects are the pro-life advocates who promote violence toward abortionists. Since 1976, when the first arson of an abortion clinic was reported, over 5,000 individual crimes against abortion providers have been documented, including seven murders and seventeen attempted murders. The first murder of an abortion provider occurred in 1993, when Michael Griffin, a participant in an anti-abortion demonstration, shot Dr. David Gunn outside a Pensacola, Florida, abortion clinic. His piety led him to first pray for the physician's soul, but did not prevent him from taking a life in the name of preventing the taking of lives. A year later, Paul Hill, once a Presbyterian minister, shot and killed Dr. John Britton and his bodyguard, Lt. Col. James Herman Barrett. Barrett's wife, June, was shot in the arm. (Hill was executed for the murders in 2003.) Other murders, such as James Kopp's shooting of Dr. Barnett Slepian in October 1998, have occurred not onsite at the abortion clinics, but in the providers' own homes, even, as with Dr. Slepian, with their children present. Conspicuously devoted? Most certainly. Do the effects of their actions support their underlying beliefs and intentions? Not so sure.

While the statistics regarding violence and disruption against abortion providers in the United States have decreased over the last decade, the sentiment that drives such behavior is still rampant. Websites such as *armyofgod.com* not only promote the use of violence against abortion providers, but celebrate those who have committed such violent crimes as "heroes of the faith."[5] Obviously they firmly believe that taking one life to save others is not only morally justifiable, but also prescriptive. Unfortunately, though they ostensibly place such monumental worth on human life, their methods defeat their objectives, and the message they intend to convey—that all human life is valuable—is thoroughly discredited by their crimes.

Even non-faith-based piety can be taken too far. Activist groups such as the Earth Liberation Front and the Animal Liberation Front (ELF and ALF, respectively) aim to protect Mother Nature and her family, but while the organizations themselves neither publicly oppose nor advocate violence, their adherents often act on their beliefs in violent and criminal ways. While neither group has taken responsibility for any violent crimes against other people, other crimes are tolerated, if not deliberately encouraged. The ALF's credo, for instance, states its purpose as carrying out "direct action against animal abuse in the form of rescuing animals and causing financial loss to animal exploiters, usually through the damage and destruction of property."[6]

On the other hand, the ELF's official position is rather ambiguous, acknowledging that "any individuals who committed arson or any other illegal acts under the ELF name are individuals who choose to do so under the banner of ELF and do so only driven by their personal conscience."[7] Seems like anything goes, as long as it's in line with the cause.

In 2001, for example, an ecoterrorist firebombed the University of Washington's Urban Horticulture Center in Seattle, where I live. As the Seattle *Post-Intelligencer* reported upon the arrest of the prime suspect,

> the apparent target at the UW center was research into the fast-growing hybrid poplar tree—a tiny portion of which were the transgenic product of DNA manipulation and had been imported from an Oregon State University lab.[8]

But the ELF attackers—who style themselves as defenders of the environment against unchecked encroachment by people—also destroyed numerous rare and endangered Northwest plants growing at the center that were intended to be replanted in the wild.[9]

Once again, the radical actions of a passionate person patently contradict the underlying intentions—in this case, destroying the very commodities they claim to want to protect. Obviously, piety itself is not an endorsement or validation of a given ideology.

The Piety of Sir Leigh Teabing

I doubt that many would label Teabing as "pious" in the religious sense—after all, his main objective seems rather to deconstruct Christianity with his evidence that precious little of its story is true. But deeply devoted he is, and his devotion to the truth of the Grail legend borders on a piety rarely seen in the religious sector. Unfortunately, his piety is grounded in preconceptions and biases. He is out to expose the truth of a two-millennia coverup, a campaign he believes in as much as the Vatican believes "these contrary documents could only be false testimony."[10]

Teabing's approach to convincing his audience of the truth consists of two parts: first, he discredits current beliefs; then, in the wake of shock and bewilderment, he pours out what seems to be a limitless collection of evidence that substantiates his claims to the falsehood of one history and the verity of the other, to which he is so adamantly loyal. It is a common method of argument, one that we all use even without trying to be surreptitious and undermining. We use it because it works. The most opportune time to convince someone that the foundation you have is more tenable than theirs is immediately after they have felt their own foundation shimmy.

But is this fair? Is it a valid form of debate? Or does it swap one set of biases for another? Teabing's statements undermining the integrity of the Bible can, indeed, be disconcerting to those who believe that "all Scripture is God-breathed,"[11] but his "conspicuously devoted" arguments are less than objective, and certainly not evenhanded. In his desire for the Grail legend to be true, Teabing has allowed his bias to color his interpretations. His observation that, when viewing *The Last Supper*, "our preconceived notions of this scene are so powerful that our mind blocks out the incongruity and overrides our eyes,"[12] is as applicable to Da Vinci's art as it is to Teabing's own arguments; his preconceived notions about the truth of Grail lore are so powerful that they block out the fact that his sources are all less than a quarter-century old, and that the foundational pieces of "historical evidence" (the Sangreal documents, the remains of Mary Magdalene, the continuing Priory of Sion) he relies upon are merely presumed to exist, not known facts. As philosopher Arthur Schopenhauer noted, "The discovery of truth is prevented more effectively, not by the false appearance of things present and which mislead into error, not directly by weakness of the reasoning powers, but by preconceived opinion, by prejudice."[13] Rather than letting truth guide him, Teabing has set his course to prove the truth he likes the best, and his pious declaration that "learning the truth has become my life's love"[14] is a hollow expression of passionate intentions leading not toward truth but toward wherever Teabing's beady little eyes are looking (which is usually at the Grail legend).

Piety and the Search for Truth

At first glance, it would seem that part of being pious is seeking the truth, even that seeking the truth is part of what makes a person pious in the first place. But is this really the case? Is piety something we can choose, or is it the outgrowth of something else?

Consider the Council of Nicaea, which Teabing alleges was made up of a group of men who voted certain aspects of Christianity into orthodoxy—holidays, leadership roles, and, most scandalously, the divinity of Jesus Christ.

But even back in Jesus' time, there were biases and prejudices, and whole groups of people whose biases and prejudices kept them from recognizing the truth of Jesus' divinity. The Pharisees and Sadducees (as a whole, though some who truly sought the truth did find it in the Christ), in particular, missed the boat entirely because they were so focused on their own expectations. This is not to say that the Pharisees and Sadducees were not "deeply pious men"—they were the religious experts, the highly educated, the men who had truly devoted their lives to the memorization, teaching, and interpretation of the Scriptures. In a word, these men embodied piety. But their piety did not serve them well once the Messiah they were seeking actually arrived. Instead, their lifetimes of study had been guided by preconceptions and prejudices about the Scriptures, and not guided by a sincere seeking of the truth. Jesus told them, "You diligently study the Scriptures because you think that by them you possess eternal life. These are the Scriptures that testify about me, yet you refuse to come to me."[15] The Jews were looking for a different kind of Messiah—one who would conquer the ruling Romans and establish an earthly kingdom that would elevate the Jews to the governing party rather than the governed rabble.

Even Jesus acknowledged the outward righteousness of the Pharisees, admonishing the people that unless their righteousness (or piety) exceeded that of the Pharisees, they had no hope of entering the Kingdom of Heaven.[16] Later, Jesus warned His disciples against the teachings of these learned men, knowing that their undying devotion had not brought about righteousness, but had only furthered their prejudices and biases.[17] Then, of course, there is the entire diatribe against the heartless practices of the Pharisees in Matthew 23, in which Jesus exposed their "piety" for what it was: an endless pursuit of personal holiness that did little more than promote themselves and mislead others.

So if the righteousness of the Pharisees didn't cut it, what hope is there? They *knew* their stuff. Much like Teabing, they had all their data ducks in a row, all their arguments Tupperware tight, all their bullet points locked and loaded. And still they lacked something.

The truth is, sometimes our personal piety can be as blinding as any prejudice. The unwavering focus on a single idea can prevent us from seeing the truth. So how should we think about Christian piety and the search for truth?

Truth and Piety: The Chicken and the Egg

If piety itself cannot guarantee a straight course in pursuing the truth, we'd better look elsewhere, right? After all, the pursuit of truth is what this whole thing is all about—truth about the Grail, truth about the historicity of the Bible, truth about the divinity of Jesus of Nazareth. If we genuinely want to be truth-seekers, we need to be prepared for what follows—which may or may not be what we expect.

Jesus' own words regarding the truth are numerous, but one thing they all lack is any sense of humankind's ability to find truth on its own. Rather, truth is a revelation, a God-given gift distributed through His Spirit. In the gospel of John, Jesus promises His disciples that He "will ask the Father, and he will give you another Counselor to be with you forever—the Spirit of truth. The world cannot accept him, because it neither sees him nor knows him. But you know him, for he lives with you and will be in you."[18] Soon after saying this, He tells them that the Spirit of truth that will be sent will guide them into all truth.[19] Apparently, the Spirit is the genesis of truth, and allowing the guidance of the Spirit of truth will, inevitably, lead to deeper knowledge of the truth.

Based on that understanding, then, it would follow that piety is not the means of seeking truth, and, in fact, piety can impair one's pursuit of truth. Instead, Jesus seems to be indicating that we seek truth in order to become truly pious, that is, righteously and humbly devoted to the Truth. And in this devotion, the fruit is evident, as we learn to love not "with words or tongue but with actions and in truth. This then is how we know that we belong to the truth, and how we set our hearts at rest in his presence whenever our hearts condemn us."[20] The evidence of being guided into truth by the Spirit of truth is an active love, not mere "conspicuous devotion." As Paul noted in his greeting to Titus, it is "the knowledge of the truth that leads to godliness"[21]— and not godliness which leads to the knowledge of truth.

When the Truth Isn't Easy to Believe

St. Augustine, the Roman church father of the fourth and fifth centuries, noted that "faith therefore is to believe that which you do not see, truth is to see what you have believed."[22] But truth isn't always easy to accept, even when one has been seeking it with all sincerity and humility. Nicodemus, the Pharisee in John 3, could not fathom the rebirth Jesus described as being necessary for salvation. His preconceived notions of birth, as well as his presumptions about the Messiah, blinded him, at least temporarily, and kept him from understanding what Jesus said.

Likewise, Jonah, the famed fish-eaten prophet of the Old Testament, had a little glitch in his truth cogs. His mission was to preach the message of repentance to the city of Nineveh, warning them that should they fail to repent of their wicked ways, the city would be destroyed by God. Now, prophets in those times were tested by the results of their prophecies—if a prophesied event did not occur, the prophet lost all credibility, and sometimes even his life. So after the great fish incident, Jonah, godly (and repentant) prophet that he was, preached his sermons, and then waited for God's wrath to come down upon Nineveh.

Only that didn't happen.

You see, Nineveh repented. They actually listened and responded to Jonah's (obviously unintentionally persuasive) words. But Jonah hadn't counted on repentance; he had counted on a good show of God's wrath, just like he'd predicted. And when God's hand was stayed, Jonah had a bit of trouble accepting the truth: that God really does value repentance, and that He is "a gracious and compassionate God, slow to anger and abounding in love, a God who relents from sending calamity."[23] Jonah wanted the truth that he had proclaimed about God's anger with Nineveh to be seen. His devotion to God's message was colored by his desires to be proven as a prophet, and his sulky response to the salvation of 120,000 people paints a sterling picture of how even the pious ones don't always like the truth that is revealed to them.

Even the apostle Peter rejected the truth when it rocked his world. In Acts 10, Peter has a vision: three times, a congregation of both clean and unclean animals is shown to him, with the directions to "Get up, Peter. Kill and eat," and, after Peter's very Jewish refusals, "Do not call anything impure that God has made clean."[24] Yet after the third instance, with the Lord clearly telling him that there is no more distinction between clean and unclean animals, Peter still lies there, "wondering about the vision."[25] Despite his known devotion to God, his role as a leader in the new church, and his genuine ambition to seek the truth, even Peter's cultural and religious biases prevent him from immediately seeing the truth that God has so clearly revealed in this vision. It isn't until after he witnesses the Holy Spirit's work in Gentile believers that he begins to fully understand and accept the truth of God's message: that, as Paul later wrote, "Here there is no Greek or

Jew, circumcised or uncircumcised, barbarian, Scythian, slave or free, but Christ is all, and is in all."[26]

So the truth, even when directly revealed by God, isn't always so readily believed. On the other hand, the truths we hold so dear are sometimes easily threatened—by skeptics, scientists, or, say, novels about conspiracy theories. When faced with a potential "threat" to our faith, we often react hastily, drumming up our defense of the truth with apologetics and our own set of faith-based "facts." But really, what are we afraid of? The truth is the truth in spite of all arguments, and in spite of all "evidence" to the contrary. As such, the truth is unassailable, and needs no defense from simple human minds. We accept the truth through which the Holy Spirit guides us, and we can pray fervently that the Spirit will guide those who oppose the truth as well. "For we cannot do anything against the truth, but only for the truth."[27] The truth about Jesus' divinity, the truth about the integrity and reliability of Scripture—such truths will continue to be true whether we (and others) accept them or not. And no amount of conspicuous devotion can change them either way.

Pious Intentions: *Jesus*

Originally intended to be merely an accurate representation of the story of Christ as presented in the gospel of Luke, the 1979 movie *Jesus* was an early docudrama of sorts. Produced by people "conspicuously devoted" to the historicity of Jesus Christ, the film has been used—to great effect, really—as an evangelistic tool. Now, obviously we can't quantify or qualify the number of "true" conversions that have occurred as a direct result of the film; nor can we document the staying power of such conversions. But for a movie that was made not for theatrical release, but for the sincere objective of showing the life of Christ on film, the effects, intended or not, have been far-reaching and evangelistically (if not financially) successful.

Yet while the movie is certainly true to Luke's gospel, and

depicts the life of Christ as read in the Bible, it lacks the drive, the compelling nature a story should have, which, perhaps, is why it never made the Oscar list, or was never released on the big screen. Why? Because the gospel was written as a historical account, a documentary of sorts, and as such lacks the narrative story arc that we have come to expect since Aristotle set it down over two thousand years ago. Consequently, the *Jesus* movie, while conspicuously devoted to the biblical text, is also conspicuously not a great movie in an artistic sense. It is a film made by pious people, depicting pious people; as a result it may very well attract those who prefer watching to reading, but it will never attract those who are conspicuously devoted to the cinema, simply because, while it *is* the greatest story, it is not necessarily well told.

Moving from "Facts" to Truth

So, presuming we're all still seeking the truth, we must start thinking about Teabing's offhand remark that "when two cultures clash, the loser is obliterated, and the winner writes the history books."[28] Soon Teabing will be barraging Sophie (and us) with a plethora of "facts" and "scientific evidence" that contradict orthodox beliefs. What will we do with them?

Quite simply, we will examine not necessarily each piece of data, but the lenses through which the data has been interpreted. And we will remember that the Truth will always be so, and that as we seek truth, the Spirit of truth has been sent to guide us. And when we reach our conclusions about these things, perhaps we will be able tie them up neatly with some pithy little saying that manages to avoid sounding so conspicuously devoted to intellectual piety.

> Teabing chuckled. "When
> two cultures clash, the
> loser is obliterated. By its
> very nature, history is
> always a one-sided
> account."

For Further Investigation
The Da Vinci Code, Chapters 55 through 60

Dig a Little Deeper

➢ What is your understanding of piety?

➢ How does a website like *armyofgod.com* influence people's ideas about Christianity?

➢ How did Teabing's "fast talking" and barrage of information discounting the historicity of the Bible and its records of Jesus' life affect you? Why did you react the way you did?

➢ How are our own interpretations of Scripture tainted by our biases and prejudices? Is awareness of our preconceived notions helpful?

➢ What happens when the truth is not what you expect? Should Christians handle such situations differently than other people?

➢ Think of an instance when your reaction to the truth closely resembled that of Nicodemus (John 3) or Jonah or Peter (Acts 10). How did you reconcile yourself with the truth?

Draw Your Own Conclusions

➤ Piety on the Web:

- www.armyofgod.com [WARNING: This site contains extremely graphic photos which appear immediately on its home page. Please exercise considerable discernment in your choice to visit the site or not.]

- www.prochoice.org provides valuable information regarding violence against abortion clinics and providers.

- www.earthliberationfront.com

- www.animalliberationfront.com

➤ Piety in Scripture:

- Matthew 5 famously recounts Jesus' "Sermon on the Mount," which examines earthly notions of piety against a more spiritual standard.

- In Acts 26:2–29, Luke records a speech by the Apostle Paul, in which the former Pharisee recounts both his piety as a Jew and as a Christian.

Part Four:
A Line of Reason

> Langdon was gone. Faukman
> hung up the phone, shaking
> his head in disbelief.
> *Authors*, he thought. *Even
> the sane ones are nuts.*

The Sane Ones Are Nuts

Jenn Wright, Lead Investigator

Let it be understood that the authors of this book are in no way attempting to abolish reason, or to denigrate the Enlightenment and all that it has brought us. On the contrary, we are committed to rational thinking, to reasonable debate, and to logical presentation. However, we also firmly believe that within the realm of reason there is a place reserved for the rational acceptance of that which we cannot rationally understand—a place reserved for mystery and wonderment, a place for faith. As Mohandas K. Gandhi declared in the mid-1920s,

147

Rationalists are admirable beings; rationalism is a hideous monster when it claims for itself omnipotence. Attribution of omnipotence to reason is as bad a piece of idolatry as is worship of stock and stone believing it to be God. I plead not for the suppression of reason, but for a due recognition of that in us which sanctifies reason.[1]

That being said, our exploration of sanity slipping from enthusiasm to fanaticism and beyond is not aimed at destroying the original (presumed sane) opinion or interpretation. Rather, we aim to investigate where the line between the logically-based conception and the fanatically-outrageous response got blurred, bent, or broken.

Fanaticism, it has been said, "consists in redoubling your effort when you have forgotten your aim."[2] Enthusiasm—even excessive enthusiasm—is not, in and of itself, a bad thing. Jesus was enthusiastic about His Father's work. We should be enthusiastic about the story of salvation. But sometimes enthusiasm crosses a certain logical line, and even the sane ones go nuts.

Keystones, Cops, and Robbers

Okay, so Saunière's secret wasn't that Sophie is a Merovingian princess—at least we get that cleared up right away. And when Teabing gets called out of the study by Rémy, Langdon continues where the knight left off—citing accounts of Grail symbolism in the works of artists from Mozart to Hugo to Disney. When Teabing returns, however, the explanations of more current legends—those of Langdon as a murderer—must begin. Only when the magic word "keystone" is thrown into the conversation does Teabing stop babbling about his own knowledge long enough to hear the revelations of Sophie and Langdon.

Once the Big News has been revealed—that Saunière was the Grand Master of the Priory of Sion, and he left the secret of the Grail (albeit encoded) with Sophie—Teabing (after recovering from the shock over someone else having more knowledge than he does) ravenously moves on with the keystone. Never mind the fact that Sophie has just told him that the murdered man was her grandfather—Teabing just wants the keystone, which Langdon produces from its very concealed hiding place underneath the couch. Silas, still lurking outside the château, finds the glass doors (through which he has been stealthily eavesdropping) miraculously unlocked, and slips silently in, gun drawn and ready to fire.

The law enforcement officers, awaiting the go-ahead from Captain Fache, are stunned when Fache orders them to wait for his arrival on the scene, presumably for his opportunity to take credit for Langdon's arrest. While fuming over his self-promoting captain's orders, Collet's men find Silas' car—and, to Collet's chagrin, the armored car Langdon and Sophie used to escape from the bank, right from under his nose. As he contemplates the two vehicles, and who could possibly be aiding Langdon and Sophie in their escape, he hears the gunshot.

While Teabing and Sophie are discussing the keystone's construction, Langdon has stepped away into better light to scrutinize the mysterious vessel—where Silas promptly knocks him unconscious with the butt of his gun. Turning the pistol on Sophie and Teabing, Silas asks for the keystone, appealing to his Teacher's ability to decipher the code. As Teabing braces himself on his crutches to hand Silas the cylinder, he fakes a fall, taking the opportunity to knock the crutch against Silas' *cilice*. As he falls, the gun fires, and Collet realizes his chance for a stealth operation has come and gone. Flaring blue police lights alert the trio of Grail protectors, and with a few tricks involving intercom systems and Java Black Pearl Range Rovers driven by intermittently allowed-to-be-present manservants, they escape through the forest behind the château—with Silas peacefully tied up in the back, and Langdon nursing a doozy of a headache.

Despite the headache, however, Langdon is able to put two

and two together, and realizes that his editor had sent a copy of his as-yet-unfinished manuscript on goddess worship to Saunière, thus unwittingly unleashing the events of the past twenty-four hours. And upon exiting the woods and entering the conveniently-placed highway five, he and his companions speed toward the airport and Teabing's privately-owned and -piloted plane, where the French/English/American fugitives make a stunning decision to become international fugitives.

Rationality Isn't Everything

One of the great difficulties in life is striking a balance between the rational/mathematical and the aesthetic/creative. Since the Enlightenment, reason and logic have been favored over intuition and faith. But are the two extremes really so polarized? Or are the right and left hemispheres still components of the same singular brain?

Of course, rationalists would love to claim that whatever cannot be logically proven cannot be true. Such an extreme position, however, taken to its logical extreme, relegates quite a large portion of human life and experience to the realm of fiction—or at least questionable value.

Consider just one concrete example—Powerball. Analyzed scientifically, the urge to play just doesn't make sense. History proves that people don't break the bank, the bank breaks people.

Yet people act on probability, even when the odds are incredibly slim. Such behavior actively behaves like faith. We act on myriad probabilities: that tomorrow will happen, for instance—personally, globally, and universally. We act on a scientific probability that a natural disaster will not occur today, despite the tsunamis, hurricanes, droughts, and floods experienced in the dramatic 2004–2005 weather year. Even though certain natural disasters occur every four hundred years or so, we forget all too soon, and then are surprised when they happen again. In spite of the scientific evidence, we seem to remember the consequences of trusting in probability only as long as the most recent data point or perceived experience.

But it only takes a few right-brain cells to understand that individual experience is not clearly identifiable as "true" or "false." Sometimes, experience just *is*.

Religious faith can fall into this category. While the Bible defines faith as "being *sure* of what we hope for and *certain* of what we do not see"[3] (emphasis mine), there is a difference between factual certainty (two plus two equals four) and faith that something is true (I am certain my husband loves me). These two "types" of certainty are not exclusive, nor are they contradictory. As Albert Einstein wrote,

> Even though the realms of religion and science in themselves are clearly marked off from each other, nevertheless there exist between the two strong reciprocal relationships and dependencies. Though religion may be that which determines the goal, it has, nevertheless, learned from science, in the broadest sense, what means will contribute to the attainment of the goals it has set up. But science can only be created by those who are thoroughly imbued with the aspiration towards truth and understanding. The source of feeling, however, springs from the sphere of religion. To this there also belongs the faith in the possibility that the regulations valid for the world of existence are rational, that is, comprehensible to reason. I cannot conceive of a genuine scientist without that profound faith. The situation may be expressed by an image: Science without religion is lame, religion without science is blind.[4]

It is the marriage, then, of the rational and non-rational, that creates the human whole. Accepting one without the other, or significantly favoring one over the other, places us in a precarious situation, in danger of losing objectivity by blinding ourselves with either fact or passion. Yes, it is a delicate balance, but a necessary one.

When Rationale Leads to Something Else

When examining human behavior, it doesn't take long to note that rational thinking doesn't always lead to rational behavior. As explored in the previous chapter, even the most pious of thinking can lead to sometimes inexplicable actions. So where do our characters depart from rationality and enter the realm of "what the heck?"

Our good albino friend, though never portrayed as a particularly rational fellow, certainly departs from good reason as he prepares to purloin the keystone from Teabing, Langdon, and Sophie. While he has definitive instructions from the Teacher to harm no one, he insists on taking a pistol to Teabing's house, using it to knock Langdon unconscious (does that qualify as "harm"?) before being taken out by Teabing himself. While we may see his "logic" in bringing a weapon to aid him in the heist, he has still disobeyed his orders, and caused more injury (to himself, to Langdon, and to the operation in general) by allowing his passion for the quest to override what is reasonable.

Likewise, Bezu Fache has crossed his own tenuous line, by wanting credit for a big arrest more than he wants true justice to be served. Rather than allow Collet and his men to move in and take Langdon while they can, Fache orders his lieutenant to hold quietly until he arrives, an egoistic instruction that not only costs him his moment of celebrity and heroism, but the apprehension of the suspect at all. How can he rationally justify not allowing his men to complete their assignment—other than the fact that that would make Dan Brown's novel into a short story?

And then, of course, there's Sophie and Langdon, who, though rationally fleeing authorities until they can muster a defense against the charges, have made a whole host of really bad decisions. They have taken the keystone from the security of a Swiss depository, stolen an armored vehicle, sat around chatting about Grail legend while the police are hot on their tails, and now have fled France to become not just fugitives, but *international* fugitives. It seems that each poor decision leads to another, and now the irrationality has really gotten out of hand. Truthfully, "if a 'line of reason' had ever existed,"[5] they had all just crossed it.

Trusting the Source

For the most part in this section of our story, Langdon and Sophie are pretty quiet—Teabing, gracious host that he is, removes the burden of conversation by talking their ears off. The ultra-rational-sounding scholar has clearly done his homework, citing numerous sources in support of his, shall we say, *enthusiastic* Grail hunt. But despite his semblance of stability, Teabing seems to have descended into slightly unbalanced ideology. While his study may be the size of a ballroom, and his resources seemingly limitless, on what does he base his actual foundation for the myriad interwoven conspiracies surrounding the historicity of Jesus? A quick glance at the list of works by "scores of historians" who have chronicled Jesus' royal bloodline "in exhaustive detail"[6] reveals that none of the texts are more than twenty-five years old (the oldest being *Holy Blood, Holy Grail*, 1982), and that two of them were written by the same scholar. So while Teabing "ran a finger down a row of several dozen books,"[7] not one is a historical document itself—they are merely books by contemporary authors setting forth their own conspiracy theories based not on actual documents but on legend, circular reference, and inference.

If Teabing's resources sound so plausible, though, and his theories seem so well documented and supported, why should we question his enthusiasm? Obviously he's not alone in his ideas— and if "scores of historians" agree, shouldn't we take notice?

Well, yes. But not because his ideas are threatening, or because we want to discredit him and all the other conspiracy theorists who seem to want to make those of us who believe the orthodox version of the Christ story appear ignorant and/or naïve. We should question the Grail speculations because it is the discerning thing to do, and we are called to exercise discernment. Paul, in his letter to the Philippians, tells them that he prays that their "love may abound more and more in knowledge and depth of insight, so that [they] may be able to discern what is best."[8] Likewise, Solomon exhorts his son to "preserve sound judgment and discernment, do not let them out of your sight; they will be life for you, an ornament to grace your neck. Then you will go on your way in safety, and your foot will not stumble."[9] After all, if the Bereans were commended for cross-examining Paul's own words with Scripture,[10] should we neglect to do the same with non-canonical conjectures and propositions?

It stands to reason, then, that the hypotheses of a fictional character in a fictional piece of work should be examined closely prior to any response, either supporting or rejecting. In this section of the novel, a host of "facts" are presented to Sophie (and the reader) that, when taken as a whole, seem plausible and, to many Christians, scandalous. But just because the data comes from a (fictional!) scholar's mouth doesn't make it any more true or real than the novel itself. The validity of sources is still an issue, if we even want to take Teabing's allegations seriously— and the sources listed in Teabing's bibliography are somewhat less than convincing.

Likewise, Langdon's own (however noncommittal) theories have questionable foundations. His claims that "works by Da Vinci, Botticelli, Poussin, Bernini, Mozart, and Victor Hugo... all whispered of the quest to restore the banished sacred feminine"[11] again sound plausible; but where is his evidence? In fact, he rather discredits his own musings immediately by declaring that "once you open your eyes to the Holy Grail... you see her everywhere. Paintings. Music. Books. Even in cartoons, theme parks, and popular movies."[12] Rather similar to that well-known phenomenon that an injured or sore part of the body will attract additional assault more than the well parts—a theory which, by experience, certainly seems true, but upon examination reveals that the nerves of an injured body part are simply more sensitive to stimuli, ergo we notice any contact with that area more than we might otherwise. We see what we want to see, and our vision is always tinted—if not completely distorted—by the lenses through which we frame our world. As educator Allan Bloom noted, "Reason transformed into prejudice is the worst form of prejudice, because reason is the only instrument for liberation from prejudice."[13]

This tendency to be more alert to particular occurrences is certainly not limited to Grail legend or stubbed toes. Romans 1 speaks of those who, despite the evidence in creation, still fail to see the hand of God. On the other hand, there are those who see Satan lurking behind every corner, and interpret every difficult circumstance in light of whether it is Satan trying to thwart God's work, or God trying to test His children. Similarly, it is no secret that medical students are quick to become nominal, if not technical, hypochondriacs—repeated reading about hundreds of diseases, conditions, and syndromes is bound to leave a person more highly attuned to changes in physiology. And how long after the dreaded phone call announcing the passing of a loved one does the heart sink every time the phone rings? Our experiences, our perceptions, and our biases—however innocent—cannot but affect what we see, and how we see it.

Langdon's symbolic Mickey Mouse watch, then, lends little credence to his speculations regarding the Grail symbols in Disney's animated features. Like the hypochondriac medical student whose body suddenly seems racked with numerous diseases, Langdon notes that "for the trained symbologist, watching an early Disney movie was like being barraged by an avalanche of allusion and metaphor."[14] Now, I'm sure that there is all sorts of Grail symbolism interwoven into *Dumbo* (something about those ears, maybe?), but once again, Langdon's own words weaken his argument. Perhaps there are vast quantities of "hidden messages… and stories of the subjugated goddess"[15] in Disney's films for those who are looking for them, but, as with any art, there are other symbols to be seen and interpreted as well, depending on who is doing the looking, and who the interpreting.

When Good Ideas Get Taken Too Far

When I was about nine years old, my sister and I attended a weekend Bible camp with some friends. They were of a different denomination (which scared me already), and consequently they prayed different prayers, taught different stories, and sang different songs from those I knew and trusted (in my denominationally-sheltered way) to be sound. But despite my guarded little ways, one song got under my skin, and gave me nightmares for nearly two decades. On an album entitled *Just Visiting This Planet*, Larry Norman had recorded a rather disturbing song based on a total of two sentences from the mouth of Jesus. Despite its rather divisive us/them mentality, "I Wish We'd All Been Ready" was a hit, and amateur Jesus Movement guitarists were able to easily pick up the chords and spread the cheery message. If a nine-year-old believer was freaked out by the prospects outlined his song, I can't imagine how a non-believer might respond.

The basic premise of Norman's vision was a hypothetical future characterized by war, lawlessness, and deprivation of a sort not too dissimilar from that of the Great Depression: mob violence, children going without bread, skyrocketing Weimar Republic-type inflation. The kicker, of course, was that the scenario was not the result of some global economic collapse. No. The chaos was due to Jesus' return, and He had taken His "worthy" followers with Him—leaving behind those nasty souls who had rejected Him. The result was a field day for demons. What else could you expect?

If that didn't scare something out of you, I'm not sure what could. Sorry, Baby, time's up, and you missed the boat. The world's a darn ugly place now—kids are dying, people getting trampled, and, well, you're screwed and I'm not.

There's the Good News for you.

Λ Screen Too Far: *Left Behind*

As an adult, I still find the song disturbing, and on more levels than just the fear that I'm going to wake up someday and my husband and cat will have been spirited up to heaven and I'll be alone in the apartment with a clean litterbox and an extra toothbrush to get me through the days without bread. What disturbs me more is that the premise of the song is literally based on two sentences that Christ spoke in the middle of a lot of other valuable information. As with Teabing and his "scores" of historical evidence and numerous supporting scholars, we must look at the sources that form the basis of the information. To take those two sentences (Matthew 24:40–41 and Luke 17:34–35, in parallel accounts) and build an entire eschatology around them not only detracts from the message of the Gospel (which does mean, by the way, "*good* news," not "frightening" or "ominous" news), but changes the focus from the Kingdom of God being here and now to being somewhere in the future, where I get in and you don't (or vice versa).

In the pop-Christian movie *Left Behind*, based on the series of novels by Tim LaHaye and Jerry Jenkins, the same premise is taken to its rather illogical extreme. The world is thrown into chaos when all of the Christian believers are suddenly taken to heaven, leaving their pathetically unbelieving loved ones (as well as their clothes) behind to fend for themselves. Fortunately, many of those who didn't make the cut have at least some prior knowledge of the theology behind the bizarre events, and for those who don't, several believers have pre-recorded messages to explain the current state of affairs. But to what avail?

Most subscribers to the *Left Behind*-version of Christ's return (pre-tribulation pre-millennialists, if you want the technical eschatological terms) believe that following the initial rapture (the taking of the chosen into heaven), there will be seven years of severe tribulation, during which the anti-Christ rules the world. Following these seven years, Jesus will return to reign on earth for a thousand years, destroying the anti-Christ and establishing His Kingdom forever. That little seven-year pocket of tribulation allows the original left-behinders to change their minds (in spite of Larry Norman's grim projections), having done their seven-year penance on earth and realized the error of their ways.

It would be nice if all that were true (and I'm not saying it's not). But again, the focus of Jesus' message was never one of insiders and outsiders, or heaven and hell—at least, not in this life. It was, and is, a message of grace and hope and love, of mercy given to those who, by definition, are undeserving, and of a God who deeply desires none to be left behind.[16] So whether the foundational eschatology of *Left Behind* is sound or not, the problem is that a single idea has been taken out of context and into the extreme, crossing that precarious line between the rational and the radical.

Staying Sane in a World Gone Nuts

So if rationality isn't everything, how can we determine what is "normal," and what is "nuts"? If we can't depend on Reason to keep us from crossing that line, what hope do we have?

This is the balance referred to at the beginning of the chapter. If Reason alone were going to save us, casinos wouldn't exist, and abuse victims would readily abandon abusive relationships. But we're human, and we have two components to our singular brains—one that processes the world rationally, and one that processes intuitively. And we must make room for both.

Objectively speaking, Teabing's passion for his "mistress" the Grail has long ago exceeded his intellectual desire for truth. Despite his claim that "learning the truth" is his "life's love,"[17] he has allowed his enthusiasm to grow into fanaticism, seeing Grail legend where he chooses to, and accepting as factual those accounts which feed his own presumptions. In spite of himself, he is taking many things on faith—the existence of the Priory of Sion, the existence of the Sangreal documents, even the authenticity and historicity of the Gnostic Gospels. Having chosen to accept these things as facts without acknowledging the choice to believe is what removes Teabing from the realm of the hyper-rational. Should he concede that all he has staked his life and work upon is still a matter of faith rather than certainty, he might actually *gain* some credit. But his unwillingness to recognize what can be proven by reason and what can only be accepted as a plausibility pulls him across that famous line.

So while Kant may exhort us, "*Supere aude!* Dare to use your own understanding! is thus the motto of the Enlightenment,"[18] we must remember that understanding involves the whole brain, not just the left hemisphere. As Paul noted in his first letter to the Corinthian church, the message of Christ embraces the rational and the intuitive:

> My message and my preaching were not with wise and persuasive words, but with a demonstration of the Spirit's power, so that your faith might not rest on men's wisdom, but on God's power. We do, however, speak a message of wisdom among the mature.[19]

Knowing the difference between fact and faith, and being okay with both, keeps a believer on the "sane" side of the line. Blur the boundaries, or refuse to acknowledge either side, and even the sane ones are nuts.

> A window of opportunity, Sophie knew, had just closed. She was leaving the country. If a "line of reason" had ever existed, she had just crossed it.

For Further Investigation
The Da Vinci Code, Chapters 61 through 68

Dig a Little Deeper

➤ Where do you draw the line between sanity and fanaticism with your faith? What are you willing and not willing to do?

➤ How would you elucidate the relationship between fact and faith?

➤ What is the difference between exercising discernment and being skeptical?

Draw Your Own Conclusions

➤ The *Left Behind* Series, by Tim LaHaye and Jerry Jenkins:

- The novels are available at most bookstores, and even Wal-Mart. They have also been adapted as a series of children's books, and several of the books have also been filmed, now available on DVD.

A Line of Reason: The Sane Ones Are Nuts

➢ The Tribulation and the Rapture:

- www.geocities.com/~lasttrumpet/
- www.catholic.com/library/Rapture.asp
- A 1991 film directed by Michael Tolkin, *The Rapture*, presented a very disturbing vision of this Christian theory. NOTE: The film includes strong sexual content to make a point about the protagonist's spiritual journey.

➢ Relevant Bible Passages:

- Matthew 24:40–41.
- Luke 17:34–35.
- Revelation 20:1–10.

> Teabing turned to
> Sophie. "This puts you in a
> position of exceptional
> responsibility. You have
> been handed a torch. A
> two-thousand-year-old
> flame that cannot be
> allowed to go out."

Exceptional Responsibility

Greg Wright, Lead Investigator

I remember quite distinctly when I discovered personal privilege.

But wait. I should back up for a minute. Prior to that moment in time, I was well-acquainted with lack of privilege. Even though my father earned a quite comfortable middle-class income, our family sure didn't live like it. Both my parents were raised in post-Depression-era households in small-town Jefferson, Oregon, my father even growing up in a house with no electrical appliances and walls that literally let the wind blow through. The one heated room in the house was the wood-stove kitchen. As my father and his brother worked their way through college, they were both stunned to learn that they themselves were, in fact, those "poor people" they were always hearing about in class. My mother was born in a logging camp near Shelton, Washington.

So my parental units, apparently, were determined to pass along to their own children something of the experience of being poor. I grew up scavenging toys and ice cream—yes, straight-from-the-dairy, past-pull-date ice cream—from landfills. When my father brought a tin of tinkertoys home from a business trip, it was a literally memorable once-in-childhood event. When I was ten, my best friend David Martin, who lived two doors down from us, ate beans and rice five times a week. David's father, a rifle, and a team of eight hounds put meat on their table. I once saw a bobcat, a whole one, in their freezer. David excitedly told me about his first birthday out-to-dinner experience: a trip to McDonald's, where he'd enjoyed a fifty-five cent cheeseburger. That made my family's once-a-week visit to King's Diner on Pacific Highway seem like sheer decadence.

I was also perhaps the most unpopular kid in my school. I was an out-and-out nerd, a skinny, unathletic runt, and I'd skipped first grade. In my district, that made me a target. Every other year, mean-spirited gossip would start circulating about the Smart Kid's age, and the bullies would start heading my way. My fifth-grade visit to Camp Cispus, for instance, was a week-long exercise in terror. My grade school, Thorndike, was mixed with another that week, and a whole new batch of bullies became acquainted with me. The Tukwila gang openly declared that they were going to beat me to a pulp. The episode culminated in a midnight raid on my cabin. They found me hiding in a locker, just as the camp counselors arrived to break things up.

Mind you, I'm not whining about any of this. Adversity sharpens us, and I'm pretty happy with who I've become. And though today I truly enjoy a very modest lifestyle—regularly shopping at thrift shops, factory outlets, and liquidation stores— I've also known the luxury of the six-figure income, conspicuous consumption, and exotic travel. It's been a good life thus far.

Ah, but that first moment when you taste real privilege. What a rush.

For a long time after my own first taste, I lusted after privilege. I sought it out and cultivated it. At the University of Washington, I created a student organization whose sole purpose, really, was to provide a life of privilege for me and my closest friends. I was the ultimate insider. People I didn't even know called me by name. My reputation was bigger than life. I was *popular*, and powerful. I was a big fish in a 30,000-member pond. It was intoxicating.

I got over it.

Getting Away with Murder

Sir Leigh Teabing also gets off on privilege, and he doesn't get over it—and that proves just as well for Langdon and Sophie, as the British knight uses his connections to spirit the fugitives out of France and over to England. With them, in Teabing's private jet, travel Teabing's lackey Rémy and the subdued and bound Silas.

Oh—and they've got the keystone, too. During the flight, the brains of the bunch wrangle over the significance of a clue found in the lid of the box, retrieved by Langdon and Sophie from the Swiss bank in Paris. Saunière had inscribed a Leonardo-like, reverse-scripted message on a wafer-thin disk of wood and inlaid it in the box's lid. The message holds the solution to the five-letter "password" for opening the cryptex that the box contains.

During the flight, Sophie also gets her sex education. While Teabing is off conspiring with Rémy, Langdon takes the opportunity to tell Sophie about Hieros Gamos, the ancient fertility ritual practiced by the Priory of Sion. It was this ritual that Sophie had once witnessed in the vault underneath her grandfather's country house.

After numerous false leads, our heroic brain trust discerns that Saunière's cryptic script is merely written backwards in English, and that its message points, through some very convoluted semantic gymnastics, to the Greek form of Sophie's name: *sofia*, wisdom. How ironic.

Sophie enters the letters onto the cryptex dials. Three hearts race loudly, in anticipation of the final revelation of the Grail's location—despite the fact that over a hundred pages remain in the book. How shortsighted could the three possibly be? Naturally, the cryptex only contains another clue. And another nested cryptex.

This time, Teabing is pretty sure he knows where the new Final Clue is leading them. After managing to outwit the local police upon landing outside London, Teabing has Rémy chauffeur the whole crew, Silas still in bonded tow, to the Temple Church, just off London's Fleet Street. Teabing, Langdon, and Sophie head inside in search of knighted tombage.

Outside, Rémy traitorously frees Silas from his bonds. The Teacher, it turns out, is in cahoots with both the butler and the monk. Teabing's treachery is about to really kick in, as the pair plot to steal the black cryptex. Bezu Fache, meanwhile, is winging his way to London in tepid pursuit, while Aringarosa finds himself in the figurative hot seat. Fache has once again informed the bishop of the latest developments, and Aringarosa knows his carefully laid power-play is self-destructing.

Responsibility and Privilege

In this section of our story, Teabing's trump card is privilege. He's a knight, after all. And he's disabled. His comings and goings between France and England are highly irregular, but his status, medical condition, title, and mien all warrant special considerations from various low-level officials. "Membership has its privileges,"[1] Teabing observes.

Ah, privilege. I didn't finish telling about my own first experience with that, did I?

In 1976, Tukwila's Foster High School got its first computer: a Wang 2200, packed with 64K of memory. Total. But thirty years ago, that was a pretty amazing thing, and when I hit my freshman year in 1977, I was all over that thing. A couple of fellow nerds and I became the school's experts, thanks to some indulgence from Janice Hiranaka, our computer "teacher." Heck, in those days, who "taught" computer skills? Mrs. H. and our gang, together, learned it all from the manuals, cranking out programs to plot multi-variable equations, simulate casinos, and speed up games of Risk.

When Mrs. H. went out on pregnancy leave during my junior year, the school was up a creek. Who could possibly supervise the computer class? Ahhhhh, privilege. I was exempted from my Health credits and given oversight of freshmen, fellow juniors—even seniors! Sweetness.

Of course, certain responsibilities came with privilege. I still had a class to "teach" and assignments to "grade." Oh, and I had to tutor Kendall Blansett, too. Tough assignment.

But that's one of the interesting things about education. While we generally think of it as a right, it's really one of the privileges of a leisure society, and with all such privileges come a measure of responsibility. Sophie, for example, receives her education about the Priory of Sion from Langdon and Teabing. The latter informs her that she is "about to step onto a path from which there is no return, regardless of the dangers involved. ... You must either fully embrace this responsibility... or you must pass that responsibility to someone else." When Sophie suggests that Teabing is surely exaggerating the situation's significance, Teabing advises, "You will be in possession of a truth capable of altering history forever. ... You will be faced with the responsibility of revealing that truth to the world."[2]

And that's one of the interesting things about teaching, which I've been doing in some form ever since that high school computer class. If learning carries with it certain responsibilities, teaching carries with it even more, as James the brother of Jesus wrote: "Not many of you should presume to be teachers, my brothers, because you know that we who teach will be judged more strictly."[3] This in itself is a truth with enough power to change the world, and one which Teabing woefully ignores.

Think of the abuse doled out by teachers in our society. Think of pastor Bob Moorehead's headline-grabbing arrest for lewd conduct with another man in a Florida bathroom. Think of the Oregon Catholic diocese bankrupted by sexual abuse lawsuits. Think of Mary Kay Letourneau and Vili Fualaau. Think of the scope of sexual assaults in our public schools, which some estimates place at ten to a hundred times the rate in the Church.

Think of the duplicity of Leigh Teabing, the "Teacher." He really isn't trying to warn Sophie; he's trying to scare her off. He secretly hopes that she'll decline the responsibility of the Grail and dish it to him. In fact, he's pretty confident that she will because he has no respect for her whatsoever, perceiving her as "light-years out of her league."[4] He consistently refers to her as "my dear," and can't possibly bring himself to use her Christian name. He knows she doesn't deserve an appellation of learning and knowledge.

But wait a second. If Teabing really buys into all that Priory of Sion mumbo-jumbo, why doesn't he respect Sophie simply by virtue of her participation in the sacred feminine? Does membership in that particular club have no privileges? In addition to being a villain, Teabing is the worst kind of hypocrite and a snob.

Even when Sophie demonstrates that she's a key player in decoding the cryptex password, she's left staring blankly as both Teabing and Langdon play free-association word-games to get from *Baphomet* to *sofia*. First, the Anglicization of the pagan fertility god's name must be Hebraicized, dropping its vowels along the way. This gets us from eight letters down to five, the number of characters in the cryptex code. Then the Atbash Cipher gets us to the correct five letters, which then must be translated to Greek via the Roman alphabet... But not before O is substituted for Vav. Of course, if Vav is often a placeholder for O, why was Pei-Vav substituted for the F sound in Baphomet, particularly since, as Langdon tells Sophie, Pei "can be pronounced F"?[5] Ah, it's all just a linguistic shell game of the variety used by interpreters of the prophecies of Nostradamus. An ironic, condescending sophistry.

Privilege and Knowing Better

What gets Langdon and Teabing from *Baphomet* to *sofia* is not methodology but intuition. They already know where they're headed, really, because Saunière's clues are riddles, not a roadmap. Every secret is easy to figure out when you already know the answer—and it's equally easy to make yourself look good when you're a master at verbal hand-waving.

When I made the leap from the Wang to the University's DEC and VAX mainframes, my professors introduced me to the fascinating scientific and philosophic underpinnings of computational theory. A byproduct of Logical Positivism, for instance, was the binary encoding of all data, a system by which information is stored as a stream of 1s and 0s. Each bit of information can be properly read and interpreted as either "true" (1) or "false" (0).

A not-so-clever byproduct of Logical Positivism has been the discovery that just about anything can be true (or false) if you just get your definitions right. For instance, Logical Positivism defines its domain as anything that can be quantifiably true. Truth, then, for the Logical Positivist, is either analytic (absolute) or synthetic (merely probable, but approaching absolute). These are the things which can be said to make sense. Ahhh, but according to the terms of Logical Positivism, messy details like morals, aesthetics, and religion are wholly outside the bounds of quantifiable truth: hence, to some practitioners, literal "nonsense." But certainly not in a pejorative sense. Of course not.

Even consider the name of this school of thought: "Logical Positivism." How can one possibly argue with that? Especially in the light of the technological explosion that it indirectly spawned? As a computer scientist myself, I certainly have to not only concede but champion the utility of the philosophy. If I were to argue against it, I would be... what? An Illogical Negativist?

169

That's a stream no one can swim against when terms are defined as they are. Membership in the club has its privileges.

Other schools of twentieth century thought followed suit. The school of artistic criticism that argued for form itself as the locus of meaning styled itself "Formal Criticism" rather than the more semantically accurate "Form Criticism"—leaving the intellectually underprivileged who disagreed to the far less academic domain of "Informal Criticism," we can only suppose. And one of the projects of the formalists has been the exposure of the "Intentional Fallacy": the idea that an author's intent is the locus of a work's meaning. Not only did Wamsatt and Beardsley argue that authorial intent is irrelevant, and that the locus of meaning resides rather in the critic's perception of a work (wholly independent of intent), they suggested that the supposed fallacy of authorial intent was deliberately and insidiously propagated. Why else would the fallacy be "intentional"? Properly speaking, Wamsatt and Beardsley argued against the "Fallacy of Intent" rather than the Intentional Fallacy.

But was such deception their intent? By the logical extension of their own rules, does their intent even matter? After all, the hermeneutic of Intentional Fallacy proponents declares that I am free to interpret Wamsatt and Beardsley's work in any way that I reasonably choose.

Such are the results when we abdicate the responsibility that comes with the privilege of something as simple as language. Definitions do, in fact, matter. Dressing up one's theories with gratuitously complementary adjectives is intellectually dishonest. Dressing up intuitive leaps as logical problem-solving is disingenuous—and with due respect to Sophie, disrespectful. Gosh, boys, she is a cryptologist, after all. You might just as easily have told her, "We can't really get from *Baphomet* to *sofia* in a way that holds intellectual water, lass. It's really just an educated guess. That's the way one answers riddles. But go ahead and try opening the cryptex anyway—it's the best guess we can come up with in three pages."

The Definition of "Is"

All political chicanery, moral flimflammery, and outright perjury aside, the nadir of this kind of word game arrived when President Clinton tried to weasel his way out of an obvious lie. Sure, he was smirking when he demurred, "It depends on what the definition of 'is' is." But I'm pretty sure that both he and Monica Lewinsky had at least agreed on the definition of "cigar" and, uh, well, "vagina." The resulting brouhaha was the very lowest of crimes and messy demeanor.

Robert Langdon is equally shifty about his definition of Hieros Gamos—"sacred marriage."

> "The ritual I saw was no marriage."
> "Marriage as in *union*, Sophie"
> "You mean as in sex."
> "No."
> "No?" she said, her olive eyes testing him.
> Langdon backpedaled. "Well... yes, in a manner of speaking."[6]

One can almost hear, once again, President Clinton sternly declaring, "I did not have sexual relations with that woman!" Oh, never mind.

Sure, Langdon, although what Sophie witnessed in Saunière's cellar "probably looked like a sex ritual, Hieros Gamos had nothing to do with eroticism. It was a spiritual act."[7] Right. One can only wonder what sexual abuses would take place in a secretive cult whose highest sacrament was "orgasm as prayer."[8] I'm not taking my kids to that Sunday School, thank you very much! (Okay, I don't have kids. But if I did...)

And really, how silly is it to claim that Christianity has systematically demonized sex? Sure, various sects at various times have tried to convince us all that the sexual act itself is a sin. But it's pretty hard to convince your parishioners of that when the Scriptures themselves contain stuff like the following:

> I have come into my garden, my sister, my bride; I have gathered my myrrh with my spice. I have eaten my honeycomb and my honey; I have drunk my wine and my milk. Eat, O friends, and drink; drink your fill, O lovers. I slept but my heart was awake. Listen! My lover is knocking: "Open to me, my sister, my darling, my dove, my flawless one. My head is drenched with dew, my hair with the dampness of the night." I have taken off my robe—must I put it on again? I have washed my feet—must I soil them again? My lover thrust his hand through the latch-opening; my heart began to pound for him. I arose to open for my lover, and my hands dripped with myrrh, my fingers with flowing myrrh, on the handles of the lock.[9]

Yup. Sounds pretty much like suppressed sexuality to me. But according to Langdon, "modern religion decries [sex] as shameful, teaching us to fear our sexual desire as the hand of the devil."[10] Huh. I'm not sure which Bible Langdon reads, but I can pretty much guess which one young Bill was reading back in Little Rock.

I have to admit, though, that teaching about sex is pretty difficult in the Church. I'll never forget an adult Sunday School class I once taught while I was still an unmarried pastor. I was going through biblical teaching on lust and sensuality and had argued from Scripture that abuse of the sexual appetite was actually no different from abuse of an appetite for ice cream, pizza, or burgers. After all, gluttony is condemned by Scripture as soundly as prostitution or sodomy. The Catholic Church even classed it as one of the Seven Deadly Sins. So I suggested that husbands and wives might consider praying over their sexual activity the way that they prayed over their meals.

Wow. Did I ever get blindsided by the response to that lesson. Some of the women were absolutely scandalized by the idea. Of course, the very idea of a normal, sexual marital relationship was purely theoretical for me at the time, so I doubt I could have anticipated the reaction to my supposedly heretical implication that the Holy Spirit watches over us even as we copulate, and that Jesus is our co-lover as much as our copilot. I've since had the opportunity, with my wife, to confirm that, yes, sex is better with prayer. It focuses the mind onto things that are really important—like, your spouse.

But is orgasm itself the avenue to "communion with God," as Langdon believes? Dan Brown's narration describes the moment of male climax as a "brief mental vacuum," a "moment of clarity during which God could be glimpsed."[11] Gosh, if thoughtlessness is the only requirement for communion with God, who needs climax? Most men spend the better part of their day there. Right, ladies?

In all seriousness, the Apostle Paul even recommended marriage as a way to morally satisfy sexual urges. So there's little question in my mind that the Kingdom of God really does encompass sex. And with that privilege come certain responsibilities. But is that the only place we can encounter God? I sure hope not. I often look for him in my bowl of ice cream, too. What's the Greek term for "sacred dairy product?"

The Kingdom of Heaven

Speaking of privileges, I was fortunate enough to be in Pasadena for press screenings of Sir Ridley Scott's *Kingdom of Heaven*. Membership really does have its privileges. The Knighted One had actually considered flying the entire press corps to a castle in England for the junket, but passports and transportation could not be arranged expediently. Alas! we were left to suffer at the Pasadena Ritz-Carlton—which, as anyone knows who has stayed there, is an exercise in sheer torture.

Of course, press junkets are in themselves quite a privilege, when you're on the invite list. Free airfare with the occasional first-class upgrade, per diem, poolside lunches with press luminaries, Jack Nicholson in the bar, elevator rides with Peter Jackson, free books from Dan Aykroyd, private parties at the top of the Empire State Building with Will Ferrell—yes, that kind of thing beats the pants off the usual editorial tasks.

But the *Kingdom of Heaven* junket was something extra special. Christian and Muslim experts on the Crusades were flown in from overseas. The entire campus of the Ritz-Carlton was transformed into a medieval encampment. Hands-on demonstrations from the costumer and armor designer were scheduled. The exotic food and beverages were endless. And the studio reimbursed us for cab fare *in cash*. What more could a journalist ask for?

Oh, yes. There was the movie, too. While I was not overly impressed with it to begin with, the medieval after-movie banquet softened me up a bit, as did the roundtable interview with Mr. Scott the following day. I pointed out to the director that the hero of the story—a bastard blacksmith named Balian, who journeys to Jerusalem hoping to find forgiveness and the hand of God— seems to learn nothing from his time in the Holy City. That was not a problem with the movie, Scott explained; it was its entire point. Balian may have gone "there and back again," as they say, but he remains unconvinced at the end of the day—just as Scott himself says he remains unconvinced. Like Balian, Scott does not find salvation in Jerusalem.

My opinion of the film rose after hearing Scott's explanation. Who among us, after all, has not at some point doubted either the existence of God or man's right standing before Him? Whose conscience has never been troubled? Balian's own crisis is both tragic and craven: in the midst of despair over his young wife's death, he angrily and impulsively murders an insensitive and greedy priest. He flees to preserve his life and to join an expedition to the Holy Land, still believing, at least, the promise that the pilgrimage may lead to his redemption.

But when all is said and done, Balian does not profit from

the knowledge that neither honor nor deceit are the exclusive property of Christianity; his faith is not restored either by high-cost chastity or through legitimate love; the world is not saved by the noble, privileged principles that guide King Baldwin, Balian's father, or knights in general; even Balian's own heroics merely delay inevitable carnage. Balian doesn't find faith or forgiveness in Jerusalem because the city is no magic talisman. No city is. Jerusalem, as Saladin tells Balian, is nothing.

Unless, of course, one has at least learned that lesson from Jerusalem. Then, perhaps, as Saladin also observes, Jerusalem may be everything. At the end of Scott's story, Balian is still just a fugitive blacksmith in search of forgiveness and the hand of God: he has not completed his journey of faith; he has simply eliminated one useless and tragic option for its completion.

When Balian murders the priest, he—like Bishop Aringarosa in that jet over Europe—knows that he needs to "change destinations."[12] And when Balian decides to join his father in the Crusades, he knows—as Sophie knows when she also decides to flee France—that a "window of opportunity" has "just closed."[13] Choices are made, and to their credit, both Balian and Sophie honorably face up to the attendant responsibilities.

Neither Sophie nor Balian begin from a position of privilege. Both have privilege conferred upon them without seeking it. Both behave more honorably than those of greater privilege, those who indeed know better—men of exceptional responsibility: men who know that it's not what you have that matters, but what you do with it.

The Price of Membership

I have to admit it. I blew it on *Kingdom of Heaven*. I enjoyed great privilege on that junket, and I fell for it all, hook line, and sinker. My review should have been lukewarm at best. But it fairly glowed.

I saw the film again last summer on a flight to Schipol. I

was bored to tears. *Kingdom of Heaven* will not be remembered as one of Scott's better films.

But I did notice one curious thing: where was the Grail in Scott's Jerusalem? Why were Scott's Templars up to nothing more than petty villainy? Why was Scott's King Baldwin not orchestrating the Priory of Sion rather than being occupied with such trivial concerns as Saladin and leprosy? Did Scott simply have his history wrong? Do Dan Brown's heroes have theirs wrong?

Is Robert Langdon wrong about Hieros Gamos, just as Balian's priest is wrong about Jerusalem? Would we be as mistaken in thinking that God can only be found in orgasmic mindlessness as in expecting to find God in Jerusalem? Is it just possible that we are very close to the Kingdom of Heaven—every day and in every place?

Certainly, we're all more or less in the same boat, regardless of our beliefs. We're all members of the same club, the same human race; and I, for one, consider that a great privilege. And I, for one, resolve to accept the exceptional responsibility that comes with that privilege.

Yes, I will seek the truth, thank you, even though I full well know the implication: "From everyone who has been given much, much will be demanded; and from the one who has been entrusted with much, much more will be asked."[14]

If we don't aspire to be teachers, after all, what other option do we have? An eternity of immaturity? That's an irresponsible abuse of privilege, to be sure.

And when we become teachers, let's remember that there's more to the abuse of power than sexual predation. Let's never use enlightenment as a club, a swagger stick, or a crutch.

> The Kent chief inspector
> felt only distaste for
> Leigh Teabing as the man
> hobbled around him in
> defiance. Men of privilege
> always felt like they
> were above the law.
> *They are not,* he thought.

For Further Investigation
The Da Vinci Code, Chapters 69 through 84

Dig a Little Deeper

➤ What are some of the responsibilities inherent in learning?

➤ How does teaching carry a higher level of responsibility than learning?

➤ In what ways, however small or seemingly insignificant, are you a teacher for others?

➤ What are some high-profile examples of teachers betraying their responsibilities? How do such examples relate to your own role as teacher?

➤ Have you ever tried to have a discussion with someone whose definition of a foundational concept within the discussion was thoroughly different from your own? How did the conversation proceed? Was it valuable?

➤ Do you feel that you are at the end of your own story arc? Or do you feel more like Sir Ridley Scott and his Balian—that you are still looking for answers?

➤ At what point should we feel like we have all the answers? To what extent do we expect others to have all the answers, too?

Draw Your Own Conclusions

➤ Hieros Gamos:

  • http://en.wikipedia.org/wiki/Hieros_Gamos

➤ Regarding Logical Positivism:

  • www.philosophypages.com/hy/6q.htm

  • *Logical Positivism*, by A. J. Ayer.

  • *Reconsidering Logical Positivism*, by Michael Friedman.

➤ The Intentional Fallacy:

  • english.upenn.edu/~jlynch/Terms/Temp/intentional.html

  • http://en.wikipedia.org/wiki/Intentional_Fallacy

  • www.christianitytoday.com/ct/2004/00732.46.html contains "'Truth on Two Hills," an article by Bob Wenz, which illustrates the social significance of the Intentional Fallacy.

➤ The Crusades:

  • *The History Channel Presents The Crusades—Crescent & The Cross* (2005).

  • *The New Concise History of the Crusades*, Updated Edition, by Thomas F. Madden.

  • http://crusades.boisestate.edu/ (a full, free online course on the crusades)

  • *Tales of a Grandfather*, Series 4, by Sir Walter Scott.

➤ Nostradamus Prophecies and "Green Language" Readings:

  • www.newprophecy.net/now1.htm (The *Nostradamus NOW* site, Michael McClellan)

➤ Biblical Recommendations for Teachers:

  • Titus 2.

> Teabing looked
> flabbergasted. He wheeled
> back toward the knights.
> "We must be missing
> something!"

More Information

Mike Gunn, Lead Investigator

Have you ever received information that really didn't do anything for you? I have, and as a matter of fact, I'm kind of a receptacle for useless information. One day I was studying weak verb conjugations in Hebrew (I know—sounds real sexy!), and there were hundreds of possibilities on the page. Instead of studying to understand how they all related to one another, and how they actually worked, I decided to just memorize the chart. Despite the fact that there were close to three hundred conjugations in the chart, I aced the test. I think I got something like four wrong. Beautiful, isn't it? Except, of course, for one thing: the information I had stored in my brain was completely useless to me. It was just raw data completely out of its context. Pretty pathetic, really, and probably the number one reason why Hebrew is still a bit Greek to me.

Now, on the flip side of that were my studies in Koine Greek. My professor took an approach that limited memorization and emphasized a more holistic, applied approach. He always said that if ancient three-year-old Greeks could learn it, then so could we. He was right. I also aced Greek, but I actually get what it says, to this day. The moral of yet another of my pithy stories is that information (hidden or otherwise) is useless without context and revelation.

Kind of like Sophie, Langdon, and Teabing wandering around in the Temple Church. No orb. "*No pillow. No armor. No tunic. No sword.*"[1] No knight.

No Sherlock.

Ah, the mind of Sophie. We come to the place in our book where the action is heating up. The mystery and suspense heighten as the "evil" Silas and Rémy, um, kidnap Teabing from the Temple Church. Yes, Silas and Rémy are actually both in cahoots with the Teacher—and Rémy, Fache's men learn, has been conducting copious surveillance from Teabing's property. So the bad guys manage to bag both Teabing and the keystone. Cryptex. Lockbox. The thing that holds the final map to the resting place of the Holy Grail. And the Teacher wants it. He has Rémy bring it to him; then he kills Rémy. Silas he gives up to the police, which also means betraying Aringarosa, who has just landed in Britain.

All that our heroes Bob and Sophie have left to go on is the cryptic poem found inside Saunière's outer cryptex, the little ditty that led them on a dead-end run to the Temple Church. It reads:

In London lies a knight a Pope interred.
His labor's fruit a Holy wrath incurred.
You seek the orb that ought be on his tomb.
It speaks of Rosy flesh and seeded womb.[2]

In a frantic race to beat the bad guys to the punch line, Langdon and Sophie show up at King's College (one of the University of London's oldest colleges and finest research centers) to do research on the poem's words in the library's immense database. A few interesting things strike me about their time in King's Research Institute of Systematic Theology (KRIST).

Search Engines Running on Empty

First, Langdon and Sophie only give half of the poem to Pamela Gettum, the librarian assisting them with the database research. They fear that she might use the information for her own purposes. After all, this woman just might have moved to London and established herself as the College's chief librarian for numerous years, going into deep cover for just this very moment when two fugitives run in with the secrets of the Holy Grail. Hmm. Possible, I suppose?

I guess when you're into conspiracy theories, everyone's a suspect. Langdon and Sophie are kind of like Mulder and Scully at this point. "The truth is out there. Trust no one." It reminds me of those NFL coaches who cover their faces when they relay the play to their earphoned quarterbacks because they fear that the other team has lip readers watching the game, stealing play calls and radioing them to their own sidelines. Weird, huh? But, not so weird in the life of the paranoid—rather like Chesterton's maniac in *Orthodoxy*.[3] But it sure sounds good when you call paranoid mistrust something like "Compartmentalized Cryptography,"[4] as Sophie does. But that strategy is used *only when the key to the code is already known*; the strategy protects the *message*, not the code.

But neither the paranoia nor Sophie's odd failure to understand cryptography was what bothered me. The ramifications of information without context were what I found troubling. Can someone truly decipher the meaning of a fragment apart from the whole? The issue might seem trivial to you; but as one who exegetes ancient texts on a regular basis, I can tell you that such methods are dangerous. They have been the most frequent causes of heretical, polemical, and lazy errors in Church history. An interesting enough irony from a book that is, in part, about problems of interpretation.

Again, is information apart from context valuable? Even evidence obtained through sensory perceptions (taste, touch, sight, sound, smell) can be misinterpreted when divorced from its matrix. Could we properly read rock strata without knowing what layers are found above and below?

One pretty decent illustration of the principle of

contextualization is found in the movie *Minority Report*. Tom Cruise's character is being accused of a crime he hasn't yet committed—it has only been seen by "precognitives" who have a high-probability clairvoyant ability to see future violent crimes. Because of such presumably clear future vision, Cruise is being hunted down to be arrested for the crime that he will obviously commit; but the movie shows us the inherent problem of supposed evidence without the proper context. What looked obvious to the Precogs and their law enforcement handlers turned out not to be so obvious when all of the facts were weighed.

Naturally, this proof-texting approach underlies a great deal of biblical misinterpretation. And such cherry-picking also undergirds skeptical dismissal of the Bible and its alleged discrepancies—which most often turn out not to be problematic at all when more information is brought to the table. So information is no doubt important—but that information has to be contextualized, and properly interpreted.

Cutting the Search Short

A second interesting issue in the library episode is how Langdon's and Teabing's presuppositions lead them astray. In their desire to see the sacred feminine behind every bush and clue, they come to the conclusion that the "Rosy flesh and seeded womb" are, once again, clear references to Mary Magdalene. But their fundamental commitment to the sacred feminine lets them down this time.

How often do we interpret things that we encounter based on our preconceived and jaded notions? For us to believe the statements of the characters of this book, for instance, we'd have to buy into their basic assumptions. Or, in philosophical terms, we'd have to agree with their epistemology. As we discussed earlier, Langdon clearly lets the cat out of Dan Brown's epistemological bag when he says that "*Every* faith in the world is based on fabrication... Those who truly understand their faiths understand the stories are metaphorical."[5]

When it comes to basic issues of information, one of the fundamental questions has to be: "How do we know anything?" One literally off-beat answer states that religious folk believe (and ultimately only know) things by faith. After all, wasn't it Augustine, a Christian thinker, who said, "Seek not to understand that you may believe, but believe that you may understand?"[6] But the "rationally-minded," enlightened free-thinkers know things through reason and facts. The mantra of one Da Vinci Code forum *habitué* is even "I don't 'believe' anything. I know." Sounds great—until such a claim is placed under the microscope of everyday life.

For instance: I just got back from Africa; and, as I write these words, I expect to travel to India next week. Be assured, I do not "know" if I will return. Based on past experience, I "trust" that I will return—and, with the current data that I have, I even believe this with a fairly high degree of probability. But such trust is placed into the hands of manufacturers, mechanics, pilots, air traffic controllers, God, and so on. I think you get the picture. There is nothing that we ultimately know for sure.

What we know is based on perceptions that aren't always accurate, or on impressions that lack the fullness of knowledge. Some people believe that there is no God, while others believe that there is a God—or that there are many gods, for that matter. Not all of us are correct, but it is safe to say that not all of us are wrong. But the belief structure to which we are committed is foundational to how we interpret the codes in our lives.

Even the things that we think we know begin with faith in an epistemological framework. Ultimately, information works its way inward through a lens of subjectivity. This certainly doesn't mean that truth cannot be discerned; but it does mean that multiple perspectives are possible given any set of information.

We saw this all too clearly during the second gulf war. If you watched Fox News, CNN, the BBC, and Al Jazeera, you might think that four different wars were being fought. Which station we watched changed the way we thought about the war. And usually, we gravitated to the information that most comfortably fit our perspective, and critically lambasted the others. We are only rarely willing to look at information that will change our minds.

Information is also rarely conclusive. After all, as we Seattleites saw in Super Bowl XL, the refs still ruled in Steelers quarterback Ben Roethlisberger's favor—because the evidence was "inconclusive"!

The insufficiency of raw, incomplete, inconclusive information was brought home to me in a recent episode of *24*. President Logan had to make a decision whether to stop a terrorist from using nerve gas in a local mall, guaranteeing the deaths of about eight hundred people, or to allow the bombing to proceed so that the perpetrators could lead the Feds back to the other terrorists and the remaining nineteen canisters of nerve gas— which could potentially kill hundreds of thousands of people. Now, that's a moral dilemma that I don't think anyone wants to face, and the arguments on both sides seemed airtight. Do we kill a few to save the many? Is it always wrong to kill? Both sides had the same information, and both perspectives seemed logical; but the truth was neither coldly objective nor obvious.

We all have opinions about the information we are given, but we often either lack further information, or we allow our subjective preconceptions to interpret the information for us. When we read a book like *The Da Vinci Code*, or watch the movie, we do the same thing. We make our judgments based on limited knowledge and our own biases—instead of taking the time to research the facts

The Broadband Effect

This leads to a third issue regarding the library sequence. Like most of us, Langdon and Sophie want their information now!

Gettum is aware of this and senses that "her guests' desire for discretion was quickly being outweighed by their eagerness for a fast result."[7] Of course, our heroes are hurrying to break the code so that they can get to the tomb before the bad guys, and then save Teabing. It's noble.

But conspiracy theories like the one in which our heroes are enmeshed are often rush-jobs, a lazy quick fix to explain issues that are actually more complex than the supposed conspiracy. Only the evidence that supports the theory and buoys the underlying claims gets examined.

And this applies to the skeptic as well as the believer. I certainly find this true of religious folk who, all too often, blame everything on anti-Christs lurking behind every rock. Christians too often live in a world defined wholly by systematic theology. Our minds desire organization; consequently, we organize and systematize "God's truths." But as with Sophie's compartmentalized cryptography, we only examine half of the information needed to make good decisions, or cast away or hide from information that might damage our preconceptions and truth claims.

We need to be less rushed when we seek ultimate answers, and seek after truth as if it were gold and silver. That means our search for truth needs to be diligent. For Christians, that means our search must be more biblical than systematic. We can't continually compartmentalize everything we do, pulling out truths from disconnected places. We need to see the Bible in its whole, and not just the parts we like. We would also do well to examine truth from cultural and external means—not as authorities over the Bible, but as part of the Bible's (and the Spirit's) context.

Skeptics and Christians alike would do well to consider John Calvin's words about the search for truth:

> Therefore, in reading profane authors, the admirable light of truth displayed in them should remind us, that the human mind, however much fallen and perverted

from its original integrity, is still adorned and invested with admirable gifts from its Creator. If we reflect that the Spirit of God is the only fountain of truth, we will be careful, as we would avoid offering insult to him, not to reject or condemn truth wherever it appears.[8]

It is well for Christians to recognize and acknowledge truth when it is promulgated by minds in disagreement with our positions, and it would behoove many of us to read and interact with material (books, movies, music, and people) that will stretch our worldviews, not echo them.

The skeptic would likewise benefit from a mirrored remedy. But it would require being loosed from a purely materialistic view, one that excludes any chance of truth resulting from a metaphysical solution. Pride and arrogance are usually on the business end of a closed mind, whether that mind is religious or not.

Bandwidth Limitations

I wonder, is full disclosure really going to matter? I don't know how many times I have heard skeptics like Bertrand Russell say that there is simply not enough evidence to believe in God. Most skeptics I talk with say that we are born without any knowledge of God, but our environment and upbringing (that is, our lame religious education) coerce us into "believing"—until we one day break free from the shackles of superstition and are thankfully enlightened into disbelief. Could more evidence alone possibly overcome such an entrenched epistemology?

A few years back a very prominent man was interviewed in *Time* magazine, and was asked if he thought God existed. He answered that he wasn't sure, and that it was possible, but he really didn't have any time to figure that one out.[9] Wow. It's really not about the information, but the attitude of a person's heart.

In the first chapter of his letter to the Romans, the Apostle Paul observes that we have plenty of information provided to us

186

in order to "know" that God exists—what is referred to in theological circles as "general revelation"—but we choose to reject that knowledge and "worship the creation instead of the creator." We have the knowledge of God inherent in us, but we reject it, because it doesn't fit our worldview. We literally "suppress the truth in unrighteousness."[10]

So who's right? Does religion coerce us into belief? Or does skepticism suppress truth?

Enlightenment has its price. "From everyone who has been given much, much will be demanded; and from the one who has been entrusted with much, much more will be asked."[11] But the issue isn't really the quantity of information, but rather what we do with the information we have. If I suddenly knew everything that God knew, would that automatically make me care more about my neighbor? History suggests, "no." Information alone does not soften hard hearts. After all, men like Judas knew Jesus very well, but still chose to reject Him. So even meeting God face to face is no silver bullet.

Belief in God, or in any ultimate truth, begins with a simple faith-like response to what has already been revealed. Einstein reportedly said that "imagination is more important than knowledge,"[12] which I believe to be true. Knowledge doesn't ultimately do anything unless that knowledge is used constructively and leads to something bigger than ourselves. And there's the rub. Our human bandwidth is limited. God runs on broadband, and we're stuck with a dial-up connection.

Limited human knowledge—scientific, philosophical, religious, or otherwise—can be (and has been) used for some of the most heinous acts we have ever seen. If might doesn't make right, neither does mere possession of information. The Bible says that "knowledge puffs up, but love builds up."[13] While information is important in recognizing the truth, information alone is not itself truth. Raw data must be interpreted, and used for a constructive purpose.

The Gospel of John & Assumptions of Christendom

A movie that negatively illustrates the point is *The Gospel of John*, a yeoman-like attempt to put the words of St. John's gospel on the silver screen. One might think that, as a Christian, I wouldn't have much of an objection to such a righteous endeavor. After all, the only words in the screenplay are the words of John's gospel, acted out by a cast of what appear to be twentieth-century frat boys and grunge musicians.

For all intents and purposes, this movie might as well have been an update of *Jesus Christ Superstar*—which at least was deliberately aiming at anachronism, cultural imperialism, and irony. Even John the Baptist is blonde. Jesus looks like Keanu Reeves with a beard, and I'm pretty sure that my mother was playing Mary. Can't anyone paint or cast a Jewish, dark-skinned Jesus without blue eyes, for Christ's own sake? I'm sorry I'm raging; but this is my pet peeve, and I think I'm over it now.

The theory behind *The Gospel of John* is obviously this: if the filmmakers could just get the actual words of Scripture out into the theaters, people would come, and they would fall on their face in repentance—or something like that. That is, if the Church can just manage to corner someone with the right information, and if it's presented in just the right, magical way, then *Voila!* you've got a convert!

But the equation is not so simple. We cannot assume that people have the proper context in which to understand or be motivated by the words. And with film, in particular, it's not just the words. The delivery of those words matters, too—inflection, facial expression, attitude. Compassion. Irony. Humor. There's the effect of music, as well, which clearly does not come from Scripture. And then, yes, there's the visual elements. And all of this can get in the way of very well-meaning words.

In this movie, for instance, the scene in which Jesus overturns the money-changers tables in the temple portrays Him like a madman—akin to some of the wackos with big signs we see frequenting sporting events. Was this portrayal maybe inspired by Fred Phelps?

In *The Gospel of John*, Jesus goes crazy, but there really is no explanation why. Those of us who actually study these stories, of course, have the luxury of examining the passage in the context of parallel biblical accounts. We can discuss the incident within the theoretical framework of John's larger narrative. We have even been able to examine the history of the temple money-changers. We realize that they were ripping off the poor by telling them their sacrifices weren't good enough, selling them "unblemished" animals for a "good" price while turning around and selling those very same "bad" beasts to the next poor person.

Context is everything. Words alone will not do.

In America, the Church is in decline. I hope that Christians increasingly realize that informational propositions alone are not enough to help people understand who Jesus was, and is. He is not an abstract concept, but a real person who really walked on this earth. It is not enough to tell people about Jesus; Christians must bring people to know Jesus.

How can Jesus be presented to a world that is reared on MTV? We have an attention span of a few minutes, and want our information in short bursts of pithy highlights. Missiologist Leslie Newbigin says that "the congregation is the hermeneutic of the Gospel,"[14] meaning ultimately that the people of God are the physical, concrete explanation for the truths of God's Word, because simple propositions are not effective in a post-Christian culture. Maybe Kanye West has it right. Jesus walks. He doesn't just talk.

Filtering the Search Results

The Gospel of John makes the assumption that people watching the movie are able to put the fragmented, pre-digested and pre-interpreted pieces of that gospel together and understand what and why everything was happening. This is simply not the case in most cultures today—including western culture. Information needs to be put into context and interpreted. And a purely western, white presentation of the Gospel is not only anachronistic, it's offensive to 70% of the world. It's as revisionist as *The Da Vinci Code*'s version of Jesus' story.

It's hard for me to get too upset with Mr. Brown when Christians have been revising the text to suit themselves for years. We always tend to create a Jesus that looks like us. At least Dan Brown continues to maintain that he is only writing fiction, while a majority of our preachers proclaim "Thus sayeth the Lord!" Any hyphenated Jesus (Feminist-Jesus, Marxist-Jesus, Republican-Jesus, American-Jesus) is a domesticated one, a savior we have invented for our own purposes—instead of the Jesus of Scripture, suited for His own purposes, and His own glory.

> **"We need to refine the search parameters further."** Gettum took off her glasses and eyed the two. **"I need more information."**

For Further Investigation
The Da Vinci Code, Chapters 85 through 95

Dig a Little Deeper

➤ What kind of information do you like to hear?

➤ How do you handle information you don't agree with? Why?

➤ What kind of information could effectively destroy your worldview?

➤ Do you believe that truth can be found solely through the

gathering of the "facts?"

➤ How would you describe or define the relationship between information and truth?

➤ In what ways do Christians tend to use information falsely?

➤ In what ways do those who disdain religion and Christianity tend to use information falsely?

Draw Your Own Conclusions

➤ Kanye West's "Jesus Walks":

- The song is available on the album *The College Dropout*, a bestselling CD widely available at most music outlets.

- The music video for the track is also available online: www.mtv.com/music/artist/west_kanye/videos.jhtml#/music /artist/west_kanye/videos.jhtml

- In addition, Kanye West has published the *College Dropout Video Anthology* on DVD, which offers alternate versions of the "Jesus Walks" video.

➤ John's Own Words About the Purpose of His Gospel:

- John 20:24–31.

- John 21:20–25.

Part Five:
Mystery and Wonderment

> Teabing's heart turned
> grave, then resolute. He
> aimed the gun at Langdon.
> "And you, Robert? Are you
> with me or against me?"

A Man of Humanity

Jenn Wright, Lead Investigator

Every family has its own set of legends—stories that are told and retold, perfected by the tellers. They may be humorous (as when my normally table-manners-scrupulous dad "passed" the hot dogs buns like miniature footballs) or poignant (like my sister sensing the presence of our late grandmother at my wedding). These stories usually link us to our heritage—emotional or genealogical—often providing a sense of history and selfhood not found anywhere else.

The recording of history has much the same effect (whether

you believe it is always "written by the winners" or not). Accounts of the events that have shaped our lives, whether personally or corporately, are an intimate component of who we are and who we become. A culture's ceremonies often shed light on its history and values, just as the stories told by a family or by an individual reveal much about what has shaped (and is shaping) them into who they are.

One significant method of corporate remembrance is through the celebration of holidays. In the United States, we have specific holidays to remember our mothers, our fathers, our military heroes, our presidents, our national independence, and even certain pivotal individuals such as Christopher Columbus and Dr. Martin Luther King, Jr. Likewise, Christian holidays are based around the remembrance of certain events: Christmas celebrates the birth of Jesus; Easter commemorates the resurrection. Celebrating these holidays helps us to remember who we are and where we came from.

The Jewish culture is a prime example of the resonance of ancient stories retold. Jewish holy days such as Purim and Passover are commemorations of God's intervention on behalf of His chosen people. This power of remembrance was established by God Himself, who created us to depend on the past for direction in the present and future. In Deuteronomy, for example, God directs His people to remember His laws, to imprint them on their own minds and hearts as well as the minds and hearts of their children:

> In the future, when your son asks you, "What is the meaning of the stipulations, decrees and laws the Lord our God has commanded you?" tell him: "We were slaves of Pharaoh in Egypt, but the Lord brought us out of Egypt with a mighty hand. Before our eyes the Lord sent miraculous signs and wonders—great and terrible—upon Egypt and Pharaoh and his whole household. But he brought us out from there to bring us in and give us the land that he promised on oath to our

forefathers. The Lord commanded us to obey all these decrees and to fear the Lord our God, so that we might always prosper and be kept alive, as is the case today. And if we are careful to obey all this law before the Lord our God, as He has commanded us, that will be our righteousness.[1]

Similarly, the Jews were commanded to remember God's deliverance during their exile in Egypt, when the angel of death passed over all Hebrews' homes whose doors had been painted with the blood of the Passover lamb:

> When you enter the land that the Lord will give you as he promised, observe this ceremony. And when your children ask you, "What does this ceremony mean to you?" then tell them, "It is the Passover sacrifice to the Lord, who passed over the houses of the Israelites in Egypt and spared our homes when he struck down the Egyptians."[2]

Much later, Esther and Mordecai established the feast of Purim, a two-day celebration of the Jews' deliverance from Haman's plot to have them destroyed during the time of King Xerxes. While the holy day is not specifically recorded as coming from God (Mordecai and Esther are credited together for the decree), Purim remains one of the holiest days of the year for Jews, as it was commanded nearly twenty-five centuries ago to

> celebrate annually the fourteenth and fifteenth days of the month of Adar as the time when the Jews got relief from their enemies, and as the month when their sorrow was turned into joy and their mourning into a day of celebration. ... These days should be remembered and observed in every generation by every family, and in every province and in every city. And these days of Purim should never cease to be celebrated by the Jews, nor should the memory of them die out among their descendants.[3]

The power of recalling the past continued to influence the Hebrews throughout their history, establishing traditions that would last millennia. In addition to observing holy days, physical tributes such as stone altars were built to memorialize miraculous or prominent events. Moses, for example, built a stone altar at the foot of Mount Sinai after receiving the Ten Commandments. Likewise, Joshua directed the Israelites to build a stone altar to commemorate God's miraculous intervention as the Israelites crossed the Jordan River into the Promised Land:

> So Joshua called together the twelve men he had appointed from the Israelites, one from each tribe, and said to them, "Go over before the ark of the Lord your God into the middle of the Jordan. Each of you is to take up a stone on his shoulder, according to the number of the tribes of the Israelites, to serve as a sign among you. In the future, when your children ask you, 'What do these stones mean?' tell them that the flow of the Jordan was cut off before the ark of the covenant of the Lord. When it crossed the Jordan, the waters of the Jordan were cut off. These stones are to be a memorial to the people of Israel forever."[4]

Clearly, history influences who we are, and who we become—as individuals, families, nations, and global communities. The stories we tell of our past, the ones we choose to continue telling, shape our consciences, both individual and collective, inevitably affecting our sense of identity and purpose.

Retelling Dan Brown's Story

Somewhat dejected by the Teacher's choice to have Rémy deliver the prize of the keystone, Silas seeks rest at the Opus Dei Centre in London. Yet he is awakened suddenly by an intuitive sense of foreboding, one which proves true when the police some crashing through the door. With some strategic moves requiring both force and flexibility, Silas is able to escape from the room, only to be shot as he runs. After Silas collides with an officer and stealthily procures his gun, a second figure emerges from the shadows, seizing Silas by the shoulders. In one quick move, Silas turns and fires—directly into Aringarosa's chest. Promising vengeance on the Teacher, who has deceived both of them into believing they would share in the grand disclosure of the Grail, Silas hefts Aringarosa's body through the driving rain into the hospital, where he learns the bishop's chances for survival are tenuous at best.

Meanwhile, Sophie and Langdon have hurried off to Westminster Abbey and the tomb of Sir Isaac Newton, having finally determined that he was the knight A. Pope (Alexander Pope) interred, and hoping against hope to reach the tomb and solve the puzzle before Teabing's captors. What they don't know, however, is that the Teacher is already there, scanning the myriad orbs and wondering which one the clue refers to. He sees Sophie and Langdon approaching, and starts to formulate his plan for leveraging just the right pressure to get their help in opening the cryptex. As Sophie and Langdon approach, they discover a note the Teacher has left behind, indicating that he has Teabing, and that they should meet him in the public garden, via the Chapter House.

Still hoping to rescue their poor scholarly friend, they rush into the Chapter House, only to have the door shut behind them, catching them in a renovation-related dead end. And, to their utter surprise, there is Teabing—with a gun leveled at Langdon.

Leigh "the Teacher" Teabing now has the two most formidable assistants for solving the cryptex at his complete disposal. After revealing the "truth" about how Saunière betrayed the Priory and the Grail by failing to reveal the Sangreal documents at the appointed time, not only does he take responsibility for Saunière's murder, he also divulges the "truth" about how Sophie's family died in a not-so-accidental accident. After completely shattering Sophie's world (again), Teabing then attempts to bring the cryptologist and symbologist on board with his own plans for solving the cryptex and exposing the two-thousand-year cover-up. As bait, Teabing hands over the keystone to Langdon, ominously asking in a scriptural allusion, "And you, Robert? Are you with me, or against me?"[5]

History and Humanism

When recalling history, we have a natural tendency to become humanist. After all, history largely records the activities of mankind, so it seems only natural that the past is often read as a chronology of the accomplishments and offenses of the human race. Embodied in the very idea "history" are wars, discoveries, assassinations, inventions, genocides, explorations, and desecrations—to each of which we often ascribe fault or credit, whether or not such charges are justified. For instance, we often credit Christopher Columbus with discovering the New World (heck, we even set aside a holiday for him), when, in actuality, no discovery was needed—the place was already well-populated, and other Europeans had landed on the shores long before he did.

Similarly, we all know that Hitler was responsible for the Jewish holocaust, right? But what about all the people who actually carried out his orders? What about the myriad people who unwittingly allowed such atrocities to happen? Clearly history is more than a chronology, and often less than the entire story. Still, it gives us a picture of what humankind is capable of—good, bad, and indifferent.

This focus on the achievements of our race is by no means new; however, the advent of the Enlightenment has most certainly enhanced our humanist tendencies. The ability of the human mind to create and discover has led to untold benefits for humanity (as well as detriments to society, the environment, and other species, but we won't get into that here)—from psychological and sociological awareness to air and space travel. Men and women have discovered exciting technologies, harnessed electricity, and created nuclear weapons. We have developed medications to treat the common cold as well as cancer. We have probed the psyche, scrutinized the nature of civilization, and examined nearly every living thing. We can predict the weather, prevent infection, and preserve embryos. In all, we are pretty darn amazing.

Except for all those things we still don't understand.

Like the nature and substance of love. Or how schizophrenia racks the brain. Or what black holes are, and how physical objects interact on an atomic level, and how all those stem cells know what to be when they grow up. Even simpler things astonish us, leaving us with a sense of wonder about the world in which we live. As Solomon muses,

> There are three things that are too amazing for me, four that I do not understand: the way of an eagle in the sky, the way of a snake on a rock, the way of a ship on the high seas, and the way of a man with a maiden. Under three things the earth trembles, under four it cannot bear up: a servant who becomes king, a fool who is full of food, an unloved woman who is married, and a maidservant who displaces her mistress. Four things on earth are small, yet they are extremely wise: ants are creatures of little strength, yet they store up their food in the summer; coneys are creatures of little power, yet they make their home in the crags; locusts have no king, yet they advance together in ranks; a lizard can be caught with the hand, yet it is found in kings' palaces.[6]

Such simple things, yet we, like the wise Solomon, are left in awe of them. So much for our amazing cranial capacities. Humanism, it seems, has its limits. We know a lot, but we are not yet all-knowing. "Humanism," wrote Simone Weil, "was not wrong in thinking that truth, beauty, liberty, and equality are of infinite value, but in thinking that man can get them for himself without grace."[7] As human history has shown, we might be able to learn and process vast amounts of data about our world, but that knowledge has yet to free us from the influences of the past, and our distinct proclivity for repeating it.

Humanism and the Individual

While confidence in the mind of mankind is certainly not unwarranted, there are obviously times when such confidence would be best curbed. "There is no prejudice so strong as that which arises from a fancied exemption from all prejudice,"[8] wrote British essayist William Hazlitt, and the prejudice toward the human mind's ability to conquer both the world around it and the world within it is most dangerous indeed.

Teabing's confidence in his own ability to discern the Grail secrets serves as a well-qualified example of such disastrous over-confidence. He claims that "a true knight learns humility in the face of the Grail. He learns to obey the signs placed before him... I am not looking for singular glory here. I serve a far greater master than my own pride. The Truth."[9] However, his behavior rather contradicts his statement. His pride in his own research, his own conclusions about Grail legend, and his own "unbiased" perspective ultimately leave him exposed; his inability to solve the cryptex, not to mention his unethical and outright criminal activities, demonstrate Alexander Pope's observation from several centuries ago:

> Of all the causes which conspire to blind
> Man's erring judgment, and misguide the mind;
> What the weak head with strongest bias rules,—
> Is pride, the never-failing vice of fools.[10]

Teabing clearly believes that the human mind (particularly his) is capable of reducing mystery and wonderment to mere pieces of data. His disregard for the Christian faith and its (by definition) impenetrable mysteries has not only biased his research and conclusions, it has cost him his freedom—both intellectual and physical.

Humanity and the Individual

The recent film *Joshua*, based on the novel by Joseph Girzone, paints an excellent picture of humanism in the context of humanity and divinity. In the movie, Joshua—a man with apparently no history at all—appears one day in a quiet little town and takes up residence. While voluntarily picking up various projects, such as rebuilding the local Protestant church, Joshua stirs up some controversy as to whether his intentions are pure or divisive. In the midst of this exploration of Jesus (the Anglicized Greek form of the equivalent Hebrew name "Joshua") visiting our world in the here and now, we are given a glimpse of how divinity interacts with humanity. In *Joshua*, at least, the divine nature of the man ultimately brings about the development and fulfillment of those individuals who allow his truth to permeate their lives— past, present, and future. The story is less about Joshua himself than about what his presence does in the life of the town and in the lives of the people. The man without a history quietly affects the development of those around him, keeping personal and societal history relevant without allowing it to be definitive.

This subtle battle between Joshua and those in the town who distrust him mirrors the conflict between the humanistic desire to believe we can transcend the past, and the divine desire to mold us within the context of history. Humanistically, we want to pull ourselves up by the bootstraps, and beat both our internal and external worlds into submission, usually by the application of strict reason. Douglas Bush pointed out the distinct foci of humanism by comparing the ideas of Bacon and Montaigne:

> The sovereignty of man, says Bacon in one of his massive phrases, lieth hid in knowledge. Montaigne would agree, but his terms would have an entirely different meaning. Bacon means that through scientific knowledge man can conquer external nature for his own use and benefit. Montaigne would mean that through study of his own inner strength and weakness man can

learn to conquer himself.[11]

But can history be so easily disregarded?

All humanistic pride aside, how does history play into a person's identity? Look no further—Sophie Neveu is, perhaps, the perfect example of history influencing the growth and maturity of an individual. After all, Dan Brown gives us Sophie's entire life story. Other than a few references to Langdon's phobia-inducing childhood trauma and Silas' rescue by Bishop Aringarosa, the formative events of the other characters' lives are apparently inconsequential, and therefore never explored. But Sophie—we know all about Sophie, and hers is the history which matters most throughout the course of the novel.

Granted, in past chapters we have been somewhat critical of Sophie—implying that her relative ignorance and mental opacity override her evolution as a character. Nevertheless, it is undeniable that, of all the characters in Brown's narrative, Sophie's personal growth provides the foundation for the entire adventure. As Brown gradually and skillfully divulges the details of Sophie's background, we may just realize that the history ostensibly being rewritten is not that of the Grail or the Christian faith, but of a young cryptologist whose self-discovery ultimately transcends more trivial revelations. Really—the Grail quest is never completed in the course of the novel; the conclusion, rather, is Sophie's discovery of her own true history, and her reunion with her past.

Just how does Dan Brown effectively tell Sophie's story? Indeed, it is so well-told that we may miss the fact that *The Da Vinci Code* is more about Sophie discovering herself than about anyone discovering anything radically new about the Grail and its legends. Her development, however, provides the narrative backbone of Brown's adventure; her life's story is revealed in bits and pieces until, at the end, we have a full portrait not of the *Mona Lisa*, nor of Robert Langdon, but of Sophie Neveu.

Sophie first comes on the scene as a highly-regarded

cryptologist, one who has quickly devised a way to get Langdon away from Fache so she can help the framed man escape. Indeed, she gives a first impression of phenomenal composure and marked intelligence. She even evokes a measure of sympathy upon her revelation to Langdon that the murdered curator was her grandfather. But it is not long before Sophie's initial intelligence gives way to a certain blankness—her complete ignorance of Grail legend, as well as her inability to recognize or solve some basic anagrams and codes, leaves the reader wondering which rock she's been hiding under. Ever so gradually, however, Brown reveals more and more of her story—the death of her family, the fallout with her grandfather, the genesis of her love affair with cryptography. Ultimately, Sophie's posthumous reconciliation with her grandfather and his pursuit of the sacred feminine, more so than Teabing's quest for the Grail, drives the narrative structure of the novel. And her story, along with Dan Brown's, is neatly tied up at the end when she reunites with her presumed-dead family.

History? Humanity?

So perhaps Dan Brown (as so many people would like to believe) is not trying to rewrite HIStory; instead, he is inventing HERstory. By delving into the spirit of a woman, and following her through the amazing discoveries of the past that have so formed her life, is it possible that our gifted author has, indeed, celebrated the sacred feminine through his development of the character of Sophie? Or has he perhaps invited us to pursue *Sophia*—Wisdom—in the same manner with which Sophie pursued her self?

> Do not forsake wisdom, and she will protect you; love her, and she will watch over you. Wisdom is supreme; therefore get wisdom. Though it cost all you have, get understanding. Esteem her, and she will exalt you; embrace her, and she will honor you. She will set a

garland of grace on your head and present you with a crown of splendor.[12]

> Turning his back to the others, Langdon walked toward the towering windows. Saunière was not a man of science. He was a man of humanity, of art, of history.

For Further Investigation
The Da Vinci Code, Chapters 96 through 100

Dig a Little Deeper

➤ What kinds of things do you find important to memorialize? Why?

➤ How effective are prescribed methods of remembrance (*i.e.*, holidays) for you? Would another approach be more practical?

➤ If it's not the "winners," who writes history?

➤ What is your opinion of Douglas Bush's summaries of Bacon's and Montaigne's views of the sovereignty of man? Is one more "right" than the other? Are there more things to consider?

Draw Your Own Conclusions

➤ Regarding Simone Weil, Holocaust Survivor and Philosopher:

- *Simone Weil: A Life*, by Simone Petrement; translated from the French by Raymond Rosenthal.

- *Waiting for God*, by Simone Weil.

Mystery and Wonderment: A Man of Humanity

➤ Humanism, Secular Humanism, and Christian Humanism:

- *Humanism: Finding Meaning in the Word*, by Nicolas Walter.
- *The Philosophy of Humanism*, by Corliss Lamont.
- www.answers.com/topic/secular-humanism
- www.newadvent.org/cathen/07538b.htm
- *Christian Humanism: Creation, Redemption, and Reintegration*, by John P. Bequette.

➤ Symbols and Remembrance in Scripture:

- Genesis 9:8–17.

> Fache paused. "My Lord, where do you go from here?" Aringarosa smiled. "A little faith can do wonders, Captain. A little faith."

A Little Faith

Jenn Wright, Lead Investigator

The seasoned storyteller is a serious craftsman, carefully honing his art as we, his very willing audience, hang attentively on every word. My brother Rick is one such storyteller. Though in other aspects relatively soft-spoken, he tells stories that are the most believable and entertaining accounts of outdoor adventures I have ever heard. (Think Patrick McManus meets your grandpa, only forty years before you were born.) His manner is quiet, never raising his voice to maintain your attention, nor flailing about wildly in efforts at physical humor. Nevertheless, his tales enchant me and the rest of my family, never failing to send us into bladder-testing gales of laughter along the way. The chronicles of his hunting and hiking escapades with his surreptitiously astute (albeit characteristically stubborn) mule, Louie, in particular, weave an almost mythical tapestry of truth and humor that never once crosses the line into fable or caricature.

Mind you, no one else in my immediate family has any such flair for legend-making. Any attempt I might make, for instance, exceeding a good one-liner, leaves my audience simply yearning for a conclusion. But Rick has that certain genius—that exquisite marriage of inborn artistry, engaging personality, and refined technique that never fails to pick you up out of your easy chair and plop you back down in the middle of an adventure.

On the other hand, many a good Bible story has been ruined by a bad storyteller. Flannelgraphs, homemade painted wood chairs with too-short uneven legs, and blatant repetition all conspire against Sunday School's child. A virtual anthology of lively historical accounts and picture-perfect parables could conceivably keep us rapt with attention from infancy to old age—yet so often it doesn't. Why not?

Perhaps for the same reason Dan Brown's story has topped the bestseller list for nearly three years: a good story isn't good unless it's well told.

The Road to Rosslyn

Once again, Langdon is confronted by a gunman—this time it's Teabing behind the trigger, demanding that Langdon choose between him (with all the attendant Grail fame and fortune) and Sophie (the "honorable" if less profitable option). The crafty symbologist stalls, choosing silence and a bit of pacing around to stimulate his overworked cerebral cells. Meanwhile, the reader is casually granted access (however unwillingly) into Teabing's mind as he recounts the entire plan—from sending Silas to murder Saunière to recruiting Langdon's help in solving the cryptex.

Finally, Langdon kneels to put the cryptex on the floor. Then, looking directly into the revolver Teabing has trained on his face, in one swift move, Langdon lobs the treasured keystone into the air. Despite his best efforts to catch it softly, the cryptex breaks in Teabing's hands, and the acidic vinegar pours sickeningly out. Just then he notices that there is no disintegrating papyrus amongst the broken glass—and that the letters are no longer randomly arranged, but neatly spell out the word APPLE. At that, Langdon suavely pulls the map from his pocket, the crippled Teabing in anguish over his loss. And just in the nick of time (which means before anyone gets shot, but after we know that Langdon and Sophie have beaten Teabing in the Grail hunt), Bezu Fache and his men rush in to save what's left of the (really long) day.

Once in custody at the police station, Teabing (perhaps unwittingly) convinces Fache that he is aiming to plead insanity—mainly because the former British Royal Historian won't stop babbling about the Holy Grail. Aringarosa, while recuperating from the unintended gunshot wound, mourns Silas' death, having tragically learned that the devoted albino monk had committed numerous crimes for the Teacher, all in the name of the Grail. And in a quiet and humble visit to the convalescing bishop, Fache returns the amethyst ring Aringarosa had used to bribe the French pilot—an oddly touching scene of two very different but broken men with uncertain futures.

Sophie and Langdon, meanwhile, have high-tailed it to Scotland and Rosslyn Chapel, where Sophie recovers long-repressed memories of visiting the ancient building with her grandfather. The young docent showing them the chapel then recognizes the rosewood box in Langdon's hand, claiming that his grandmother, the head of the Rosslyn Trust, has an identical one. In yet another touching moment, Sophie and the young docent realize that they are siblings, both having been told the lie that their entire family perished in a car accident. And finally, Sophie feels "at last that she [is] home."[1]

Components of a Well-Told Story: Miracle Maker

Perhaps part of the reason that Bible stories often lose their sense of wonderment is that in the telling and retelling, we have somehow lost the ability to communicate the inexplicable. In our heroic efforts to present the stories as the historical accounts we believe them to be, we emphasize the facts, and consequently undersell the supra-human foundation upon which every account rests. Enlightened as we are, we want to make the Bible as rational as possible, accepting miracles where we must, but analyzing the characters and their behaviors until we think we can fully understand their motives and intentions. The problem is that human nature itself is never fully explicable (as we discussed earlier in "The Sane Ones Are Nuts"); how, then, can we expect to follow the story of the ultimate account of the metaphysical interacting with the physical—an interaction which, by definition, transcends our understanding?

Without the inherent mystery and inexplicability of the foundations of Christianity (go ahead, try to logically explain the need for blood sacrifice, or the resurrection), faith would not be faith—it would be knowledge. The difference? Perhaps philosopher Soren Kierkegaard explained it best:

> It is easy to see, though it scarcely needs to be pointed out, since it is involved in the fact that Reason is set aside, that faith is not a form of knowledge; for all knowledge is either a knowledge of the eternal, excluding the temporal and historical as indifferent, or it is pure historical knowledge. No knowledge can have for its object the absurdity that the eternal is the historical.[2]

It is faith, then, that must lead us to the eternal—not well-reasoned historical accounts, nor carefully investigated "evidence" of the metaphysical. When we, in our hubris, forget that we are incapable of understanding everything that goes on in the world through the "reliable" lenses of our five senses, we have lost our grasp on the eternal, and become as unmovable and impenetrable as the "rock" of certainty to which we have chained ourselves.

The Miracle Maker, an animated account of Christ's work on earth, provides some insight into how the incomprehensible can be presented in the context of verifiable history. Centered around the miraculous resurrection of a centurion's daughter, *Miracle Maker* makes no attempt to portray Jesus and his followers as either ultra-rational or ultra-intuitive; rather, the events and the people are what they are—composites of the explainable and the unexplainable, the logical and the illogical, the literal and the aesthetic. While a cartoon version of the life of Christ may be difficult to take seriously (despite stellar performances from Ralph Fiennes and William Hurt), the movie subtly portrays the delicate balance between what we can see and hear and touch, and what we believe as a result of—or despite—such tactile evidence.

In the context of the story (recorded in the gospels of Mark and Luke), Jairus, overwhelmed by his daughter's progressing illness, must decide whether or not to trust in the healing power of a local controversial teacher. While the child is fascinated by Jesus, clearly undeterred by the grownups' skepticism, Jairus himself is torn between the knowledge of his daughter's incurable condition and the hope that Jesus can do something about it. In his indecision, his friend, Cleopas, assures him that "no one ever lost their soul by *listening* to a liar. Only by believing him and following him. But if he speaks the truth... We have nothing to fear from the truth, do we?"[3] Ultimately, when his daughter is literally dying, Jairus chooses to act on his hope rather than his logic, declaring with full conviction, "I will go to Jesus and you will be healed by his power."[4] This hope—this faith—that he has chosen transcends his own physical understanding, persisting even when he is informed that his daughter has already died. And in response to his choice to believe, Jesus revives the young girl, encouraging Jairus and the attendant witnesses to "keep on believing."[5]

As *The Miracle Maker* demonstrates, there is no need for heavy-handed manipulation in defense of either reason or faith. Instead, the movie effectively portrays how faith and reason necessarily intertwine, and how, once again, we must engage both hemispheres of the unified mind in order to effectively navigate the seas of sense and experience. Michael Ramsey, Archbishop of Canterbury, described the relationship in an address to future priests, stating that "Reason is an action of the mind; knowledge is a possession of the mind; but faith is an attitude of the person. It means you are prepared to stake yourself on something being so."[6]

There is that which we can justify using our five senses, and that which steps outside the reaches of the definable, and one without the other is like a waltz without a partner: arms absurdly encircling the air in a ridiculous mockery of the very nature of the art.

The Da Vinci Balance

Brown's narrative also illustrates the necessary balance between the logical and the mystical. The "foundation of the Grail legend," that "you do not find the Grail, the Grail finds you"[7] ascribes almost a living, organic nature to the celebrated treasure. While hyper-rational in his research and study, Teabing, in his desperation to recruit Sophie and Langdon to help him "uncover the truth and make it known," leaves reason behind and appeals instead to the enigmatic side of the Grail quest, whispering dramatically, "Listen. Can you hear it? The Grail is speaking to us across the centuries. She is begging to be saved from the Priory's folly."[8] The Grail quest, the novel suggests, is based neither entirely on reason, nor entirely on faith.

So it should come as no great surprise that after four hundred pages of intertwining games of cops and robbers, hide and seek, hot potato, and hangman, all in pursuit of legends and secrets, the stories of our two protagonists have two very different endings. For Sophie, the Grail mystery is of little consequence, now that a familial mystery has been solved; the discovery of her natural family is enough to satiate her thirst for the Grail. Once she learns that her own bloodline thrives, she apparently loses interest in the ostensible holy bloodline that has dominated the scene, content in the knowledge that she is not "so alone in the world."[9]

For Langdon, however, the mystery continues, with little

more than a woman's intuition to console him. Apparently his only option is to return home to further ponder the current whereabouts of the Grail, trusting the treasure to reveal its secrets through whatever mystical means it chooses (perhaps a dream?), guiding him through the codes and riddles until he unravels the last strand of the yarn. Marie Chauvel merely offers her condolences, telling Langdon that she is "sorry that after all your hard work, you will be leaving Rosslyn without any real answers. And yet, something tells me you will eventually find what you seek. One day it will dawn on you."[10] With that, she shrewdly bids him keep any revelations secret, just as Saunière did, and thus, it seems, endeth our Grail quest.

This double denouement merely accentuates the relationship between faith and logic that Brown has illuminated throughout his novel. The fact that Sophie's Grail quest begins and ends in less than twenty-four hours is rather surprising; yet the fact that it ends with the very natural, very human comfort she finds in discovering her family resonates with her humanistic foundation, her very career being built on the power of the human mind to solve problems. Langdon's empty hands, however, with the Grail mystery so close to being solved, leave him (and us) with that sense of "mystery and wonderment that serve our souls"[11] intact. It seems that Brown would seek to satiate our appetites for both the rational and the non-rational.

The Reason for Faith

So perhaps it is no wonder that Brown's novel concludes with a juxtaposition of faith and logic. The waltz of the two extreme partners dances before us numerous times throughout the novel, never really settling on one as the lead. As we explored in previous chapters, Brown certainly celebrates the enlightened mind (the intellect-bending codes and riddles reinforcing our faith in the human power of reason), yet the very fact that the Grail, the Priory of Sion, and myriad other foundational aspects of the plot are based in rumor and legend leaves the audience—as well as the characters—taking quite a bit on faith.

Thomas Merton, the author and poet, made the following analogy:

> One might compare the journey of the soul to mystical union, by way of pure faith, to the journey of a car on a dark highway. The only way the driver can keep to the road is by using his headlights. So in the mystical life, reason has its function. The way of faith is necessarily obscure. We drive by night. Nevertheless our reason penetrates the darkness enough to show us a little of the road ahead. It is by the light of reason that we interpret the signposts and make out the landmarks along our way.[12]

Interestingly, this analogy is reproduced almost perfectly earlier in the novel, after Sophie and Langdon have procured the armored vehicle and are frantically seeking sanctuary until they can prove Langdon's innocence. Having damaged the vehicle by hitting a tree in his haste to leave Vernet behind, Langdon struggles to navigate the weighty truck, its lone functional headlight "casting a skewed sideways beam into the woods beside the country highway."[13] His attempts to remedy the situation are futile; "like an eyeball dangling from its socket,"[14] the remaining headlight is simply useless.

And it is here, with the headlights of reason broken and misdirected, that Langdon makes a fateful leap of faith: to seek asylum with Sir Leigh Teabing.

In his desperation, Langdon can only think of one "professional" who can help them—the knight and former British Royal Historian whose life work has been focused on revealing the truth about the Holy Grail. Sophie is a hard sell, unwilling to trust just anyone, but Langdon is convinced that his faith in Teabing is well founded. Relying on his brief collaboration with the eccentric man, Langdon acts not on Teabing's proven character; rather, "instinct told Langdon that Teabing would be totally trustworthy. An ideal safe harbor."[15] Not only does he trust Teabing to protect them, he firmly believes that Teabing "would probably trip over himself to help them as much as possible,"[16] particularly after hearing Sophie's claim that her grandfather was the Grand Master of the secret society Teabing has been earnestly trying to reveal for decades.

But is Langdon's faith well placed? Of course, at this point, we know that his blind drive down that highway proved unwise; the signposts and landmarks of Teabing's avaricious nature were left unilluminated. Sophie, on the other hand, "was hesitant to involve a total stranger. Considering the information potentially enclosed, the instinct was probably a good one."[17]

Instinct. Trust. A gut feeling. Faith. Call it what you will, Brown's novel is full of it. And not as the fall guy for stupidity or naïveté. "Faith must feed on reason," historian Reinhold Niebuhr observed. "But reason must also feed on faith."[18]

Clearly, faith has its place—right in the open arms of reason.

A Rational Place for Faith

John Henry Newman, nineteenth-century British theologian, noted that science

> gives us the grounds of premises from which religious
> truths are to be inferred; but it does not set about
> inferring them, much less does it reach the inference;
> that is not its province... This is why Science has so
> little of a religious tendency; deductions have no power
> of persuasion. The heart is commonly reached, not
> through the reason, but through the imagination, by
> means of direct impressions, by the testimony of facts
> and events, by history, by description. Persons influence
> us, voices melt us, looks subdue us, deeds inflame us.
> Many a man will live and die upon a dogma; no man
> will be a martyr for a conclusion.[19]

The realms of science and faith each have their respective places, and they are not at opposing ends of the spectrum, as we would often make them seem. Faith might be understood, then, as the *continuance* of reason, the next natural step, rather than either the end or the antithesis of what is logical or rational.

For Langdon—as for Brown, apparently—there is room for both faith and reason on the dance floor. At the close of the book, Langdon is on a path to discovery—but not one based on evidence or facts or symbological interpretation. Instead, he must wait for the Grail's location to "dawn" on him, at some unknown point in the future. After spending so much time and energy solving all the riddles and codes while still winding up at Rosslyn with empty hands, Langdon's only choice is to accept that some things defy rational explanation—like waking up someday and "knowing" where the Grail resides; and that inexplicability in doing so does not make such realizations any less true or vital.

Langdon does not need to believe that the answer will come to him through more diligent research and painstaking devotion to codes and symbols. He merely accepts that "there remained some facet of this mystery yet to reveal itself."[20] The confidence that mysteries are able to anthropomorphically reveal themselves again points to the conclusion that not everything can be explained or justified by the five senses. Such is the way of the mystical—the "glorious unattainable treasure that somehow... inspires us."[21]

Is faith, then, in and of itself, the savior? Or does the object of faith make a difference? A classmate of mine (in French class, oddly enough) boldly proclaimed that faith itself was a causative entity: if enough people truly believed a thing was so, then it was. Now, he couldn't quantify the relationship between the number of people believing and the truth of a statement or the actual occurrence of an event. (Would procuring a resurrection require the same collective force of faith that producing a rainstorm would?) But he was fervent in his belief. (So, by a somewhat circular logic, I suppose that if enough people believed that his tenets were legitimate, they would be.) Such faith in faith seems like a dog chasing its tail—but is it so different from trusting anything else?

In the phenomenally engaging movie *Serenity*, the captain of the titular Firefly-class spaceship, Malcolm Reynolds, prides himself on his rationality and pragmatism. Despite the efforts of the once-resident preacher, Shepherd Book, Mal refuses to acknowledge faith in anything beyond what he can see and understand—particularly in relation to any Higher Power at work in the 'verse (for the non-Browncoats out there, that's *Firefly*-speak for "universe").

Mal's reluctance to trust seems confirmed when, as the Shepherd lies dying on a ravaged terraformed planet, he implores Mal: "I don't care what you believe. Just believe it."[22] What with all the wreckage and destruction—and the apparent injustice of the Shepherd's violent death—it's no surprise that his last words are shrugged off by the captain. Later, though, we all breathe a collective sigh of satisfaction when Mal ultimately confesses that he has found a belief for which he is willing to die. As Aringarosa tells Fache from his hospital bed, "A little faith can do wonders."[23]

And that's where we leave Langdon at the end of this section of our text—with little more than faith that the Grail will reveal itself to him, someday, somewhere. The interdependence of the rational and the mystical, illuminated once and for all through the disparate endings of Langdon's and Sophie's once-united quest, leaves no question as to the author's acceptance of—and even advocacy for—the balance. As with the overemphasized balance between the sacred masculine and the sacred feminine, the sensible, tangible conclusion of Sophie's story interweaves with the ethereal, aesthetic end of Langdon's journey—a balance struck with both the reasonable and the mystical firmly intact.

When the Grail does reveal itself to him, Langdon is ready,

hearing "a woman's voice... the wisdom of the ages"[24] calling to him from beneath the miniature pyramid. In a gesture of both reverence and triumph, Langdon kneels, demonstrating in a single motion how "Faith must not be slow to reason, nor reason to adore."[25]

Faith and reason—complementary components of a good story well told.

> Marie Chauvel gazed up at Rosslyn. "It is the mystery and wonderment that serve our souls, not the Grail itself."

For Further Investigation
The Da Vinci Code, Chapters 101 through 104

Dig a Little Deeper

➤ Who are the best storytellers you know? What makes them so good? What draws you into their stories?

➤ How can a story be best told in order to communicate both its truth and its mystery?

➤ Do you find Cleopas' advice for Jairus in *The Miracle Maker* sound? Why or why not?

➤ How much should we be content with "mystery and wonderment," and how much should we pursue further concrete knowledge of the spiritual?

➤ Is faith itself sufficient? Or does the object of faith matter?

Draw Your Own Conclusions

➤ According to filmmaker Norman Stone (*Shadowlands*) his friend Murray Watts, screenwriter of *The Miracle Maker*, says that films "make an audience feel so much that they can't help but think."

➤ The Bible itself walks a fine line between metaphysical mysteries and revealed truths. Consider the words of the Apostle Paul in Ephesians 3:4–12 and 4:1–24.

> Marie Chauvel paused. "You
> are writing a manuscript
> about the sacred feminine,
> are you not? Finish it, Mr.
> Langdon. Sing her song.
> The world needs modern
> troubadours."

Modern Troubadours

Mike Gunn, Lead Investigator

Our final act finds Langdon and Sophie in Roslin as directed by Saunière's final message: "The Holy Grail 'neath ancient Roslin waits." We are told that Scotland's Rosslyn (originally spelled Roslin) Chapel has become a site for "mystery seekers" wanting to "absorb the lore of the Holy Grail."[1] The only mystery that gets resolved here, as we noted in the last chapter, is that of Sophie's life story. Her grandmother and apparently nameless brother are not really dead, but had gone into "hiding" when Sophie's parents were killed in a suspicious car wreck—this to protect them from the insidious Opus Dei and other alleged Grail suppressors. And what better place to hide under an assumed name than as curator of one of Grail lore's principal pilgrimage sites? Perhaps the protection they really needed was from poorly written conspiracy theory stories?

In spite of learning the "hidden" truth regarding Sophie's lost grandmother and brother, and in spite of finding out that the Grail didn't exist in Rosslyn, and quite possibly didn't exist at all, Langdon is nonetheless cajoled by grandma "Marie Chauvel" to sing the song of the sacred feminine. She wants Langdon to tell the story of the sacred feminine and make the world aware of her "truth."

Now if it's "mystery and wonderment that serve our souls,"[2] as Chauvel says, then why would we want that "song" revealed? Wouldn't that demystify the mystery and throw a wet blanket on the wonder? What song is it, anyway, that needs to be sung? Just the mystery, but without the truth? Only Langdon and Chauvel, apparently, know for sure—and it's clearly more than simply paying homage to the sacred feminine. And how would that story "serve our souls," especially since "the Grail can be deceptive,"[3] as Chauvel warns? The whole story is an ambiguous, "ethereal," and "unattainable" sham isn't it? But isn't that the point? According to Marie, the sacred feminine's story is being told through "art, music, and books" (books such as *The Da Vinci Code*, I suppose), and the "pendulum is swinging."[4] But does the search for truth need a pendulum swing, or just a course correction? A gnomon, as we discussed earlier, doesn't swing like a pendulum. It wouldn't be of much use if it did.

Still, if we want to interpret the culture and its story, it's always good to know what direction the wind is blowing. The story Marie wants told, however, is not moored in concrete facts; it's anchored, as Marie says, in "our souls,"[5] and our desires. As such, it conveniently makes no specific, defensible claims and levels only the vaguest of demands, so it's easy to tell without repercussion. Still, even though the story is a dead end, isn't it worth proclaiming in the hope that it will topple the tyranny of the dominant metanarrative? Isn't that the supposed objective?

Pursuing the Mystery

This appears to be the Holy Grail behind the postmodern hermeneutic. Language is simply a mutable tug-of-war symbol set disconnected from reality, and metanarratives don't deserve to exist—at least, not oppressive male-centered ones. Is this the only absolute truth in Dan Brown's fictional dreamland—the rule by which Magdalene's alternate story becomes as true as any other? Perhaps this is his truth serum, his personal secret code. Perhaps this is why he needs to sing his siren song, and why so many respond: they are mesmerized by a message that allows us to customize our own interpretations of symbols. It seems that the truth of the story is not important, or at least not as important as the telling of the story itself, or even the feelings that the story evokes.

As Erwin Lutzer describes this cultural urge, "Some historians say that history should no longer be the quest to find objective facts and then, as best we can, interpret them. History… should be revised to bolster self-esteem and to foster politically correct agendas."[6] In other words, postmodern historians aren't looking to find objective reality but a subjective alternative reality. Creatively, this approach plays out in films like *Jakob the Liar* and *A Beautiful Life*, tales about soothing lies that bring hope and comfort to an otherwise untenable situation. After all, isn't it better to tell good stories that bring forth hope (even if those stories aren't true) than to be discouraged by the reality of a meaningless or horrible life? Maybe reality is either too boring or too horrific for us to want to know the truth.

I can't help but suspect that this is Dan Brown's point after all, no matter how conspiratorial we want to be. He critiques not only the oppressive deceptions of the Church, but the empty promise of reactionary countermyths. Otherwise, how could he end his book—which has made so many bold statements regarding the "truth" of the Grail story, which has as its keystone the suppression of that truth by the early Church—with such weak evidence of the tale's reality? Marie Chauvel seems to concur with Karl Marx's assessment that "religion is the opium of the people."[7]

Maybe we are ripe for this sort of thing. Aren't we all too ready to hear "tales" that make us feel good, that tell us evil is "out there" and that the truth is "within us?" What about the stories that lead us to the truth about ourselves, that tell us that the truth is out there and that the biggest evil we need to confront is not only on the doorstep but within—the stories that bring us to despair before they can build us a foundation of hope? *The Da Vinci Code* wishes to bring us to hope, but does so largely via disdain, rather than via despair. But what if true hope and inspiration can only begin in pain and death, in a story of Paradise gone awry and in need of redemption from outside of ourselves?

Singing the Christian Song

What if there were a truly transcendent and mysterious kingdom that has been hitherto unavailable to us because of our rejection of its King? What if we are responsible to that King, a King who is greater than ourselves, and greater than our corrupt desires to create alternate kingdoms—desires that have put us at odds with Him? What if that King has been seeking His own, seeking those who have been enslaved to alternative kingdoms? What if that King has vowed to destroy all who oppose Him and have caused harm to His people? And what if that King has laid down His own life to establish a lasting pact with all who would like to abandon their own petty fiefdoms and join His Kingdom?

Isn't that a story (if it were true) that we ought to trumpet from the rooftops? Shouldn't we blow our horns in announcement of that King's presence, warning those who oppose Him, and guiding those who love Him and seek Him? Or are we just willing to succumb to preachers who tell good stories, rather than preachers who tell true ones? Such preachers, of course, are not confined to stuffy and staunch cathedrals, or to churches with empty pews. There are many pulpits in the world, and not all of them are found in churches.

Every media format we turn to, be it books, music, TV, or movies, trains us and teaches us like a personal mentor on the mountaintop of humanity's hope. And in a culture begging for ratings, it's easy to be like the Dalai Lama on Barbara Walters' special *Heaven*, to come out looking so cuddly and cute because what you have to say fails to critique the dominant culture, mimics the status quo, and connects us all to the goddess within. Though you're not trumpeting anything challenging or convicting, you can still sound so profound and lovely—while utterly failing to move anyone toward the real problem that besets all humans: sin—knowing what's right and not doing it!

Three Steps Back?

Devotion to the sacred feminine sounds so nice, but it failed in the second and third centuries. It's impossible to know precisely why today, but it was ultimately swallowed up in the truth of God's complete story, one which continues to cut across cultural and economic barriers because it is a comprehensive story of the creation, fall, redemption, and future consummation of the cosmos—a metanarrative explaining the entirety of the human story.

Whatever the cause of its demise, ancient worship of the sacred feminine certainly bore little resemblance to that proposed by Langdon and Chauvel: a horizontal, humanistic mysticism devoted to our "inner woman," little more than a disjointed conglomeration of naturalistic and apocryphal earth-bound legends which isn't the least bit interested in verifiable history or the truly transcendent that it ostensibly champions. The goddess story complements a genial egalitarian climate, but that still doesn't address the reality of the human problem. Restoring gender balance won't calm the savage wrath of Mother Earth, and the best we could hope for is a momentary balance as Chauvel's pendulum passes the point of equilibrium and begins to swing too far the other direction. That's what pendulums do.

The real-world irony of Dan Brown's supposedly enlightened Priory of Sion—whose "*senechaux* were traditionally men"[8]—is its similarity to the male-dominated cultures of India, which to this day promote the sacred feminine through many forms of goddess worship and fertility rites, yet treat their woman as second-class citizens.

By contrast, nations with firm traditions in both the Enlightenment and nominally patriarchal Christianity are those which have raised the value and cultural status of women to their highest place. Is the job done yet? Probably not. But the trend began long before the "rediscovery" of the sacred feminine in the latter half of the twentieth century.

In any event, elevating women to godhood is not the answer to raising their standard of life in any culture, as history has shown: poor ideas ultimately get swallowed up by better ones no matter how much the better idea co-opts aspects of the inferior. Yes, as Marie exhorted Langdon, the world does need troubadours, but it needs troubadours who are speaking with the courage of conviction and espousing the truth of the human condition. Our stories shouldn't settle for the merely gnostic, hidden, and ethereal; they should be contextual and clear, leading us outside ourselves and toward the only Being in the universe who can truly satisfy the soul.

Yes, Marie, mystery and wonderment can serve our souls, but they do so when solid substance acts in concert with truth as the compass to guide us there. Without substance there is no true wonderment. Any truth about the Divine, be it in relation to the masculinity or femininity of its nature, will drive us to ask more questions and continue our adventure. Any "truth" that tells us we are sufficient unto ourselves, that tells us we are okay right where we are, is no adventure at all and is as empty as the dead-end crypt in Saint-Sulpice. Such truth would be a mystery in which we search for clues that we wrote ourselves and which are never correct—and which never lead to another clue.

Real clues reveal a mystery that is both true and transcendent, not denigrating the clues, yet elevating the mystery. And the best mystery may lead us to more mystery, but with real clues that buoy our hope and connect it to an anchor for our souls. What is it that is both true and transcendent, and what is worth the calling as troubadour? A mere *"quest to kneel before the bones of Mary Magdalene"*?[9] In the end, Robert Langdon is no better than a pilgrim genuflecting before a sacred relic. How progressive.

The Truth About Emptiness

When I was traveling through Jerusalem and Israel in 1999 while ministering in Jordan, I went, as most tourists do, to many of the "holy" sites, which were indeed cool to see. But what struck me was how commercial the venture was. In reality, many of the "authentic" sites were merely conjectured and up for archaeological grabs. The merchants clamored for your money, and much of the experience lacked any real spiritual connection— except the garden tomb of our Lord Jesus Christ. As our tour group walked into the site, I felt something different from what I had felt when I walked into the others. It was in stark contrast to the "Church of the Holy Sepulchre," for instance, which our guide (a friend who lived in Jerusalem) didn't even want to bring us to because of its three-ring commercial atmosphere. No, this was anything but. It seemed off the beaten path, and when we walked in, we were greeted by a British volunteer guide in his fifties or sixties.

During the tour he made the case for why they think Jesus had been buried there, instead of the traditional site inside Jerusalem (a doorway with a rock inside, over which the Church of the Holy Sepulchre had been built). The garden tomb, in contrast, is a relatively new archaeological find, and is completely intact just outside of the walled Jerusalem—much as the Bible describes it. And it is right next to the ancient winepress of an obviously wealthy man. This would also fit with the Bible's account of Jesus being buried in a grave owned by Joseph of Arimathea, a member of the ruling Sanhedrin. The tomb is also located in a garden, once again fitting the biblical description, and as far as anyone knows, it is right next to Golgotha, "The Place of the Skull" (also a new find reminiscent of the biblical description). It even has a huge trough in front of the site, which archaeological evidence suggests was used to roll large stones in front of the entrance.

But what struck me was not the site so much as this man's narrative. Unlike other sites' guides, he consistently admitted many times throughout his presentation that we simply do not know where Jesus was buried; but as he ended his tour, he said this: "Even though I do not know for sure if this is the place where Jesus lay after His death, I do know this one thing for sure, though, that when you go into that cave you will not find Him there, because we serve a risen Savior."

Even though the guide spoke with conviction with regard to the details of the site, he left its conclusion in mystery. He, like Marie, and like the angel in the biblical garden, knew that the "Grail" we sought wasn't there. Yet while Marie Chauvel leaves us with a myth that is true "only in Spirit,"[10] this composed British man left us with a myth that rang of truth, conviction, and reality. We walked away in reflective awe, contemplating the One who fulfilled all of man's prototypes and symbols, who rose from the grave and brought forth the redemption we all crave.

The historical Jesus has no doubt perpetuated mystery, and every attempt to come to terms with His person aside from revelation from God has ended in futility—has found a Jesus who is also real only in spirit, only symbolically real. But Jesus said that God is not just real *in* spirit, but, in fact, *is* Spirit, and His worshipers must "worship in spirit and in truth."[11] Only truth can achieve this type of awe, folklore, and true worship—a worship that strikes at both our heads and our hearts, at both our spirits and our search for truth. We, like those who walked the Emmaus road with Jesus in Luke 24, have had our hearts burn with passion for our Savior, who has changed our hearts to settle on Him as the fulfillment of all our symbols and myths, no matter how prolifically and in what form they persist.

Skeptics may object: "But the Christianity you describe differs little from the goddess worship that Marie Chauvel advocates." Just so. Shouldn't a worthwhile alternate story offer something more unique than just a change of gender allegiance and a disingenuous aversion to truth claims? The onus is not on the established story to offer something new, but on the challenger. Chasing after the new and the fashionably correct tells us a lot more about ourselves than it tells us about the ancient and the traditional.

The Matrix and the Use of Symbols in Art

Dan Brown isn't the first artist, and certainly won't be the last one, to use symbols in his storytelling. As we saw in the very beginning of our investigations, symbols abound in art, as they are sometimes the only way to communicate the transcendent reality that exists around us. Jesus Himself used symbols, parables, and metaphors to explain the unexplainable, and here we are here two thousand years later drinking in the depth of meaning in these pithy sermons.

Symbols are useful and important to communication, but in the twentieth century, they had been relegated to second rate storytelling by a Modernist approach that favored literalist realism. This approach saw reality defined by universal, rational and *a priori* presuppositions, redefining symbolism as fanciful myths and tales of ancient, irrelevant struggles. Joseph Campbell indicated the same when he said that symbols and myths represent the collective human spirit, and are not transcendent of the mythmaker. "We keep thinking of deity as a kind of fact, somewhere; God as fact. God is simply our own notion of something that is symbolic of transcendence and mystery."[12] According to such an approach, the only transcendence possible is the transcendence of romanticism, which is ultimately a mysticism formed from a collective human consciousness, not from a reality greater than our own minds.

Are symbols multi-layered? Are symbols truths with veils on, or are they intended for multiple interpretations? And in this sense, is there meaning in any form of text or story outside of the hearer's personal construct? The problem of non-transcendent symbols is confusing if everything is, in fact, open to interpretation and if there are multiple, but equally valid and contradictory, stories.

We see this problem in full force in *The Matrix*, Warner Brothers' blockbuster hit from a few years ago. It used symbols and metaphor to tell the story of an alternate world, one which could be led to freedom if the people would follow their controversial leader to their own personal Zion. The three-part story sequence had promise, and many artistically gifted minds in the "emerging church" saw in the first installment an incredible and powerful metaphor for the truths of the Christian faith. That all seemed to fade away into an increasingly pessimistic hopelessness as the multi-layered story leaped into symbols on steroids.

People of every faith—from Scientologists to Zen Buddhists, postmodern pilgrims, and secular humanists—jumped on board to claim the film's vision as their own. Books have been written about the philosophical message of *The Matrix*. The University of Washington even ran a class on *The Matrix* to study the media's influence on philosophy. By the end of the trilogy, most of the supporters from the evangelical camp jumped ship, claiming that the Christian message was neutered in a sea of relativism. There were "too many layers of nuance" in order for one to find meaning in a story that was obviously intended to be meaningless. "It was an existential nightmare."[13] Many believed that *The Matrix* had simply reflected the cosmology of the Hindu and Buddhist gods, especially as portrayed in common Buddhist *thankas*.[14]

In spite of the overpopulation of symbols and metaphor in

the movie, it still told a story of love. Neo, the obvious messiah figure in the story, did not come from the gods but instead developed as the trilogy moved on. Didn't Jesus grow, too, in favor with God and man? But Neo was different; he began as "Mr. Anderson" and became Neo—became "new," anagrammatically became the "One." He began as a self-centered individual, melancholy over his seemingly meaningless existence, knowing deep inside that there was more to life; and through a series of events he became embroiled in a cosmic fight for freedom and righteousness.

But it wasn't the fight that motivated him; it was the love of "Trinity" that compelled him to move on and proceed to lay down his life for the sake of that love. The theme is developed, repeated, and mirrored throughout the three films, and becomes the source of narrative tension in any scene with Persephone[15] and the Merovingian. Later, in the third installment's epic battle between Agent Smith and Neo, Smith says,

> Could it be for love? Illusions, Mr. Anderson, vagaries of perception. The temporary abstracts of a feeble human intellect trying desperately to justify an existence that is without meaning or purpose. And all of them as artificial as the Matrix itself, although only a human mind could invent something as insipid as love.[16]

The Matrix, in spite of it propensity to kill its own metanarrative through the overuse of symbols, still tells a story that deserves to be trumpeted. Love is, indeed, more than a feeling, as Boston sang, and in its truest form is more sacrificial than it is self-serving. It is deeper than sex, though it is certainly expressed beautifully within the sexual context by people who are committed to more than self-gratification. *The Matrix*, and its portrayal of love, is a beautiful story for the ages, told incredibly and artfully by the Wachowski brothers. This is the kind of story that a narcissistic, self-gratifying culture needs to hear.

The number one shortcoming of *The Matrix* is that it

desires to find this love outside of the context of supernatural redemption. Yes, Neo fulfills his role through selfless, redemptive love. But that, in and of itself, is not enough to save Zion. He needs the help of the machines, too—and they are truly Deus ex Machina. But they are all machine and no God, all mind and no heart, all reason and no spirit. What's worse, they're man-made, not transcendent. This is nothing more than our own very human gospel, which claims that we, in fact, created God, and have within us the ability to save ourselves.

Similarly, *The Da Vinci Code* desires to redress a wrong done to women in a male-dominated culture of oppression by deconstructing the dominant cultural narrative Dan Brown believes is at the root of that oppression. While this is a noble cause, it is naïve. *The Matrix*, at least, recognizes that slavery and subjection can at best be kept at bay in human society. *The Da Vinci Code*, however, doesn't even leave us with that pragmatic compromise, or with anything redeeming to take its place. Instead, all we get is a dubious and cryptic conspiracy of truth, and a pendulum swinging like a grinning guillotine.

Whatever the true merits of Dan Brown's book—a subtle advocacy of harmony between polar extremes, an appealing personal journey for Sophie, even a well-thought-out structure for examining a wide range of theological, historical, and philosophical developments—it still explicitly trumpets a secret knowledge that will unlock the mysteries of our time and bring forth a new hope. Like it or not, his book is true to the human condition: we reject the narrative found in the Bible because it doesn't agree with our own desires, and we fabricate our own— though we are by nature limited to the concrete knowledge of our own matrix.

So Dan Brown has it partially right. We all desire hidden knowledge that will raise us beyond our problems. Some find that knowledge in religion, some find it in science, and some, like Mr. Brown's characters, at least, try to find it in deconstruction and conspiracy. Brown is seeking redemption, but his tale does so on a modernist model that says "We will find it on our own." It's an ideal that promises much, but has always delivered little—just a handful or two of bootstraps.

Of course, many in this camp continue to tell themselves that they are creating a better world, but my guess is that they either don't travel, don't follow world news, or haven't seen *Serenity*.

We are free to interpret symbols as we please, but ultimately the only way that we can discover the meaning and truth behind them is by having the author reveal the meaning intended. Wouldn't it be nice if Dan Brown would just tell us clearly what he's up to? Wouldn't we rest easier if we knew which of his characters really represent his own thinking? Couldn't we all relax if he would just admit that Langdon's adventure with Sophie—with Wisdom—was all just a revelatory dream? Or would that all just ruin the story? Maybe we should simply grant the author the wisdom of saying, "Figure it out for yourself. I've given you enough clues. You're big kids now." Or would that allow him too much of a godlike status?

We are finite and in need of revelation. Every story has an author, and if we are going to continue to tell ourselves that our story in this cosmos has no author, the tale will end without meaning—a lot like Robert Langdon's dead-end quest for the Grail, an alternate story about the Christ in which Jesus doesn't have to be much different from ourselves. If Brown's tale—if any tale—could only connect in a meaningful way with a transcendent metanarrative, it would actually offer hope.

Symbols are only as good as the truth behind them. The Bible tells us that Jesus is that revelation, is that truth. He interprets God to us in a way previously unknown. He connects all symbols and archetypes by revealing the truth. The sacred feminine only makes sense in the wake of a real God who created men and women equally in His own image. If we want to know

God and His story, we must know Jesus who claimed to be God, and raised women to a level of equality in Him. It is His story that we must trumpet from the housetop, because that story ultimately makes sense in a nonsense world. It is the one myth, as C. S. Lewis says, that happens to be fact, and makes sense of the rest of our stories and symbols.

Dan Brown gives us a gift much like the gift that Arius gave the Church in the fourth century. Arius opposed the truth with an alternative story that made the Church stand up and take notice, that made the Church clear the dross and cobwebs from its beliefs and crystallize the truths that it knew to be true. And if this is really the point of Dan Brown's project, he is to be congratulated. Sometimes reform can only be driven from the outside, as Martin Luther demonstrated.

This is why books like *The Da Vinci Code* are not to be feared, but rather engaged, seriously examined and thought through—even by the Church. With a biblical lens allowing us to separate fact from fiction, the Church can engage such alternate stories for the sake of finding and testing truth; otherwise it ends up being the institution that artists and crusaders like Dan Brown rightly expose for suppressing that which merely opposes its worldview.

If what we believe is true, we should have no problem facing alternate worldviews head on, knowing that we can both grow from the challenge—knowing that we can equally challenge those who challenge us.

Symbols do abound, and many stories are being told; so why should we believe our story over the other stories? This is a question we must always ask ourselves. But it should also be asked by men and women like Robert Langdon, Sophie Neveu, and Leigh Teabing, who choose to believe an alternative story not because of the evidence but because of their presuppositions and prejudices.

With that observation, please feel free to read (or re-read)

Dan Brown's book. Get to know Teabing, Langdon, and Sophie. Ask good questions. I think you will find the truth there somewhere—maybe as a hidden code?

> **Robert Langdon awoke with a start.**
>
> **He had been dreaming.**

For Further Investigation
The Da Vinci Code, Chapter 105 through Epilogue

Dig a Little Deeper

➤   Why should we engage books like *The Da Vinci Code*?

➤   Is there such a thing as Truth?

➤   How does one arrive at the truth in a pluralistic world?

Draw Your Own Conclusions

➤   Regarding Modernism and Postmodernism:

  • www.as.ua.edu/ant/Faculty/murphy/436/pomo.htm

  • *From Modernism to Postmodernism: An Anthology*, by Lawrence E. Cahoone.

➤   On Popular Perceptions of Heaven:

  • The ABC special *Heaven—Where is it? How Do We Get There?* (2005) is available from the online ABC News Store.

  • Diane Keaton's documentary *Heaven* (1987) is also available on DVD.

➤   On the End of Jesus' Story, and the Ascension:

  • Acts 1:6–11.

Notes

We have employed dual citations for Dan Brown's *The Da Vinci Code* in the following notes. The first page number cited refers to the first Doubleday hardback edition, and the second page number, following the slash, refers to the Anchor mass market paperback edition. (The larger-format Anchor trade paperback edition, released at the same time as the mass market edition, employs the same pagination as the Doubleday hardback edition.) Thus, the citation "Brown, *Code*, 253 / 273," refers to page 253 in the Doubleday hardback, page 253 in the trade paperback, and page 273 in the Anchor mass market paperback.

The Power of Symbols

1. Edward O. Wilson, *Consilience*, 146–147.
2. Sharan Newman, *Real History*, Introduction, x.
3. Dan Brown, *The Da Vinci Code*, 257 / 278.
4. Al Pacino, in *The Devil's Advocate*.
5. Wilson, 235.
6. "Edutainment is a form of entertainment designed to educate as well as to amuse… Most often, edutainment seeks either to tutor in one or more specific subjects, or to change behavior by engendering specific socio-cultural attitudes." See "Edutainment," *Wikipedia*.
7. Michael Moore, in Roger Ebert, "Answer Man."
8. Oliver Stone, Graduation address, 2.
9. Stone, Graduation address, 4.
10. Brown, *Code*, 341 / 369.
11. See Matthew 22:37, for instance.
12. Michel Foucault, in Hubert Dreyfus, *Michel Foucault*, 106.
13. Michel Foucault, in Paul Rabinow, *The Foucault Reader*, 350.
14. Dan Brown, in *Jesus, Mary and Da Vinci*.
15. Jack Finnegan, *Myth and Mystery*, 15.
16. C. S. Lewis, *God in the Dock*, 67.
17. Brown, *Code*, 16 / 17.

18. Brown, *Code*, 35 / 39.
19. Lewis, *God in the Dock*, 66–67.

Newly Emerging Power

1. Brown, *Code*, 9 / 10.
2. According to *The Da Vinci Code* (16 / 16) Landon and Vetra were supposed to meet every six months; but it has already been a year, and he is now into his new conquest. It seems his love, concern, and respect for women is too much to be contained in one relationship?
3. Peter Jackson's film-trilogy adaptations of *The Lord of the Rings* had everyone from fundamentalists, environmentalists, and pacifists claiming symbolism in the movies for their causes.
4. See Dale Peterson and Richard Wrangham, *Demonic Males*.
5. Fabienne André Worth, *"Rameau's Nephew."*
6. Brown, *Code*, 15–16 / 16.
7. Brown, *Code,* 15 / 16.
8. Brown, *Angels and Demons*, 243.
9. Brown, *Code*, 157–161 / 171–175.
10. Brown, *Code*, 38 / 42.
11. Brown, *Angels*, 243.
12. See "Euhemerus," *Wikipedia*.
13. See Hebrews 4:15.
14. 1 Corinthians 1:23.
15. Philippians 1:20–21.
16. Friedrich Nietzsche, in Walter Kaufmann, *Portable Nietzsche*, 95.
17. Hebrews 4:15.
18. Brown, *Code*, 246 / 267.
19. Brown, *Code*, 37 / 41.
20. John Dunphy, "A Religion for a New Age," 26.
21. Luke 17:33.

Powerful Motivators

1. 2 Corinthians 6:8–10.
2. 1 Timothy 6:10.
3. Matthew 6:24.

4. Brown, *Code*, 157 / 171.
5. Brown, *Code*, 45 / 50.
6. Revelation 22:1.
7. Attributed to St. Francis of Assisi.
8. Brian Martin, "Scientific Fraud."
9. As popularized by cable television network evangelists.
10. Bruce Wilkinson's book *The Prayer of Jabez* popularized the prayerful pursuit of greater material wealth and temporal influence—inspired by an obscure Old Testament figure who asked of God, "Enlarge my territory!" See 1 Chronicles 4:9–10.
11. Roger Ebert, "The Passion of the Christ."
12. Henry Scougal, *The Life of God*, 62.
13. Romans 5:8.
14. C. S. Lewis, *Weight of Glory*, 26.
15. Blaise Pascal, in *The Columbia World of Quotations*, no. 43679.
16. Philippians 1:20.
17. 1 Corinthians 13:13–4:1.

Λ Gnomon

1. Brown, *Code*, 106 / 114.
2. Brown, *Code*, 107 / 115.
3. Brown, *Code*, 232 / 252.
4. Freke and Gandy are authors of *The Jesus Mysteries: Was the "Original Jesus" a Pagan God?* (New York: Three Rivers Press, 1999), which is dedicated to "The Christ in You," revealing their clear biases against orthodox Christianity.
5. Brown, *Code*, 106 / 114.
6. No, not the boxer. But wouldn't *that* be a conspiracy!
7. Teabing is correct in saying that there are more gospels than the four found in the New Testament; but the number is far less than the eighty he proclaims (231 / 251), and all of the non-canonical gospels originated well after any eyewitnesses could have been alive—which made them irrelevant to the conversation about the Christ. Teabing is also quite misinformed (or disingenuous) when he says that "The Bible, as we know it today, was collated by the pagan Roman emperor Constantine the Great" (231 / 251). The

manuscript evidence disproving this claim is overwhelming. In contrast, all of the books accepted into the canon of the NT were written before 100 CE, and were heavily quoted by early church fathers writing before 150 CE, whereas only a few of the other gospels were mentioned by the same writers, and were never used in the context of worship. Justin Martyr actually wrote a treatise against the "Mystery Religions" and Gnostic literature and practice in 160 CE, claiming they were stealing Christian symbolism and rituals like baptism and communion. How ironic is that?

8. Brown, *Code*, 98 / 105.

9. Brown, *Code*, 96 / 103.

10. See Langdon's description of Teabing and other Grail enthusiasts in his words to publisher Jonas Faukman in Brown, *Code*, 163 / 177.

11. David Shugarts, in "The Plot Holes and Intriguing Details of *The Da Vinci Code*," *Secrets of the Code*, Dan Burstein ed., 269.

12. Dan Burstein, *Secrets of the Code*, 283.

13. Brown, *Code*, 230 / 249.

14. Hebrews 5:11, NASB. The NIV translates the phrase, "slow to learn."

15. Rodney Stark, *For the Glory of God*, 2.

16. Ibid.

17. Graham Chapman, in *Monty Python and the Holy Grail*.

18. Graham Chapman and John Cleese, in *Holy Grail*.

19. John Cleese, in *Holy Grail*.

20. Brown, *Code*, 341 / 370.

A Campaign of Propaganda

1. Brown, *Code*, 121 / 130.

2. Ibid.

3. Genesis 1:27.

4. See, for instance, John 4:24.

5. Genesis 1:31.

6. Brown, *Code*, 126 / 135.

7. See, as examples, Exodus 34:12, Deuteronomy 12:3 and

Deuteronomy 16:21.

8. Galatians 3:27.

9. Creed, "One," *My Own Prison*.

10. See 1 Corinthians 11.

11. See 1 Timothy 2:13, for instance.

12. Sharan Newman, *Real History*, 259.

13. Eva Cantarella, *Pandora's Daughters*, 101.

14. Joseph Campbell, *Transformations of Myths*, 2.

15. Although these heinous events indeed occurred, they were not nearly as destructive as Langdon leads us to believe (five million dead), and they weren't just directed at women. There probably were less than 100,000 killed, and many of them were men (see Sharan Newman, 319–324).

16. Galatians 3:28.

17. Title track of Switchfoot's *New Way to be Human*.

18. Attributed to St. Francis of Assisi.

A Pristine Truth

1. Brown, *Code*, 154 / 167.

2. Brown, *Code*, 158 / 171.

3. Timothy Freke made these comments on a CNN message board attached to articles by Allan Dodson posted on September 21, 2000. CNN has since made this message board unavailable.

4. Oliver Stone, Interview by Gavin Smith, 39.

5. Michael Moore, Interview by Harlan Jacobson, 23–24.

6. Ibid., 23.

7. G. B. Shaw, in *The Columbia World of Quotations*, no. 53707.

8. Brown, *Code*, 158 / 172.

9. I made these comments on a CNN message board attached to articles by Allan Dodson posted on September 21, 2000. CNN has since made this message board unavailable.

10. André Gide, in *Simpson's Contemporary Quotations*, no. 5032.

11. Brown, *Code*, 169 / 183.

12. See, for instance, Brown, *Code*, 24 / 26.

13. Brown, *Code*, 25 / 27.

14. Brown, *Code*, 163 / 177.

15. Brown, *Code*, 169 / 184.
16. Brown, *Code*, 38 / 42.
17. Brown, *Code*, 341 / 369.
18. Brown, *Code*, 157 / 170–171.
19. Brown, *Code*, 161 / 175.
20. Brown, *Code*, 165 / 179.
21. As Brown similarly writes of Leonardo in *Code*, 170 / 184–185.
22. Brown, *Code*, 171–172 / 186.
23. Brown, *Code*, 163 / 177.

Welcome and Keep Out

1. Brown, *Code*, 171 / 186.
2. Brown, *Code*, 176 / 191.
3. Brown, *Code*, 177 / 192.
4. Brown, *Code*, 187 / 203.
5. Ibid.
6. Brown, *Code*, 57 / 62.
7. Brown, *Code*, 195 / 213.
8. Brown, *Code*, 201 / 219.
9. Brown, *Code*, 157 / 170.
10. Brown, *Code*, 182 / 197.
11. Brown, *Code*, 199–200 / 217.
12. Brown, *Code*, 45–46 / 50.
13. Brown, *Code*, 181 / 196.
14. Brown, *Code*, 177 / 192.
15. John Turturro, in *Barton Fink*.
16. Brown, *Code*, 194 / 210.
17. John Goodman, in *Barton Fink*.
18. Brown, *Code*, 201 / 219.
19. Brown, *Code*, 184 / 200.
20. See, for instance, Brown, *Code*, 91 / 97.
21. Brown, *Code*, 197 / 215.
22. Patrick Janson-Smith, quoted in Katy Papineau and Salome Wagaine, "Da Vinci case."
23. Brown, *Code*, 202 / 220.
24. Ibid.

25. Brown, *Code*, 177 / 191.
26. Brown, *Code*, 196 / 213.
27. Brown, *Code*, 194 / 211.

If You're Smart Enough

1. Greg Wright, *Strange Things Done*, 58.
2. Brown, *Code*, 205 / 223.
3. Brown, *Code*, 206 / 224.
4. Richard Leigh, in *Beyond the Da Vinci Code*.
5. Jean-Luc Chaumeil, in *Beyond the Da Vinci Code*.
6. Leigh, in *Beyond the Da Vinci Code*.
7. Chaumeil, in *Beyond the Da Vinci Code*.
8. Leigh, in *Beyond the Da Vinci Code*.
9. See *The Forgotten Monarchy of Scotland*, xxv.
10. Sir Walter Scott, *Tales of a Grandfather*, 211.
11. Brown, *Code*, 205 / 224.
12. Brown, *Code*, 229 / 248.
13. Hazel Borst, in Greg Wright, *Strange Things Done*, 139.
14. Brown, *Code*, 111 / 119.
15. Worth, *"Rameau's Nephew."*
16. Ibid.
17. Ibid.

Deeply Pious Men

1. See "Pious," *The American Heritage Dictionary*.
2. Brown, *Code*, 244 / 264.
3. Brown, *Code*, 255 / 275.
4. George Bush, White House press release.
5. See the Army of God website.
6. See the Animal Liberation Front credo.
7. See the Earth Liberation Front website.
8. Paul Shukovsky, "Ecoterrorism Suspect."
9. Ibid.
10. Brown, *Code*, 235 / 255.
11. 2 Timothy 3:16.
12. Brown, *Code*, 243 / 263.

13. Arthur Schopenhauer, *Parerga*, vol. 2, ch. 1, sct. 17.
14. Brown, Code, 242 / 262.
15. John 5:39–40.
16. See Matthew 5:20.
17. See Matthew 16:12.
18. John 14:7.
19. Ibid.
20. 1 John 3:18–20.
21. Titus 1:1.
22. Augustine, in *The Columbia World of Quotations*, no. 55101.
23. Jonah 4:2.
24. Acts 10:13, 15.
25. Acts 10:17.
26. Colossians 3:11; see also Galatians 3:28.
27. 2 Corinthians 13:8.
28. Brown, *Code*, 256 / 276.

The Sane Ones Are Nuts

1. Mohandas K. Gandhi, in *The Columbia World of Quotations*, no. 24394.
2. George Santayana, *Birth of Reason*, introduction, xxvii.
3. Hebrews 11:1.
4. Albert Einstein, *Later Years*, 26.
5. Brown, *Code*, 293 / 317.
6. Brown, *Code*, 253 / 273.
7. Ibid.
8. Philippians 1:9–10.
9. Proverbs 3:21–23.
10. See Luke's discussion of the Bereans and the Thessalonians in Acts 17.
11. Brown, *Code*, 261 / 282.
12. Ibid.
13. Allan Bloom, in *The Columbia World of Quotations*, no. 7604.
14. Brown, *Code*, 261 / 282.
15. Brown, *Code*, 262 / 282.
16. See 2 Peter 3:9.

17. Brown, *Code*, 242 / 262.
18. Immanuel Kant, in *The Columbia World of Quotations*, no. 32015.
19. 1 Corinthians 2:4–6.

Exceptional Responsibility

1. Brown, *Code*, 328 / 355.
2. Brown, *Code*, 293–294 / 319.
3. James 3:1.
4. Brown, *Code*, 299 /325.
5. See chapter 77 of Brown, *Code*, for the discussion of the Atbash cipher.
6. Brown, *Code*, 308 / 334–335.
7. Brown, *Code*, 308 / 335.
8. Brown, *Code*, 309 / 335.
9. Song of Songs 5:1–5.
10. Brown, *Code*, 310 / 336.
11. Brown, *Code*, 309 / 335.
12. Brown, *Code*, 313 / 339.
13. Brown, *Code*, 293 / 317.
14. Luke 12:48.

More Information

1. Brown, *Code*, 354 / 382.
2. Ibid.
3. See Chapter 2 of G. K. Chesterson, *Orthodoxy*.
4. Brown, *Code*, 378 / 406.
5. Brown, *Code*, 341–342 / 369–370.
6. Attributed to Augustine of Hippo.
7. Brown, *Code*, 381 / 409.
8. John Calvin, *The Institutes of the Christian Religion*, Book 2, 236.
9. The point here is not who would say such a thing; and the billionaire who once actually believed such things has now changed his heart fairly radically. And that's the point.
10. Romans 1 indicates that creation itself reveals God to man, but man rejects the truth of the creator in favor of the creation (compare with Psalm 19).

11. Luke 12:48.
12. Attributed to Albert Einstein.
13. 1 Corinthians 8:1.
14. Leslie Newbigin, *The Gospel in a Pluralist Society*, 222ff.

A Man of Humanity

1. Deuteronomy 6:21–25.
2. Exodus 12:25–27.
3. Esther 9:21–22, 28.
4. Joshua 4:4–7.
5. Brown, *Code*, 413 / 445.
6. Proverbs 30:18–19, 21–28.
7. Simone Weil, in *The Columbia World of Quotations*, no. 63561.
8. William Hazlitt, in *The Columbia World of Quotations*, no. 27492.
9. Brown, *Code*, 410 / 441.
10. Alexander Pope, *Essay on Criticism*, part ii line 1ff.
11. Douglas Bush, in *The Columbia World of Quotations*, no. 9387.
12. Proverbs 4:6–9.

A Little Faith

1. Brown, *Code*, 441 / 475.
2. Soren Kierkegaard, *Philosophical Fragments*, 50.
3. Daniel Massey, in *Miracle Maker*.
4. William Hurt, in *Miracle Maker*.
5. Ralph Fiennes, in *Miracle Maker*.
6. Michael Ramsey, in *Simpson's Contemporary Quotations*, no. 4253.
7. Brown, *Code*, 273 / 297.
8. Brown, *Code*, 412–413 / 444.
9. Brown, *Code*, 441 / 475.
10. Brown, *Code*, 447 / 482.
11. Brown, *Code*, 443 / 479.
12. Thomas Merton, in *The Columbia World of Quotations*, no. 39389.
13. Brown, *Code*, 213 / 231.
14. Brown, *Code*, 214 / 233.
15. Brown, *Code*, 217 / 236.
16. Ibid.

17. Brown, *Code*, 218 / 237.
18. Reinhold Niebuhr, in *The Columbia World of Quotations*, no. 41474.
19. John Henry Newman, *An Essay*, 92–93.
20. Brown, *Code*, 438 / 472.
21. Brown, *Code*, 444 / 479.
22. Ron Glass, in *Serenity*.
23. Brown, *Code*, 431 / 464.
24. Brown, *Code*, 454 / 489.
25. Lakdasa J de Mel, Anglican Metropolitan of India, in *Simpson's Contemporary Quotations*, no. 4103.

Modern Troubadours

1. Brown, *Code*, 433 / 465–466.
2. Brown, *Code*, 444 / 479.
3. Brown, *Code*, 446 / 481.
4. Brown, *Code*, 444 / 479.
5. Ibid.
6. Erwin W. Lutzer, *The Da Vinci Deception*, 31.
7. Karl Marx, in *The Columbia World of Quotations*, no. 38123.
8. Brown, *Code*, 444 / 478.
9. Brown, *Code*, 454 / 489.
10. Brown, *Code*, 446 / 481.
11. John 4:24.
12. Joseph Campbell, *Transformations of Myths through Time*, 16.
13. Such were the words of many of my film geek friends and fellow pastors.
14. In Buddhist art, *thankas* depict a circle representing the cosmos, and an evil God (Yama) holding the circle. Within the circle is a story representing the seasons of birth-life-death-rebirth, reflecting *samsara* (endless cycles of life). Six facets of life are usually depicted. The bottom three represent hell and evil, while the top three represent the gods, angels, and heaven. Between are the three important sins that Buddhists see behind worldly attachments (greed, hatred, and pride), which prevent us from seeing the cosmos as it is. As a result, we live in endless cycles of

illusion (*maya*) instead of being released into *nirvana* and *moksa*.

15. It is interesting that the movie referenced the mythological Persephone (goddess of the underworld)—a beautiful woman who was used by men for her beauty and ultimately manipulated by Hades to stay with him for three months of the year. During that three months' time, Demeter (Persephone's mother) cursed the ground so nothing would grow, creating winter. The myth symbolized the budding and dying of the seasons.

16. Hugo Weaving, in *The Matrix*.

Works Cited

Albany, HRH Prince Michael of. *The Forgotten Monarchy of Scotland: The True Story of the Royal House of Stewart and the Hidden Lineage of the Kings and Queens of Scotland*. Boston: Element Books, 1998.

American Heritage Dictionary of the English Language, The. 4th Edition. Boston: Houghton Mifflin, 2000.

Animal Liberation Front. Ann Berlin, 2006. http://animalliberation front.com

Army of God, The. Donald Spitz. http://armyofgod.com

Bartlett, John, comp. *Familiar Quotations*. 10th ed. rev. and enl. by Nathan Haskell Dole. Boston: Little, Brown, 1919. Online Edition. *Bartleby.com*, 2000.

Barton Fink. Directed by Joel Coen. Circle Films, 1991. Videocassette. FoxVideo, 1992.

Beyond the Da Vinci Code. Directed by Will Ehbrecht. The History Channel: 2004. DVD. 2005.

Brown, Dan. *Angels and Demons*. New York: Pocket Books, 2000.

———. *The Da Vinci Code*. Mass Market Edition. New York: Anchor, 2006.

———. *The Da Vinci Code*. New York: Doubleday, 2003.

Bush, George. White House speech transcript press release. June 18, 2002. http://www.whitehouse.gov/news/releases/2002/06/2002 0618-1.html

Calvin, John. *The Institutes of the Christian Religion*. Trans. Henry Beveridge. 2nd. ed. Grand Rapids: Eerdmans, 1995.

Campbell, Joseph. *Transformations of Myths through Time*. New York: Harper & Row, 1990.

Cantarella, Eva. *Pandora's Daughters: The Role and Status of Women in Greek and Roman Antiquity.* Trans. Maureen B. Fant. Baltimore: Johns Hopkins University Press, 1987.

Columbia World of Quotations, The. New York: Columbia University Press, 1996. Online Edition. *Bartleby.com,* 2001.

Creed. *My Own Prison.* CD. New York: Wind-up Records, 1997.

Devil's Advocate, The. Directed by Taylor Hackford. Warner Bros., 1997. DVD. Warner Home Video, 1998.

Dreyfus, Hubert and Paul Rabinow. *Michel Foucault, Beyond Structuralism and Hermeneutics.* 2nd ed. Chicago: University of Chicago Press, 1983.

Dunphy, John. "A Religion for a New Age." *The Humanist* vol. 43 no. 1 (Jan.–Feb. 1983) 23–26.

Earth Liberation Front. http://earthliberationfront.com

Ebert, Roger. "Movie Answer Man." Chicago *Sun-Times.* April 6, 2003. http://rogerebert.suntimes.com/apps/pbcs.dll/article?AID =/20030406/ANSWERMAN/304060303

———. "The Passion of the Christ." Chicago *Sun-Times.* Feb. 24, 2004. http://www.suntimes.com/output/ebert1/cst-ftr-passion 24.html

Einstein, Albert. *Out of My Later Years.* Revised reprint edition. Secaucus, NJ: The Citadel Press, 1956.

Finnegan, Jack. *Myth and Mystery: An Introduction to the Pagan Religions of the Biblical World.* Grand Rapids: Baker Book House, 1989.

Jesus, Mary and Da Vinci: Discover The Truth Behind the Mystery. ABC Television, 2003.

Kaufmann, Walter. *The Portable Nietzsche.* New York: Viking Press, 1968.

Kierkegaard, Soren and Johannes Climacus. *The Philosophical Fragments or A Fragment of Philosophy.* Princeton: Princeton University Press, 1946.

Works Cited

Lewis, C. S. *God in the Dock*. Grand Rapids: William B. Eerdmans Publishing, 1970.

———. *The Weight of Glory*. 3rd ed. San Francisco: Harper Collins, 1980.

Lutzer, Erwin W. *The Da Vinci Deception*. 2nd ed. Carol Stream: Tyndale Publishing, 2005.

Martin, Brian. "Scientific Fraud and the Power Structure of Science." *Prometheus* vol. 10, no. 1 (June, 1992), pp. 83–98. http://www.uow.edu.au/arts/sts/bmartin/pubs/92prom.html

Matrix, The. Directed by the Wachowski Brothers. Warner Bros., 1999. Videocassette. Collector's Edition. Warner Home Video, 1999.

Miracle Maker, The. Directed by Stanislav Sokolov and Derek W. Hayes. BBC, 2000. DVD. Artisan, 2000.

Monty Python and the Holy Grail. Directed by Terry Jones. Handmade Films, 1975. DVD. Columbia/Tristar, 1999.

Moore, Michael. Interview by Harlan Jacobson. "Michael and Me." *Film Comment* November–December 1989: 16–26.

Newman, John Henry. *An Essay in Aid of a Grammar of Assent*. London: Burns, Oates, & Co., 1906.

Newman, Sharan. *The Real History Behind the Da Vinci Code*. New York: The Berkley Publishing Group, 2005.

Newbigin, Leslie. *The Gospel in a Pluralist Society*. 2nd ed. Grand Rapids: Eerdmans, 1996.

Norman, Larry. "I Wish We'd All Been Ready." *Only Visiting This Planet*. LP. Salem, Oregon: Solid Rock Records, 1972.

Papineau, Katy and Salome Wagaine. "Da Vinci case has no hope, says publisher." London *Times Online*. March 15, 2006. www.timesonline.co.uk/article/0,,923-2087503,00.html

Peterson, Dale and Richard Wrangham. *Demonic Males: Apes and the Origins of Human Violence*. New York: Houghton Mifflin, 1996.

Pope, Alexander. *Essay on Criticism*. Originally published anonymously May 15, 1711. Whitefish: Kessinger Publishing, 2004.

Rabinow, Paul ed. *The Foucault Reader*. London: Penguin, 1984.

Santayana, George. *The Birth of Reason and Other Essays*. Reissue edition. New York: Columbia University Press, 1995.

Schopenhauer, Arthur. *Parerga and Paralipomena*. New edition. New York: Oxford University Press, 2001.

Scott, Sir Walter. *Tales of a Grandfather, Fourth Series: Tales from French History*. Last revised edition. Philadelphia: Porter & Coates, undated. Originally published 1830.

Scougal, Henry. *The Life of God in the Soul of Man*. 3rd ed. Harrisburg, Virginia: Sprinkle Publications, 1986.

Secrets of the Code: The Unauthorized Guide to the Mysteries Behind the Da Vinci Code. Ed. Dan Burstein. New York: CDS Books, 2004.

Serenity. Directed by Joss Whedon. Universal, 2005. DVD. Universal, 2005.

Shukovsky, Paul. "Ecoterrorism suspect may be charged in 2001 UW arson." Seattle *Post-Intelligencer*. December 14, 2005. http://seattlepi.nwsource.com/local/251991_indict 14.html

Simpson, James B., comp. *Simpson's Contemporary Quotations*. Boston: Houghton Mifflin, 1988. Online Edition. *Bartleby.com*, 2000.

Stark, Rodney. *For the Glory of God*. Princeton: Princeton University Press, 2003.

Stone, Oliver. Graduation address at Berkeley. October 13, 2000. globetrotter.berkeley.edu/Stone.html

———. Interview by Gavin Smith. "The camera for me is an actor." *Film Comment* January–February 1994: 26–29, 37–43.

Switchfoot. "New Way To Be Human." CD. Brentwood: Chordant,

Works Cited

1999.

Wikipedia, The Free Encyclopedia. Wikimedia Foundation, Inc. http://en.wikipedia.org

Wilson, Edward O. *Consilience: The Unity of Knowledge.* New York: Vintage, 1999.

Worth, Fabienne André. *"Rameau's Nephew,* Godard, and *Mona Lisa*: Uncovering the Veil of Gender in the Undergraduate Classroom." *ADFL Bulletin.* Vol. 19, no. 2 (January 1988): 20–23. www.mla.org/adfl/bulletin/v19n2/192020.htm

Wright, Greg. *Strange Things Done: A Biography of Robert Irvine Wright.* Privately published, 1998.

Index of Film Titles